FREEDOM'S
POWER

FREEDOM'S POWER

The True Force of Liberalism

PAUL STARR

BASIC
BOOKS

A Member of the Perseus Books Group
New York

Books published by Basic Books are available at special discounts for bulk
purchases in the United States by corporations, institutions, and other
organizations. For more information, please contact the Special Markets
Department at the Perseus Books Group, 11 Cambridge Center,
Cambridge MA 02142, or call (617) 252-5298 or (800) 255-1514, or
e-mail special.markets@perseusbooks.com.

Design and composition by Trish Wilkinson
Set in 11-point Goudy

Library of Congress Cataloging-in-Publication Data
Starr, Paul, 1949–
    Freedom's power : the true force of liberalism / Paul Starr.
        p.   cm.
    Includes bibliographical references and index.
    ISBN-13: 978-0-465-08186-8
    ISBN-10: 0-465-08186-X
    1. Liberalism. I. Title.
JC574.S73 2007
320.51—dc22

                                                        2006031409

10 9 8 7 6 5 4 3 2 1

To ABC and all our children

Contents

Part I
CONSTITUTIONAL LIBERALISM

Part II
MODERN DEMOCRATIC LIBERALISM

PART III
THE LIBERAL PROJECT OF OUR TIME

For more discussion about the book and its ideas, go to
www.freedomspower.com.

Preface and
Acknowledgments

———

EXPLAINING HIS RELIGIOUS BELIEFS, JOHN DEWEY ONCE WROTE THAT HE was "skeptical about things in particular" but had "faith in things in general." The liberal view of politics is analogous. Liberalism has always been a gamble on freedom and public argument, made out of a willingness to entertain doubt about all things in particular, a belief in robust criticism and competition, and a general confidence in the outcome. Recent history has surely tried that confidence, but liberalism has survived darker times than these, and the odds, I believe, still favor the gamble that liberalism invites us to make. The free encounter of conflicting ideas, the methods of organized skepticism, and the system of economic and democratic political competition have been rich sources of knowledge, abundance, and human possibility. They are part of the story of freedom's power.

This book, however, is also about what some may regard as the counterintuitive propositions that freedom requires power in the form of a strong and capable constitutional state and that modern democratic liberalism—by enlarging that state in some respects while constraining it in others—makes it possible for a society to achieve both greater power and greater freedom. In these pages I offer a historical interpretation of the liberal project and a defense of its modern inclusive and egalitarian form. Liberalism does not call only for rights that place limits on the state. Rights inevitably imply corresponding individual and social responsibilities, and as I try to show in these pages, liberalism is as much a method of creating power as of limiting it. This is the lesson of the immediate aftermath of the great classical liberal revolutions (1688 in England, 1776 in America) as well as liberal revolutions of more recent vintage (1989 in eastern Europe). In a sense, the liberal state and its laws *are* freedom's power, the indispensable basis of freedom's survival. Liberalism isn't just a set of fine aspirations. Historically, it has emerged from the pressures of political conflict, domestic and international, not least of all from the pressures of war. *Freedom's Power*, therefore, is about both the power that free societies generate and the power that they demand.

This book may be read both as a rebuttal to contemporary conservatism and as a corrective to some currents of liberal thought and progressive politics. I set about writing it because it seemed to me that there was no cogent, concise, accessible, and up-to-date account of the liberal project, at least not as I understand it. I hope to persuade you that there is a better way to think about liberalism—truer to the tradition and better suited to the world's realities—than what you may previously have understood. Although I have by no means tried to address every aspect of liberalism, I have ranged widely here, dealing with both history and ideas, philosophy and politics, international relations and domestic policy. While acknowledging the different strands of thought that make up the tradition, I have tried to give a sense of its coherence and integrity. Unlike those who see a sharp discontinuity between classical and modern liberalism, I see the two as closely related—the latter growing out of the former in response to historical experience, changed social conditions, and a more democratic politics. Both conservatives and liberals in the United States see themselves as bearers of the nation's founding ideals. This book argues that liberals have the better claim.

In the face of attacks, some liberals advise using the term "progressive," not necessarily to indicate any change in beliefs, but merely to escape the abuse that conservatives have heaped on liberalism. Rebranding may work in marketing, perhaps even in marketing political candidates, but it is a pointless dodge in the contest of ideas. No one would be fooled, and giving up an identification with liberalism would mean sacrificing the felt connection to a rich heritage of political thought. In any event, this book reflects a different impulse—not getting away from the past, but returning to it to get straight what liberalism is about and to set straight what has gone wrong with it in recent decades.

It is impossible here to discharge all the debts I have accumulated in the process of writing this book. In a sense, those debts extend back to my undergraduate teachers at Columbia, especially Fritz Stern and Daniel Bell, who have been models of wide learning and high intelligence. Some twenty years ago, I hoped to write a book about liberalism with my friend Stephen Holmes; that book never happened, but I have learned a great deal from him about both classical liberalism and contemporary politics in the former Soviet Union and eastern Europe. I am also indebted to many of my Princeton colleagues who have given me advice and ideas and commented on various chapters in progress. I particularly want to thank Stephen Macedo, Andrew Moravcsik, Daniel Rodgers, and Kim Scheppele. Through years of collaborative work on *The American Prospect*, I have learned immensely from my fellow editors Robert Kuttner, Robert Reich, Christopher Jencks, and Michael Tomasky. I had thought originally that some of the articles that I published in the *Prospect* would become chapters in this book; in the end, I used only bits and snatches, but the process of working through so many issues in connection with the magazine has been invaluable, particularly in thinking about "The Liberal Project Now" (the title of an article of mine in the *Prospect*'s fifteenth anniversary issue). I also want to thank my family, especially my wife Ann, who, as a literary scholar—on no less a figure than Milton—has helped me to understand the history of ideas in a more complete way.

Paul Starr
November 2006

Introduction
The Liberal Project

LIBERALISM IS DEEPLY ROOTED IN AMERICAN SOIL, SO MUCH SO, IN FACT, that in the years after World War II many historians and social scientists regarded the liberal project and the American civic creed as more or less identical. The two share the same aspirations. The proposition that each of us has a right to "life, liberty, and the pursuit of happiness" remains as good a definition as anyone has ever come up with of liberalism's first principle and America's historic promise. For some time, however, contemporary liberalism has been under political siege in the United States, and liberal ideas have lost the high ground they once commanded in moral argument and public life. The popular conservative media paint dread images of liberal beliefs and values that are unrecognizable to liberals themselves, while critics on the left in the academy are equally severe in their denunciations of liberalism, by which they usually mean something entirely different from what the conservatives are attacking. A loss of clarity is part of the difficulty. Even liberals at times appear uncertain about their convictions. In recent decades, national political leaders who are unquestionably liberal have often been unwilling to say so and unable to articulate a compelling public philosophy, while public opinion surveys show that many Americans who support liberal positions do not identify themselves as liberals. The problem is not only in the name. There is little

1

familiarity with the larger tradition of ideas that lies behind contemporary liberalism. And there is great confusion about how that tradition can be refashioned to provide guidance in the world ahead.

At its heart the liberal project is what it has always been: to create a free, fair, and prosperous society. But the ways and means of achieving that end have necessarily evolved. Every living political idea must be tested against new experience and periodically clarified and revised in light of it. Even philosophies that claim to adhere to eternal truths and original meanings quietly adjust themselves to new moral understandings and social facts. A readiness to adapt to new conditions is all the more necessary in a philosophy that asks to be judged by its real effects on human freedom and happiness and the power and peace of nations. Mere gestures toward a good society are of no interest beyond a seminar room. Liberalism stands not only for the principle that we all have an equal right to freedom but also for the hypothesis that this is a workable ideal—indeed, that liberalism, properly understood, can produce the power and wealth that make a free society more than a dream.

Liberalism is notoriously difficult to define. The term has been used to describe a sprawling profusion of ideas, practices, movements, and parties in different societies and historical periods. Often emerging as a philosophy of opposition, whether to feudal privilege, absolute monarchy, colonialism, theocracy, communism, or fascism, liberalism has served, as the word suggests, as a force for liberation, or at least liberalization—for the opening up of channels of free initiative. But liberalism in its oppositional and even revolutionary moments has not necessarily been the same as the liberalism of established parties and governments. In different countries, depending on their particular histories, parties bearing the name "Liberal" have variously ended up on the right or left and thereby colored the understanding of what liberalism means as a political philosophy. This book primarily reflects the understanding of liberalism in Britain and the United States, though it has been conceived in substantially different ways even in the Anglo-American world.

Two conceptions of liberalism chiefly concern us, as they help organize the argument in this book. In its broader meaning, liberalism refers to the fundamental principles of constitutional government and individual rights shared by modern liberals and conservatives alike, though often differently interpreted by them. This tradition of *constitutional liberalism*—classical political liberalism—emerged in the seventeenth and eighteenth centuries, culminated in the American and French Revolutions, and continues to provide the foundation of the modern liberal state. The classical liberals themselves were a diverse group, but they generally stood for freedom of conscience and religious liberty, freedom of thought and speech, the division of governmental powers, an independent civil society, and rights of private property and economic freedom that evolved in the nineteenth century into the doctrine of laissez-faire. This cluster of ideas is the principal subject of the first part of this book. The second part turns to *modern democratic liberalism*, which has developed out of the more egalitarian aspects of the broader tradition and serves as the basis of contemporary liberal politics. The relationship between liberalism in these two phases has been predominantly cumulative: while rejecting laissez-faire economic policy, modern democratic liberalism continues to take the broader tradition of constitutional liberalism as its foundation. That is why it is possible to speak not only of the two separately, but also of an overarching set of ideas that unites them.

In everyday language, "liberal" also has a meaning that predates but still bears on its political use. "Liberal" often refers to such qualities as a tolerant and open frame of mind, generosity of spirit, breadth of education, lack of prejudice, willingness to acknowledge others' rights, acceptance of disagreement and diversity, and receptiveness to innovation. These are exemplary liberal virtues, and a liberal society will promote them if it is true to its ideals. As a political doctrine, however, liberalism means something more particular—or rather, it has come to refer to a series of things, all of which, taken together, make up a design of power in support of freedom.

A great deal about that design, including its theoretical foundation, has been subject to dispute. Philosophically, liberals have started from different premises—some, for example, from a belief in natural law and natural rights; others from a utilitarian commitment to the greatest good for the greatest number; still others from a theory of history; yet others from moral principles based on equality of respect and concern for individuals and an acceptance of diverse values. Some liberals believe in the possibility of identifying a few rational and consistent principles for a just society, while others hold that politics and moral life are inherently tragic and pose choices between rival values that no philosophical system can resolve. No matter—at least for the purpose of determining what counts as liberalism. Liberals are defined more by their shared political principles than by agreement on the ultimate grounds on which those principles rest.[1]

One of those political principles, as I earlier suggested, is an equal right to freedom, where freedom has been successively understood in a more expansive way: first, as a right to civil liberty and freedom from arbitrary power; then, as a right to political liberty and a share in the government; and finally, as a right to basic requirements of human development and security necessary to assure equal opportunity and personal dignity.

Although I have described these ideas as a series of rights, they imply corresponding responsibilities that a liberal society expects of its members, individually and collectively. Inasmuch as individuals enjoy rights to civil liberty and freedom from arbitrary power, they are responsible for their own actions and what they make of their lives. Inasmuch as citizens enjoy a right to political liberty and a share of their government, they have the responsibilities of citizenship to make democracy work. And inasmuch as the members of a liberal society have a right to basic requirements of human development such as education and a minimum standard of security, they have obligations to each other, mutually and through their government, to ensure that conditions exist enabling every person to have the opportunity for success in life.[2]

The liberal project may be defined, in a preliminary way, as the effort to guarantee these freedoms and to create the institutions and forms of character that will lead a people to assume responsibility, not as an external burden imposed upon them, but from a force within. This is only a preliminary definition, however, because liberties come into conflict with each other and with other interests, and there must be a way of adjudicating among them consistent with the deepest interests in freedom and the public good. Moreover, liberalism consists of principles not only for a just society but also for the design of a state capable of sustaining that society in a world that is far from ideal.

Liberalism did not originally support an equal right to vote or policies aimed at assuring everyone an equal chance in life, but neither did it call for a "weak" state. From its origins in the seventeenth and eighteenth centuries, constitutional liberalism was concerned with both the creation and the control of power. If liberalism were antistatist at its core—that is, if it one-sidedly emphasized rights and conceived of them solely as claims against the state—the power of liberal states would be a puzzle. Liberal states have proved successful, however, not only economically but also militarily, even against regimes that were more devoted to martial values. War has not been incidental to the development of liberal democracy; the requirements of surviving in a world with other states that were armed and dangerous shaped constitutional liberalism from the start, and the pressures of war have repeatedly provided the stimulus for the expansion of democratic citizenship.

Constitutionalism itself, and even more so a liberal constitution with its emphasis on the protection of individual rights, is a system of enabling constraints. Freedom from arbitrary power implies the rule of law, and a government that abides by its own laws is more likely to abide by other commitments, such as paying its debts. Anyone who makes a promise and keeps it, even at great cost, knows that this is the only way to build up and retain trust. By binding those in power, making their behavior more predictable and reliable, and thereby increasing the trust and confidence of citizens, creditors, and investors, constitutionalism amplifies the long-term power and wealth of a state. Constitutional liberalism imposes a further discipline by dividing power within the state and between state and society and requiring public disclosure and discussion of state decisions—all of these serving as limits on the ability of officials to pursue their own private interests and enabling the citizens to control their government. Liberalism wagers that a state so constructed can be strong yet constrained—indeed, strong *because* constrained.[3] This is the classical theory of freedom's power.

Although early constitutional liberalism was not democratic, modern liberal democracies have been built on the ground that it prepared. Although classical economic liberalism did not favor extensive state intervention in the economy, modern liberalism has developed within the framework of a capitalist economy whose logic the classical economists were first to grasp. The liberals of the eighteenth century would find the technological world we live in today as strange as another planet, but the constitutional principles of modern liberal governments to be recognizably their own. The basic characteristics of liberalism—its individualism, egalitarianism, universality, and meliorism—have made it capable of extension and adaptation. Early constitutional liberals did not acknowledge all members of society as full citizens, but the groups denied equal rights were able to claim them on the basis of general principles that liberals had laid down. In providing for representative institutions and a free press, moreover, constitutional liberalism established a model for public supervision of the state that unlike the classical polis of ancient city republics proved amenable to democratic extension in large-scale modern societies. Engineers use the term "scalability" to refer to a feature of systems that can work effectively at increasing dimensions. Because constitutional liberalism proved to be scalable, it also proved adaptable and durable under conditions that its original exponents could not foresee.

A series of changes during the nineteenth and early twentieth centuries pushed liberal politics and thought toward their modern form. At the heart of this shift was the democratization of liberalism. A few eighteenth-century liberals were genuine democrats, but early liberal thought typically justified limiting political participation only to men with property on the grounds that they alone had both an independent will and a stake in a well-ordered society. Liberalism without democracy, however, proved an unstable combination in the face of the social and economic changes and popular movements accompanying industrialization and economic growth, and by the early twentieth century liberals generally stood for the political equality of all citizens, men and women. Democracy was workable, liberals believed, only through the extension of education and the creation of civic organizations that would promote responsible citizenship and political cooperation across class lines. Political inclusion, in this view, involved not just extending the right to vote but integrating new voters into the traditions of constitutional government and social reform.

A second development was the emergence of a positive conception of freedom based on the idea of self-determination. Liberalism would never have been as attractive a set of ideas if it had consisted only of a negative conception of freedom or a purely rational understanding of the self. Influenced particularly by German idealism and the romantic movement, liberals during the nineteenth century came increasingly to view freedom as self-realization and to emphasize the claims of individual expression and the cultivation of the aesthetic and moral faculties. Liberalism was already identified with the idea that the young, rather than following a course prescribed by tradition and their elders, ought to be free to choose their occupation, spouse, and path in life. Eighteenth-century liberalism, however, tended to see the passions as a derangement of reason. Liberalism in a romantic key restored the passions to a legitimate role in politics, emphasized an ideal of authenticity—of faithfulness to one's inner nature—and demanded changes in society to allow the flowering of the individual personality. Some liberals also conceived the same ideals as applying to entire peoples. Just as individuals ought to be free to determine their lives, so ought every nation to be free to determine its future and develop its own culture. While some liberals in the nineteenth and early twentieth centuries were drawn to imperialism, others offered a vision of a peaceful international system made up of self-determining peoples, held together not by conquest but by free trade.

Both the democratization of liberalization and the growing emphasis on freedom as self-determination worked in favor of a third movement—the liberal advocacy of more positive government. As the right to vote was extended, liberals had to appeal to wider constituencies among the working class and the poor in competition with socialists and others to their left, and this competition led them to become more sympathetic to demands for substantive as well as formal equality, to endorse the rights of labor unions, and to support more active intervention in the economy. The conception of freedom as self-determination favored universal public education and other means of achieving equal opportunity. In Britain during the nineteenth century, support for much of the early regulation of factories and working hours cut across the Conservative and Liberal Parties, and an administrative revolution inspired greater confidence in the capacity of government to undertake new functions. Doctrinaire laissez-faire was already outside of the mainstream of British liberalism by the 1880s; by the turn of the century, the dominant New Liberalism called for state intervention to achieve greater social equality and to protect individuals against downturns in the economy and other adverse turns in life that could destroy their independence. The older liberals, including the classical economists, had supported a limited role for government in advancing social equality, primarily through education. What was new was liberal support for such policies as workers' compensation, unemployment insurance, national health insurance, and old-age pensions, which in continental Europe originated with conservative, Catholic, and social democratic parties. Britain's New Liberals saw that these pillars of the welfare state could be constructed on liberal lines; contributory insurance programs, for example, preserved the concept of individually earned benefits. Progressives in the United States began to adopt these ideas in the early 1900s, while calling for new measures such as antitrust legislation and financial regulation to control the growing power of private corporations and concentrated wealth. Liberals also increasingly favored progressive taxation and, still later, government spending to manage the business cycle and reduce unemployment. The almost continuous crisis of the twentieth century from World War I through the Depression, World War II, and the Cold War played a crucial role in consolidating liberal support for an enlarged state.

Yet that long crisis also had the effect of strengthening liberal commitments to individual freedom. The creation of a governmental propaganda machine and the suppression of dissent during World War I and its aftermath proved a turning point in the liberal view of the state and led to the establishment of organizations to protect civil liberties. In the United States, those who had earlier called themselves "progressives" now began describing themselves as "liberals," partly to emphasize continuities with the philosophical traditions of liberalism and an affinity with Britain's

New Liberals. (Ironically, the adoption of the term "liberal" in the United States during the post–World War I era came just as Britain's Liberal Party imploded and gave way to the Labour Party.) The mid-twentieth century saw a continued double movement: the growing regulation of the economy, along with stronger protections of civil liberties and the deregulation of culture and private life. Even as liberals favored a wider role for government in social and economic policy, they sought to impose constraints on the discretionary use of political power—for example, through the development of professionalism within government; protections for the independence of science; checks on government performance through empirical social research and independent, professional journalism; and a strong role for the courts as guardians of constitutionally protected freedoms. In short, while liberalism came to support new powers for the state, it also embraced new ways of checking and limiting those powers.

Through the mid-twentieth century, liberalism occupied the political center, offering a middle way between communism and socialism, on the left, and conservatism and authoritarianism, on the right. That is not to say all liberals were moderate. A liberal in nineteenth-century Britain who advocated universal public education, full equality for religious minorities, and equal rights for women was a radical for the time; so too an American in the mid-twentieth century who advocated universal health insurance, full equality for racial minorities, and—some issues don't go away—equal rights for women. These goals, however radical they may have appeared, remained firmly within a liberal framework insofar as they called for equal rights to freedom under a constitutionally limited, democratic government with a predominantly private, market-driven economy. Socialists often said liberals were objectively no different from conservatives because they both supported capitalism, while conservatives often said liberals were tantamount to socialists because they both supported collectivism. But socialists wanted to replace capitalism with collective ownership of industry and finance, whereas liberals wanted to reform capitalism while preserving private ownership. And whereas conservatives generally defended the inequalities produced in the market and the interests of corporations and private wealth, liberals wanted to limit the extreme disparities of wealth and power that threatened to make a mockery of the ideals of democratic government and equal opportunity.

As liberalism has evolved, so has conservatism—and the grounds of conflict between them have changed. The classical opposition in the eighteenth century was between a liberalism that upheld the principles of individual freedom and equality against a conservatism that defended a more hierarchical, paternalistic, and tradition-minded society. Beginning with the embrace of laissez-faire in the early nineteenth century, however, conservatives in the Anglo-American world underwent their own liberalization, even as they continued to uphold the values of tradition, authority, and social hierarchy. The conversion of conservatives to universal suffrage came more slowly in Britain than in America. But in both countries, especially the United States, modern democratic conservatism has become a combination, in varying degrees, of devotion to the free market and social traditionalism. Each side of conservatism has provided a justification of inequalities that liberalism has attempted to reduce or eliminate. The two political philosophies offer contrasting ways of resolving conflicts among liberties. Conservatives have generally given higher priority to property rights and, accordingly, to the rights of those with property; liberals have given higher priority and broader scope to other constitutional liberties and civil rights, often those of the historically disadvantaged. In struggles over rights and equality, conservatives have generally opposed the liberal enlargement of freedom of expression and other civil liberties and the extension of rights to subordinate social groups, though they have usually assented at least to formal rights after the fact.

By the mid-twentieth century, most conservatives had also accommodated themselves to the public provision of education and social and economic security. The liberal consensus of the post–World War II era extended considerably beyond the foundations of constitutionalism and democracy. It encompassed public education, most elements of the welfare state, progressive taxation of income and estates, Keynesian management of the business cycle, and the regulation of finance and such industries as communications where, it was generally agreed, unregulated markets suffered from endemic problems of inefficiency, inequity, or instability.

In the United States, the liberalism of the 1950s and '60s was both a governing and a reforming philosophy. Liberals had helped to fashion the domestic order created during the New Deal, and after World War II they had shaped America's international commitments aimed at containing communist expansion and avoiding war. Liberals also sought, however, to compel a government that espoused liberal principles to confront its own contradictions and limitations. That meant, among other things, dealing with the national shame of racial oppression, the persistence of poverty, the hidden problems of environmental degradation, and the threat of nuclear catastrophe.

The liberal project of the post–World War II era was to awaken the public to long-ignored problems, to make liberal government bolder, and to get its leaders to take political risks. In the public mind, liberalism was the innovative and outward-looking force in American politics; conservatism, the stodgy and parochial source of resistance. And, in fact, liberalism did bring about important changes in American life, particularly in racial and gender relations, though at great political cost. Perhaps no one should have expected otherwise.

Although the erosion began during the turmoil of the 1960s, the political foundations of the liberal consensus took decades to collapse. Until 1980, liberals had an effective presence in both major political parties, but they achieved their goals primarily via the Democrats. By the century's end, not only had the Democrats lost their status as the majority party, primarily as a result of their loss of the South and of white men in all regions. The Republican Party had also become far more conservative. The decline of the Democrats and the conservative revolution within the Republican Party transformed the relationship of ideology and power in the United States. Benefiting from a close though uneasy relation with the Democrats, liberalism had long been the ideologically active force in American politics. Now conservatism became the source of ideological energy as the Republicans took the intellectuals of both the free-market and religious right into a governing partnership.

The conservative reaction began with a backlash against the liberalism of the 1960s but turned into a wholesale repudiation of the mid-twentieth-century liberal consensus. In domestic affairs, conservatives sought to undo the progressive taxation of incomes and estates; to privatize government services, including Social Security and schools; to deregulate markets, including finance, communications, and energy; and to reverse the framework of constitutional interpretation dating to the 1930s and covering such issues as federal powers and relations of church and state. In foreign policy, conservatives rejected liberal internationalism in favor of a unilateralist foreign policy with more emphasis on military force. In the collapse of the Soviet Union, conservatives saw a vindication of these policies, and in the aftermath of September 11, 2001, they saw grounds for renewing them. The collapse of Soviet communism and socialism generally also contributed to a triumphalist belief in free markets and the unrestrained exercise of American power. And the same triumphalist spirit encouraged some conservatives to bring the Cold War home in a war on liberalism.

During the mid-twentieth century, liberals had power to the extent that they could bring about change, while conservatives had power to the extent that they could stop it. Now the relationships have been reversed, and liberalism risks getting defined, as conservatism once was, entirely in negative terms. Although liberals need to defend liberal accomplishments, they cannot allow themselves to become merely defensive and oppositional. The challenge they face today is to avoid this trap, to make the case for liberalism's first principles, to renew the work of liberal innovation, and to convince their fellow citizens to make the American project a liberal project once again. Clarity about what liberalism stands for is an essential step in awakening the force of its ideas. That, in any event, is the premise of this book. The more fundamental the challenge that liberals face, the greater is the need to explain the grounds of liberal commitments and to give Americans good reasons to make those commitments their own. Liberalism's own power begins within.

I
CONSTITUTIONAL
LIBERALISM

———

1

Liberalism and the Discipline of Power

———

THE CHARGE USED TO BE LEVELED BY FASCISTS AND COMMUNISTS; NOW it comes chiefly from conservatives. Liberalism, they say, is a kind of weakness. If the charge were true—if liberal institutions and political leaders were unequal to the demands of national defense and personal security—it would have been a catastrophe for liberal democracy during the great crises of the twentieth century, and the world would look altogether different today. But this has not been the historical experience: liberal government has repeatedly proved stronger and more durable than its adversaries expected. And therein lies a critical lesson about liberalism, at least liberalism rightly understood.

The core principles of liberalism provide not only a theory of freedom, equality, and the public good, but also a discipline of power—the means of creating power as well as controlling it. This discipline has been a singular achievement of constitutional liberalism, dating from the late seventeenth and eighteenth centuries, and of modern, democratic liberalism as it has evolved roughly since the late nineteenth century.

Liberal constitutions impose constraints on the power of any single public official or branch of government as well as the state as a whole. The constraints protect citizens from tyranny, but that is not all they do. They also serve to protect the state itself from capricious, impulsive, or overreaching decisions. A central insight of liberalism is that power

15

arbitrarily exercised is destructive not only of individual liberty but also of the rule of law. Limiting arbitrary power encourages confidence that the law will be fair and thereby increases the state's ability to secure cooperation without the imposition of force. Limiting the scope of state power increases the likelihood of its effective use as well as the ability of society to generate wealth, knowledge, and other resources that a state may draw upon in an hour of need. That, at least, has been the theory of power—of freedom's power—implicit in constitutional liberalism. And the historic rise of liberal states to become the most powerful in the world suggests that the theory has worked astonishingly well in practice.

Constitutional liberalism is the common heritage of both modern conservatives and liberals, as those terms are understood in the Anglo-American world. In the eighteenth century, however, constitutional liberalism was far from fully democratic. Britain and the early American republic excluded the majority of people from the franchise and other rights, and even after working-class men gained the right to vote, liberal governments in Europe and North America continued to reject the claims of women and racial minorities. Modern democratic liberalism diverged from its conservative sibling, however, as it embraced the claims of historically excluded groups and a more comprehensive vision of equality. Even with the basic disputes over the franchise and civil rights long resolved, the line between liberalism and conservatism continues to be drawn partly on this basis.

In addition, modern liberals have split from conservatives on the role of the state in the face of depression, war, and economic insecurity. Liberals have insisted that government can take on broader functions without sacrificing individual freedom as long as the law provides strong safeguards against arbitrary power. Democratic liberalism, therefore, has called not just for broader social protections but also for stronger guarantees of civil liberties. Conservatives and liberals have also responded differently to a phenomenon that did not exist in the eighteenth century when constitutional liberalism took shape: the modern corporation. While conservatives have treated private corporations as analogous to individuals and deserving of the same liberties, liberals have regarded corporations as a phenomenon of power, needing control like government itself. The discipline of power that constitutional liberalism imposes upon the state modern liberalism attempts to impose on the corporation, albeit not in the same way.

Divisions between conservatives and liberals over foreign policy and national security also reflect different theories of power. In general, conservatives have put greater emphasis on military power, been quicker to resort to force, and regarded international institutions warily, whereas liberals have sought to create an international order that helps to safeguard national sovereignty, enlarges the sphere of liberal democracy, and minimizes the need for force. While conservatives have often regarded international law and institutions as subtracting from national power, liberals have seen them as adding to it. Just as liberalism has historically sought to protect individual rights through the rule of law and limits on unbridled power at home, so it has sought to project those same norms of respect for law, life, and liberty into the international arena—conscious, however, that force may ultimately be necessary for self-defense and that force spent unwisely may undermine security rather than ensure it.

In short, like constitutional liberalism, modern democratic liberalism seeks to promote the creation as well as the control of power. Rights for the unpropertied, racial minorities, and women are not simply a check on the powerful; full inclusion also promotes a more creative and productive society. The expanded sphere of state action has enabled liberal governments to contend successfully with war and other crises and to promote economic growth and stability. In disciplining the market as well as the state, the central liberal objective has been not just to circumscribe power in private hands, but also to make the market more productive within its appropriate scope. A liberal international order promises to conserve and augment national power as well as properly regulate it. Power disciplined is not necessarily power reduced. Discipline may impart greater legitimacy, a sharpened focus, and more judicious direction to power—to a kind of power, moreover, that supports freedom instead of destroying it.

POWER AND LIBERTY

Power is essential to liberty, yet power is also inimical to liberty—it all depends on the kind of power and its use, and on our understanding of liberty. In a generic sense, power is the capacity of an individual, group, state, or some other agent to bring about effects. Power in this general sense—"power to"—encompasses whatever capacity a society or any other collectivity may have to realize common values or purposes. To say that an individual or some other agent is powerful, however, usually means that it can bring about one particular kind of result: It can prevail over others—it can get them to do something they do not want to do, defeat them in a conflict, or perhaps even shape their understanding and desires.[1]

Whether this kind of power—"power over"—is compatible with liberty depends on whether it is subject to law, norms of fairness, and public accountability. Liberal principles for the discipline of power have a threefold purpose: to constrain "power over" that is arbitrary, despotic, and overweening; to establish rules for the legitimate exercise of power; and to enlarge the overall capacities of both individuals and societies. The central liberal hypothesis about power is that constraints on despotic "power over" contribute to greater societal "power to." Or, as the political theorist Stephen Holmes has put it, limited power can be "more powerful than unlimited power."[2]

Liberal constitutions, for example, call for checks and balances, public deliberation, periodic elections, and other institutional mechanisms to prevent state power from becoming despotic. But constitutions are not purely negative in purpose or effect. They also provide a plan for the exercise of legitimate powers and a conceptual framework for politics. Indeed, constitutions may become the very basis of national identity and patriotism and thereby an instrument for building nations as well as their governments. Or to put it in other terms, some constitutions are constitutive of both a nation and its state, not merely regulative of a state's conduct.

If well designed, liberal constitutions create states with advantages in power and performance over their illiberal rivals. Public deliberation invites ideas and information that autocrats do not receive or are unlikely to heed. A state with checks and balances and public accountability for governmental performance will be more likely to correct its mistakes. And those who lose political conflicts after discussion and voting are more likely to be reconciled to the outcome and to cooperate with the winners than if they are excluded from participation. To be sure, public deliberation may slow down decisionmaking in urgent situations, and elections may produce inconclusive results. The art of constitutional design lies partly in minimizing the chances of paralysis where decisions are imperative. The liberal premise is that although these risks are real, the advantages of constitutional government outweigh them.

Liberal principles also aim to bar private forms of despotic power by, for example, prohibiting slavery and regulating predatory and abusive aspects of commercial and even domestic relationships. Again, laws embodying liberal principles are not purely negative; to some extent, they also prescribe rules for legitimate transactions and relationships to ensure that they are entered into freely and observe minimum standards of fairness. Moreover, just as liberal principles call for checks and balances within government, so they call for a wide dispersion of power in both the private economy and civil society. Concentrations of private power undermine the effort to keep *political* power divided and limited; hence, even apart from concerns about economic efficiency, liberals from the eighteenth century to the present have often called for breaking up monopolies, broadening the ownership of land, and extending literacy and education.

These commitments follow from the recognition that liberty is most likely to be preserved when citizens themselves have the power to preserve it. When freedom does its work, it creates a self-reinforcing cycle. Free speech and freedom of association, for example, empower civil society, and the private organizations that grow up on that basis can then use their power to sustain their rights. Newspapers, for example, become jealous guardians of the freedom of the press. But monopoly turns this process on its head; if the press itself becomes monopolized, those who control it may become too great an arbiter of political life, inhibiting free discussion rather than enabling it. Modern democratic liberalism differs from its free-market rival partly in its support for stronger measures to decentralize private power and stronger guarantees against private forms of domination—for example, by calling for countervailing rights to private corporations, such as the rights of workers to collective bargaining and of consumers to information about corporate practices. In the same spirit, modern liberalism has also sought to extend to the private economy guarantees of equal treatment of racial and religious minorities, women, and other groups that have historically suffered from discrimination.

These measures to decentralize and limit private power and to combat discrimination require state intervention in the private decisions made in the market and civil society. But liberalism, according to some of its exponents and many of its critics, conceives of liberty only as non-interference by the state. This notion may suggest that liberals resist state power at every instant, despite the manifest fact that liberal states have been immensely powerful. The conception of liberty as non-interference does fit libertarian thought, but it does not express the full understanding of liberty and power even in the classical liberalism of the eighteenth century, much less in its modern democratic forms.

Liberty is a species of power—the power to make choices about what is rightfully yours, free of removable hindrances.[3] But while anxious to guard a sphere of individual choice and private life from state control, liberalism has never stood for the anarchist and romantic view that all state power is inherently repressive. Liberals have typically supported a state strong enough, at a minimum, to defend itself against external enemies, to enforce the rule of law, to provide for public goods inadequately produced in the marketplace, to control anticompetitive practices, and to uphold the rights of individuals against such internal threats to their liberty as private oligarchs, local overlords, and religious sects or clans capable of fanatical cruelty toward each other and their own members.

It is not only to the state that liberals are concerned liberty may be lost. Rights of free speech and free assembly also vanish where the fear of mobs or thugs prevents people from speaking freely or meeting together. Weak states undermine the foundations of liberty as much as the foundations of order; even "negative liberty" depends on the state's active presence in society, not merely on the "silence" of the law. Rights have no meaning except within the context of a state capable of upholding them. No state, no rights. No law, no liberty.

But by the same token, modern liberalism holds that insofar as government acquires more power, it ought to be held accountable, checked internally, and balanced by a countervailing recognition of rights. Modern liberalism does not sacrifice liberty to power. It raises the equilibrium of power and liberty to a higher level.

HOW LIBERALISM WORKS

Much political analysis assumes that if one group or individual has more power, others must have less, and that is true in certain contexts. In a war, greater military power on one side necessarily means less power on the other. But not all social life is war. Some social arrangements make it possible to expand the sum of social power, particularly over time. Liberal states have been precisely that—exceptionally productive systems of power creation.

Law lies at the base of this system, simultaneously constraining power and enlarging it. The rule of law—a first principle of liberalism, though not exclusive to it—demands, among other things, that laws be general, public, unalterable retroactively, and applied the same regardless of the individuals involved.[4] These requirements, insofar as they are realized in practice, give individuals leverage to resist arbitrary acts of state, but states also derive a benefit from them. By upholding the rule of law, including a commitment to apply the law to themselves, rulers may be better able to attract investment, obtain credit, and sustain popular loyalty and cooperation. They may also be able to reduce power-depleting rivalries among clans and factions by convincing them that the state represents an impartial arbiter of their claims and discouraging those who feel wronged from adopting private alternatives to law, such as by seeking revenge for crimes or personal affronts. Where private vengeance rules, some individuals or groups certainly have more power than others—they can prevail over them. But violent feuds deplete society of the power necessary to achieve collective ends. The rule of law offers an alternative to private justice that instead of consuming power increases it.

The rule of law also offers a model of how states can advance individual liberty along with societal powers. For when the law is general, public, stable, and so on, individuals are not only less subject to arbitrary power but also at greater liberty to plan their lives. And insofar as their plans include long-term investments, the society may be more prosperous and the state capable of raising greater revenue. This is the virtuous cycle of power and liberty that the rule of law allows and that constitutional liberalism ideally extends.

In a different way, guarantees of religious toleration and freedom of conscience exemplify the logic of liberalism as a foundation for a stable polity. Internecine religious conflicts and wars of religion, like revenge feuds, deplete the powers of states and societies. Religious toleration serves not only to allow people to worship differently but also to reduce conflict, facilitate economic exchange, and create a wider pool of talent for productive work and the state itself. By dividing religion from law— that is, by excluding religion from any binding social consensus—states guaranteeing religious freedom allow people of different faiths to cooperate under a political order that does not threaten to extinguish any of the various theological doctrines they support.

Religious toleration has also served as a paradigm for the state's acceptance of pluralism in other cultural and moral controversies. Where divisions over the meaning of the good life are deep and irreconcilable, the state's neutrality among competing perspectives furthers mutual forbearance, cooperation, and the growth of societal powers. The neutrality of the liberal state, however, does not apply to all matters of moral judgment. Liberalism not only regards people as worthy of being treated equally but holds that each individual life has positive value, and the laws and policies of a liberal state ought to embody that principle, though citizens may well disagree about how to interpret it. As each life has value, so do the health and well-being of the community: liberal policies in support of public health and a salubrious and sustainable environment stem from commitments that are moral in their inspiration. And because education necessarily cultivates character as well as intelligence, a liberal society will properly use its schools to pass on to the young such moral qualities as integrity, perseverance, empathy, and personal and civic responsibility. But just as liberalism excludes religion from a binding social consensus, so it accepts a diversity of cultural and moral practices that cause no harm to others. The framework of a liberal society is only a framework—that is, it provides space for free development, allowing for differences and promoting cooperation. We may justify religious freedom and cultural diversity on the grounds of individual rights and autonomy or the equal respect due people of different faiths and values. But the potential of liberty to promote stable cooperation and state power helps to explain why states that adopted religious toleration continued to maintain it and why they have expanded the scope of pluralism.

These kinds of effects on societal power are crucial in accounting for liberalism's historical rise. The liberal hypothesis is not that each and every constraint on power serves the utilitarian purpose of enlarging societal powers, much less that every rule should be tested solely on that criterion. Rather, the hypothesis is that liberal constraints on power, when taken as a whole, have created stronger self-corrective political mechanisms, a more innovative and productive economy, broader societal cooperation, and other formidable advantages. Mechanisms of this kind help to explain why liberal ideas became the basis of enduring liberal states.

THE ORIGINS OF CONSTITUTIONAL LIBERALISM

Constitutional liberalism emerged in the late seventeenth and eighteenth centuries, expounded in the writing of, among others, John Locke, Montesquieu, and the framers of the U.S. Constitution (particularly James Madison), and later in the work of such figures as Benjamin Constant, Alexis de Tocqueville, and John Stuart Mill. Government based on the rule of law, separation of powers, popular consent through representative assemblies, religious toleration and freedom of conscience, protection of the rights of property, and guarantees of freedom of the press and other liberties—these were the core ideas of constitutional liberalism. Each of the elements making up this cluster had a prior history, often extending back to the medieval or even the ancient world. But they came together as a coherent philosophy in the eighteenth century.

According to historical convention, England's Glorious Revolution of 1688—a victory, albeit qualified, for constitutional government, religious toleration, and property rights—marked the beginning of liberalism's influence on politics and government. "Early classical" or simply "early" liberalism is the term I use to describe the phase of liberal politics and philosophy running through the American Revolution and first stages of the French Revolution. In liberal thought, this is the century bracketed, at one end, by the publication of Locke's *Two Treatises on Government* and *Letter on Toleration* (1690) and at the other end by the American Declaration of Independence and Adam Smith's *The Wealth of Nations* (both 1776), the U.S. Constitution and the *Federalist Papers* (1787–88), and the French Declaration of the Rights of Man and of Citizens (1789).

The publication of Smith's work toward the end of this period marked the beginning of an important turn. Although early liberalism was vitally concerned with property rights and economic freedom, the idea of a self-regulating economy came later. Classical economics and the politics of laissez-faire were largely a nineteenth-century development, a branching off from the main trunk. The earlier tradition of constitutional liberalism was concerned with the creation as well as the control of legitimate and effective state power. And it is from those foundations that the strongest continuities may be found connecting liberalism throughout its history, down to the present.

Early liberalism overlapped with another set of political ideas in the early modern world: the neo-Roman, or civic republican, tradition revived in Florence and other cities of the Italian Renaissance and later taken up in Britain and its American colonies by forces resisting the claims and impositions of the British state. Although some historians of ideas set republicanism and early liberalism in stark opposition to one another, the two were intermingled in political thought. Both abhorred despotism and aimed to protect liberty through independent representative assemblies and other checks on executive discretion. The neo-Roman tradition portrayed political life as a contest of corruption and virtue. The villains of the republican story were self-aggrandizing rulers and their servile courtiers; its heroes were landowning gentlemen who because of their property and civic-mindedness were able to act independently and courageously in defense of freedom against the ever-threatening encroachments of power. The neo-Roman tradition held that to be free a man had to live in a free state—individual liberty was bound up in civic liberty—but the republican conception of the political community was limited to an exclusive, landowning elite. During the seventeenth and eighteenth centuries, radical opponents of the absolutist state used republican arguments to call for strengthening parliamentary powers or doing away with monarchy altogether on the grounds that any submission to the arbitrary will of a king constituted enslavement.[5]

Although the neo-Roman tradition provided an influential frame for early-modern political thought, it was anchored to an agrarian past and hostile to emerging capitalism. Liberalism, in contrast, welcomed modernity, science, innovation, and commerce and by the late eighteenth century offered a theory of economic development and historical progress. Liberalism emerged during the Enlightenment and reflected its influence, and many of the leading figures of the Enlightenment figured prominently in the shaping of liberal ideas through their historical imagination, commitments to reason and skepticism, sense of expansive human possibility, desire to reduce cruelty, and practical interests in reform. But the Enlightenment and early liberalism were not identical, especially in regard to political philosophy. Much of the Enlightenment was conservative and illiberal, and some of the leading philosophes were apologists for hereditary privilege and "enlightened despotism," an idea wholly antithetical to liberal constitutional principles.

Constitutionalism itself is older than liberalism, dating back to ancient Greece and Rome, but the most direct influences come from the medieval world. Under feudal charters such as the Magna Carta, rulers guaranteed rights and immunities to particular estates and corporations and agreed to abide by limitations on their powers exercised from time to time by the estates' representatives. During the sixteenth and seventeenth centuries, however, "medieval constitutionalism" collapsed in

much of continental Europe as monarchs increasingly governed by prerogative and effectively put the traditional consultative assemblies to
sleep. England remained the great exception to this pattern. The liberal theory of constitutionalism, as developed by Locke, Montesquieu,
and the American founders, drew on the English tradition but involved
more than a reassertion of checks on executive power and demand for
the rule of law. Constitutional liberalism called for generalizing and extending such principles as separation of powers and guarantees of life,
liberty, and property far beyond their old boundaries.[6]

England, the United States, and France exemplified three different
paths toward constitutional liberalism. The English acquired their
liberties—the plural is important here—through a long process of accre-
tion, without any single comprehensive or abstract formulation. By the
late seventeenth century, they conceived of their unwritten constitution as a balance among king, lords, and commons that protected their
liberties while maintaining harmony, hierarchy, and order. This constitution, however, existed only as an inference from the laws; it did not
antedate or stand above them, and thus it could be changed through ordinary legislation. Working within this framework, English liberalism
sought, one reform at a time, to eliminate the legal vestiges of feudalism,
to extend the sphere of individual liberty, and, if not to limit the state,
then to subject its expansion to a constitutional discipline.

The United States built its legal system on English foundations, incorporating English liberties into the Bill of Rights and adopting the
common law, but Americans radically changed the idea of a constitution. They invented the practice of writing constitutions through spe-
cially convened assemblies and submitting them to public discussion
and ratification. The U.S. Constitution, unlike England's, prospec-
tively created the state, established the conceptual framework of politics, and became a regulative standard above ordinary legislation. In
proposing and adopting a comprehensive structure of government created afresh, America's founding generation displayed a breathtaking
confidence in the human capacity for rational design of the state that
was utterly foreign to the English belief in the cumulative genius of political tradition. In the Declaration of Independence, the Americans of

the Revolutionary era also inscribed abstract ideals of liberty and equality into their national creed. In short, while English constitutionalism grew out of the historical and particular, American constitutionalism added to it elements that were rational and universal.

The French Revolution took that rationalism and universality one step further, repudiating the traditional liberties of the Old Regime as mere privileges and overthrowing them entirely in the name of abstract ideals of liberty and equality. In the same spirit, France's revolutionaries saw the Anglo-American devotion to separation of powers as a medieval vestige and placed full sovereignty in a single assembly. But the Revolution's uprooted abstractions and unified structure of the popular will proved no protection against terror and despotism. In the United States, constitutional liberalism was the legacy of a successful revolution that became the basis of a national creed (although it would take the Civil War to overcome the contradiction between slavery and freedom that had been left unresolved at the nation's founding). In France, constitutional liberals were merely a political faction during most of the nineteenth century, and constitutional liberalism remained the disputed lesson of a revolution that had failed to institutionalize itself.

The conservative reaction triggered by the French Revolution and its aftermath weighed heavily on liberalism in England and on the continent well into the nineteenth century. Liberal parties generally subscribed to the principles of religious toleration and constitutional government, but in the wake of the French Revolution they tended to be wary of democracy and to interpret political liberties such as free speech in narrow terms. The cause that became of greatest importance to them was economic freedom. With the rise of classical economics and laissez-faire came a conception of liberalism as being devoted to an ideal of negative liberty and a general hostility to the state. But this economic liberalism of the nineteenth century represented a shift from the more complex view of the state expressed in earlier liberal political thought. Constitutional liberalism sought both to create and to contain power—and nowhere was that dual interest more evident than when the foundations of the liberal state were built in seventeenth-century England and eighteenth-century America.

2

The Creative Reluctance of Liberal Statecraft

———

Why did constitutionally limited states ever become more powerful than states with unlimited powers? If constitutions primarily restrict rulers—and if classical liberalism, as many conceive it, was mainly antistatist—states with liberal constitutions should have been history's weaklings. Yet the two countries that originated constitutional liberalism rose successively to world power, first England in the eighteenth century, then the United States in the twentieth. Of course, no simple equation of constitutionalism and power and no iron law of progress guaranteed their achievements. History offers us too many contingencies, and the future too many uncertainties, to warrant any confidence that constitutional liberalism was inevitable or that it is irreversible, much less that it will forever remain internationally dominant.

Still, the record of the past three centuries is impressive. Circa 1700, compared to the major continental European powers, England had what many historians have described as a small, even weak state. Indeed, the English prided themselves on their government's limits during the next two centuries even as their country exerted power abroad that was vastly out of proportion to its population and resources. And before the twentieth century, the United States was sometimes said to have no state whatsoever, at least none in the proper, European sense. But appearances, even national self-images, can be deceiving. Britain and the

29

United States did not suddenly emerge as superpowers from no power at all. At critical points of constitutional formation, they established a machinery for both creating and controlling power that ultimately proved a source of immense political advantage.

But perhaps a simple economic explanation accounts for the rise of English and American power: power comes from wealth. Liberal regimes, you may say, enjoyed higher rates of economic growth than did absolutist states because they left the private economy alone, and the resulting wealth translated into higher tax revenues, greater military strength, and finally international power. Although power is partly a function of wealth, this argument runs into two difficulties. Economies do not—and did not—develop in a political vacuum merely by being left alone, and wealth never automatically yields state power. Some nations have historically suffered from what an Englishman in 1784, after the decline of the Dutch Republic, called the "Dutch disease," a condition that makes a people "rich perhaps, as individuals, but weak, as a state."[1] Rather than becoming dominant, such a state may prove a tempting takeover target for its neighbors or be repeatedly overrun by greater powers. For wealth to become the basis of power, a state must be capable of extracting resources, using them efficiently, and directing them expressly to desired political ends. In short, wealth equals power only if a state has the capacity to convert one to the other—wealth to power, and power to wealth.

But once we set aside the simple economic explanation, we meet a second, more sinister possibility. Perhaps constitutional liberalism has been only a facade obscuring a deeper, invisible, and therefore more effective system of domination. Oh, yes, you may acknowledge, a liberal constitution may promise individual freedom, but those promises are mere words. The true nature of domination lies elsewhere, at the level of everyday assumptions, systems of knowledge, and social practices that suppress subversive ideas and troublesome behavior, creating a disciplined and regulated society, prepared for empire. This view is also not wholly incorrect. Social discipline, like wealth, is certainly a factor in power. A state has less need to expend force in a society where ingrained patterns of conduct and thought produce a high level of compliance with the law. Discipline conserves and magnifies power, and this is no hidden secret. The architects of limited government well understood that it can flourish only with a complementary culture of self-restraint, and the rise of liberal constitutionalism might have been impossible without a prior "disciplinary revolution."

But is social discipline always the enemy of freedom? In some respects, yes—if discipline, to take an extreme case, prevents slaves from fighting for their own liberation. No free people, however, can do without law, and only discipline can make law workable. To equate discipline with domination is to see discipline operating only in one direction, as an imposition of power upon liberty. But a liberal constitution imposes discipline on the state itself, and that discipline—and the freedom it allows—brings power into clearer view. By opening up courts, legislatures, and political debate to the public at large and insisting on public justification of decisions, constitutional liberalism has made power more transparent and subjected it to scrutiny and disagreement. Power in the liberal state has not grown up unnoticed; it has been questioned, criticized, resisted, and constrained—and, as a result, made more legitimate.

Recognizing that dynamic affords a better understanding of the relationship of constitutional liberalism and power. Liberal states have emerged amid a characteristic tension: the expansion of state powers has typically met demands for limitation and accountability. The peculiar internal tension of liberal constitutions is that they constrain power even as they authorize it—that is, they attempt to curb the despotic power and ambitions of individual rulers and officials and, by doing so, to permit stronger systemic capacities. The sociologist Michael Mann proposes that we think of modern states as "despotically weak" but "infrastructurally strong."[2] Despotic "weakness," however, is another name for legal and constitutional limitation, and it is actually not weakness at all. By constraining those who exercise state power, liberal constitutions make a state more predictable and reliable, hence more worthy of trust by creditors and investors as well as citizens. Constitutional liberalism thereby enhances the capacity of the state to borrow, tax, and conscript—all of which contribute to "infrastructural" strength—without suffocating private initiative and economic growth. Far from simply be-ing antistatist, constitutional liberalism has turned out to be an excep-tionally effective strategy for state-building. If we want to know why states with limited powers became more powerful than states with un-limited powers, this is where we have to look—to the creative reluc-tance of liberal statecraft.

CONSTITUTIONALISM AND POWER IN ENGLAND

It is one of the seeming paradoxes of English history. The Glorious Revo-lution of 1688–89 brought only modest change, hardly amounting by it-self to a historic turning point. One monarch gave way to another when James II, a Catholic who had alienated both Whigs and Tories, lost con-fidence in his soldiers' loyalty and fled to France in the face of an invad-ing Dutch army led by his Protestant nephew and son-in-law, William of Orange. Meeting initially as a Convention (a meeting of representatives not called by a king), Parliament conferred the crown on William and his wife Mary (James's daughter), reasserted traditional English liberties in a Declaration of Rights, and adopted a Toleration Act that extended the right to worship freely to most Protestant dissenters but not to Catholics or members of other faiths. Some historians have seen in these developments little more than a coup d'état that was neither glorious nor much of a revolution. What were William's motivations? Primarily to bring England to the Dutch side in a war with Louis XIV and to secure his wife's claim on the throne. And whose liberties, after all, did the rev-olution protect? Primarily those of the propertied classes.[3]

As the years immediately afterward made clear, however, England had changed not only a king but the monarchy itself. Before the revo-lution, James II decided when and if Parliament would meet, enjoyed a lifetime right to certain tax revenues, maintained a standing army, and by royal prerogative dispensed not just individuals but whole groups from legal obligations, suspended laws entirely, purged the judiciary, and claimed all mineral rights on private land. After the revolution, Parliament sharply curbed the royal prerogative powers, denied the king the power to dismiss parliaments or to replace judges at pleasure, took firm control of the government's purse strings, asserted its supervision of the military, and strengthened property rights. Despite the limitations of the Toleration Act, the Anglican Church effectively lost control not only of religious practice but also of education and publishing; in 1695 Parliament abandoned licensing (and therefore prior censorship) of the press, and the next year restricted prosecutions for treason. Newspapers and political agitation spread. During the next twenty years, there were ten intensely competitive parliamentary elections and a substantial expansion of the electorate. And here is the seeming paradox: these changes limited the power of the monarchy, the established church, and in some respects the state itself. Yet this was precisely the moment when England launched itself on the way to become Europe's most powerful nation.

England's constitutional road to the creation of a modern state has long been recognized as different from the path followed by states in continental Europe. On the continent, the typical pattern by the seventeenth century was the centralization of power in absolutist monarchies. In the medieval world, power had been fragmented among a multitude of political units, often with no monopoly of violence even within their own territory. Feudal lords had maintained their own forces, and walled cities their own defenses. Then changes in weapons technologies, tactics, and the scale and cost of armies—the so-called military revolution—gave a decisive advantage to larger and more centralized states, though crucially not to any empire encompassing Europe as a whole. Guns first appeared in Europe in the early 1300s, but it was the development of mobile siege artillery during the late 1400s that severely undercut localism. "Wherever the new artillery appeared," the historian William McNeill writes, "existing fortifications became useless." Rulers who could afford the new weapons gained power over "neighbors and subjects" who couldn't; the result in Europe was "to dwarf the Italian city-states and to reduce other small sovereignties to triviality." By 1520 Italian cities discovered how to use earth walls, ditches, outworks, and dozens of cannon to contrive a new kind of defense capable of thwarting artillery-supported sieges. These new fortifications blocked any single power from controlling all of Europe, but they were hugely expensive. So were the larger armies of the sixteenth and seventeenth centuries, new firearms and other weapons (by 1630 it cost five times as much to equip a soldier as it had a century earlier), and the increased training needed for executing coordinated volleys of gunfire and other new tactics. In other parts of the world, gunpowder weapons led to the expansion of empires (Russian, Ottoman, Mughal, Chinese), but weapons technology then stagnated, whereas in Europe no empire arrested the competition among states and the arms race continued. The net result of this spiral of force was to strengthen national states at the expense of local centers of power and smaller sovereignties and to give Europeans an edge in the technology of war over other peoples.[4]

States achieved military superiority internally and over their rivals only if they were able to mobilize the necessary financial resources. In many areas of Europe, a king was traditionally expected to "live of his own," that is, off the income from the royal domain and other chiefly hereditary sources of revenue. The exception was in wartime, when he could call on a consultative assembly representing the estates for approval of extraordinary taxes; this check on the king's power was a key feature of medieval constitutionalism. With the military revolution and persistent warfare, however, monarchs in much of continental Europe created standing armies, made taxation the routine basis of state finance, and overrode the old representative institutions. According to an influential argument by the German historian Otto Hintze, England was able to maintain its constitutional system and a smaller state, while bureaucratic absolutism rose on the continent, for geopolitical reasons. As an island nation, England was sheltered from the pressures of land warfare on the continent and could rely on its navy for defense. In this view, English constitutionalism was rather like the unusual species discovered by Darwin on the Galápagos Islands—a survival from another age that had escaped continental predators. This analysis assumes that constitutionalism was ordinarily a source of weakness and vulnerability. But as the historian John Brewer has shown, after the Revolution of 1688–89, England created a "fiscal-military state" of enormous proportions at the same time as it strengthened its constitutional system. And the navy, far from lightening the tax burden, was actually far more expensive to build and maintain than a comparable land force.[5]

Geopolitical differences do help to explain why continental states suffered from endemic problems that England was better able to overcome. In early modern Europe, particularly between 1559 and 1660, the major continental states were embroiled in continual warfare not only with each other but also internally. The religious conflicts of the Reformation, great-power rivalries, and local resistance to monarchical control and new taxes were especially fertile sources of discord. Although the military revolution favored the centralization of power, war did not always make states stronger. Indeed, it frequently exhausted their resources, devastated their economies, and led them to sacrifice their long-term interests for their immediate ones. Even after increasing taxes, monarchs often spent beyond their means. They borrowed funds but then later repudiated debts or suspended payment, setting off financial crises until they came to terms with lenders and ensuring, by their own unreliability, that they and their successors could obtain future credit only by extortion or at high interest rates. To obtain revenue quickly, rulers sold the right to collect particular taxes to private entrepreneurs ("tax farmers"). In exchange for money or loyalty, they also gave individual state officials the right to treat their positions as private property, to pocket fees or other income, and to sell their offices or pass them on to their heirs. Like tax farming, this practice—venality of officeholding—came at a considerable long-term cost to the state in unity of control and administrative efficiency.

Although England shared some aspects of this history, the timing of developments was different. For two centuries after 1453 (when it lost its last foothold in France), England generally avoided full-scale participation in continental wars and therefore escaped the intense fiscal pressures endemic on the continent. Partly as a result, it never generated venal officeholders in the vast numbers that France spawned. The military revolution finally came to the British Isles in the mid-seventeenth century with the Civil War and England's conquest of Ireland and Scotland, and these wars replicated the continental process of state-building in one respect but not in others. They led to new taxes but did not result in the loss of parliamentary power or the privatization of state offices. With no king during the Interregnum, Parliament maintained its right to approve taxation, and it kept that authority even after the monarchy was restored in 1660, although both Charles II (1660–85) and James II (1685–88) sought to rid themselves of parliamentary constraints. The policies of the Restoration had critical effects on the state's structure and capacities. On the one hand, seeking to make the most of authorized taxes, Charles II ended tax farming, put state officials directly in charge of most tax collection, and centralized financial control in a single department, the Treasury. These measures strengthened the state institutionally. On the other hand, in 1671 Charles II stopped payment on his debt, ruining his private bankers and damaging the state's credit, and James II undermined confidence in the rule of law in more fundamental ways. Faced with opposition to his policies, James prorogued Parliament and never called it back, and within three years his suspension of statutes, disregard of precedent, and purging of judges and other officials had put the question squarely as to whether England would be governed by prerogative or by law.

The nature of monarchical power was the fundamental source of the split that emerged in this period between Whigs and Tories, England's first political parties. Before James II became king, the Whigs had sought to exclude him from the throne; they held that the monarchy existed for the nation's benefit and could be altered accordingly. Indeed, the more radical Whigs claimed that obedience was due a ruler only if he fulfilled his part of a contract with the people, and they justified the Revolution of 1688 on the grounds that James had violated that contract. In this view, parliamentary powers over taxation and a standing army were the means of enforcing the people's contract with their ruler. The Tories, in contrast, upheld the monarch's divine right to rule, the subjects' duty of "passive obedience," and strict adherence to the hereditary principle. The Tories who supported the 1688 revolution, or at least acquiesced in it, did so on grounds that they shared with many moderate Whigs: in this view, James's flight simply left the crown vacant and his daughter Mary was a proper, Protestant heir. But while the Tories rejected the idea of government as a contract (and no contract was explicitly imposed on William), they too believed in the rule of law and wanted to limit the crown's ability to raise taxes and to take England to war. In these respects, the two parties shared the same understanding of the English constitution.

After the 1688 revolution, Parliament used its control of finance as leverage to sustain its power in relation to the crown. "When Princes have not needed Money, they have not needed us," one member of the Convention Parliament declared. However grateful to William, therefore, Parliament refused to give him a blank check, approving revenue only in limited amounts for limited periods. Furthermore, instead of leaving the uses of revenue open-ended, it began making appropriations for specific purposes, and to ensure that William would need Parliament to meet annually, it declined to appropriate funds for the military for more than a year at a time. These actions were the practical basis on which a limited, constitutional monarchy was established.

But limitations on monarchical prerogative did not necessarily mean a small or weak state. Besides the split between Whigs and Tories, there was a second axis of conflict in British politics, setting the "Court," that is, members allied with the government at a given time, against the "Country," consisting of those not only out of power but typically suspicious of it. Country forces—sometimes Whig, sometimes Tory, often independent—resisted the expanding power of the state and raised persistent accusations of corruption.[6] The Glorious Revolution had a Country inspiration, but it put England in a new international position that entirely changed the domestic politics of taxation and spending. France was now backing James in his effort to regain his throne (and would later back James's son, raised a Catholic in exile). To prevent a Catholic restoration—and English Protestants at the time equated Catholic rule with absolutism—Parliament saw no alternative to war with France, as William wanted. Even the Country forces, despite their aversion to state expansion, voted William higher taxes for an enlarged military to defeat Louis XIV. The decision for war in 1689 proved to be a historic turning point. After long escaping continental entanglements, England (Britain after the 1707 union between England and Scotland) entered into a war with France that would last, with various intermissions, until the defeat of Napoleon in 1815.

So it was that a revolution limiting monarchical power produced political agreement on a vast expansion of fiscal, military, and bureaucratic capacities. At the core of the transformation was a series of developments now known as the "financial revolution," which involved interrelated changes in government borrowing, taxation, banking, and private investment. Although some of these changes began earlier in the seventeenth century (and the Dutch were the first to pioneer the system), the years after the Glorious Revolution saw the major breakthroughs in England as the government shifted to long-term borrowing, guaranteed its creditors payment from specific taxes, and then consolidated its various loans into a single public or "national" debt. The conceptual change in the debt was crucial; it became an obligation of the state itself, backed by the fiscal powers of Parliament. This was a "funded" debt: instead of paying both interest and installments on the principal, the government paid interest only, which reduced the annual costs. And instead of the creditors being a small group of private financiers, they became a wider group of investors mediated by a quasi-public institution. In 1694 Parliament authorized the subscribers to a long-term government bond to incorporate themselves as the Bank of England, which was given the right to deal in bills of exchange. The bank raised the capital for government borrowing from a base of investors, middle-class as well as aristocratic, for whom the nation's debt became a form of wealth. These "gilt-edged securities" were to serve both as a cornerstone of economic security for many affluent families and as a further basis for their attachment to the state. None of this would have worked, however, if Britain had not raised taxes to service its debt reliably. And so it did: from 1688 to 1783, while its population rose 46 percent, Britain increased taxes 600 percent, of which more than three-quarters went to paying for war or for debts incurred on account of war. New taxes and higher tax rates were the two factors chiefly responsible for this increased revenue; economic growth was third in importance. Because taxes were reliably collected and the government was punctilious in its payments, England after the Glorious Revolution enjoyed exceptionally good credit. Between 1689 and 1713, the interest rate paid by the English state fell from 8 percent to 3 percent, the lowest in Europe.[7]

England's fiscal advantages were critical in enabling it to achieve military superiority in the long series of wars with France that began in 1689. The two countries were not evenly matched. At the outset, France was four and a half times as large in population, and it was a more formidable military power. As a result of the financial revolution, however, Britain assumed a far larger debt than it otherwise could have supported, and contrary to the usual images, it also raised more in taxes than France did—indeed, Britain became the most heavily taxed country per capita in western Europe. But while a fiscal crisis was a key factor in the French Revolution, high taxes were accepted in Britain. Parliamentary power, far from making Britain a weak state, made it a stronger one by securing the consent to taxation of the propertied classes. And political representation wasn't the only reason why taxes in Britain enjoyed more acceptance than taxes in France. While the French fiscal system was riddled with conspicuous exemptions for the nobility and specific regions, British taxes were legally uniform across all classes and the nation as a whole; aristocrats often did benefit from underassessment of their land, but the chief sources of public revenue were fairly and efficiently collected taxes on domestic manufactures and imports. And whereas the French state clothed its finances in secrecy, British fiscal arrangements were more transparent because they were subject to parliamentary approval and investigation. In 1691 Parliament established the Commissioners of Public Accounts to ensure that money was spent for its appropriated purpose; according to the historian Mark Kishlansky, the commissioners "browbeat department heads, terrorized junior ministers, and uncovered scandals in procurement and supply." Contemporary observers suggested that this public scrutiny contributed to the success of British public finance by assuring investors as well as taxpayers that their money was not being stolen.[8]

With the Revolution of 1688, England had chosen the rule of law over prerogative, and in doing so it created a state of limited powers that was stronger than one ruled by prerogative. The changed nature of public debt was the financial correlate of the rule of law, and the lower interest rates were the payoff for the trust that the government earned. The conflicts between the parties, and particularly the suspicious view that Country forces had of state expansion, put the management of the state under continual examination. "The war against the state," Brewer writes, made it "both more public and accountable," paradoxically strengthening its powers rather than weakening them. "Public scrutiny reduced peculation, parliamentary consent lent greater legitimacy to government action. Limited in scope, the state's powers were nevertheless exercised with telling effect."[9]

The Glorious Revolution did not result in a democratic government; the vast majority of the English remained excluded from political representation. Moreover, it did not take long, despite the protests of Country critics, for the government to gain sway over the parliamentary opposition, in part through appointments to the expanded state bureaucracy. The freedoms achieved in the 1690s were also later compromised in other ways. Although it never reinstituted licensing of the press, the government later used taxes, prosecutions for seditious libel, and outright bribery and intimidation to squelch opposition publications. Perhaps most important, the era of intense electoral competition came to an end in 1716 when a Parliament under control of the Whig oligarchy voted that elections had to be held only every seven years (instead of every three), an act that Thomas Paine would later cite as evidence that Britain had no true constitution at all. But unlike other major European states, Britain continued to have a limited parliamentary monarchy, which for all its drawbacks became a model of constitutionalism to Montesquieu, Voltaire, and other early liberals.

In 1689, when it adopted the Declaration of Rights, the Convention Parliament maintained the fiction that it was only recognizing ancient liberties, though many of the rights enumerated in the Declaration (later enacted as a Bill of Rights) had not actually been settled law. To say that the Glorious Revolution merely affirmed a constitution that had medieval origins is to miss the crucial point that there were two opposed conceptions of that constitution—one patriarchal and authoritarian, the other contractual and liberal—and 1688 resolved which conception would prevail. And though English constitutionalism looked back in time for its legitimacy, it also anticipated something new, even if the innovators did not acknowledge the innovation. By holding officials publicly accountable for their performance, the British were creating a new kind of constitutional government that was at once more liberal and powerful than its antecedents.

The year after the revolution, when he published the *Two Treatises on Government* that he had written seven years earlier, John Locke gave theoretical expression to the Whig theory that government rested on a contract. For Locke, however, this was a contract not between the rulers and the people, but among the people prior to any government.

Locke did not anchor his theory in historical reasoning; he spoke only of natural rights, not of ancient ones. And in saying that government rested on consent, he did not conceive of consent as being given forever at one moment in the past. Rather, consent had to be periodically renewed, which meant that it could be a means of controlling and renewing power.

Locke held, moreover, that if government violated its obligations and did not rest on consent, the people had a right of revolution. This theory was too radical even for most Whigs in 1688, but nearly a century later it would suit another generation of Whig revolutionaries just fine.[10] When these revolutionaries came to set up their own government, they built into it even more extensive limits on state power than the English had established in 1689. And after some initial missteps, they also followed the English example in creating a state that would have far greater capacities than a government of unlimited powers could have achieved.

CREATING AND CONTROLLING
POWER IN AMERICA

Like the Glorious Revolution, the American Revolution has sometimes been described as no revolution at all but only a defense of traditional English liberties. Yet if that view understates the changes in England following 1688, it utterly fails to capture the far greater transformation of state and society that America experienced as a result of its revolution. The Americans followed the example of Britain in creating a form of constitutional government, but they gave a new meaning to constitutionalism and a new structure to government. While the English consolidated a form of "mixed government" incorporating king, lords, and commons, the Americans founded a republic based wholly on the principle of representation, without any hereditary class, under a Constitution and Bill of Rights that, unlike Britain's, were beyond the reach of ordinary legislation. The American founders did not create a democracy in the modern sense of enfranchising all citizens. They failed to abolish slavery or to prevent its spread south of the Ohio. But the polity they fashioned was pluralistic, transparent, and competitive, and the guarantees of freedom of religion, expression, and association were more comprehensive than the qualified advances in religious toleration and freedom of the press in England after 1688. Moreover, the laws and policies regarding landownership, inheritance, indentured servitude, education, and communications that emerged from the Revolution gave rise, in the northern and western states, to a society that was more fluid, open, and egalitarian than any in Europe.[11]

Although the American Revolution had more profound social and ideological ramifications than the Revolution of 1688, the two upheavals were fundamentally similar in one respect. Both gave rise to powerful states in an ideological climate that was deeply suspicious of state power. That climate affected not only the opponents of stronger political authority but even its architects. The Americans of the Revolutionary era were not eager state-builders; they came to the task reluctantly, and it was partly their reluctance that led them to invent new ways of organizing and thinking about government.

There was a direct line from 1688 to 1776, and the revolutionary generation in America was conscious of it. In their resistance to British imperial policy, the colonists looked for inspiration and ideas to the Glorious Revolution and to later radical Whig and Country writers who claimed that the British government had betrayed the principles of 1688. It was from these writers, as well as from their own experience of colonial rule, that the American revolutionaries derived their understanding of power and its dangers. Power, in this view, was antithetical to liberty, and "jealousy of power" was the proper attitude in constitutional design: power needed to be divided, limited in scope and duration, and kept under vigilant watch.[12] This was the understanding that dominated the state constitutions written during the Revolutionary War, and it was also reflected in the first constitution of the United States, the Articles of Confederation. But the early experiences with these constitutions revealed the perils of having too weak as well as too dominant a state, and it was not long before the leaders of the founding generation concluded that they needed to endow government with greater powers—and then to limit those powers even more clearly than they had before.

The authors of the first state constitutions, like their Whig forebears in Britain, focused their distrust on the executive power in government. During the colonial era, elected assemblies had faced off against royal governors, and the revolutionaries continued to think of legislatures as protecting the people's liberties and governors as threatening them, even though governors would now also be elected, usually by the legislature. The new constitutions typically limited governors to a one-year term, required rotation in office, denied them any veto over legislation, gave them no power to appoint or remove judges, and generally sought to reduce their role to that of a mere "administrator," as Thomas Jefferson described it in regard to a draft constitution for Virginia in 1776. The Pennsylvania constitution that year, the most radical of the Revolutionary constitutions, took this view to the logical extreme of having no governor at all but rather an executive council. Legislatures, particularly their assemblies (several states had no upper houses), became the center of power in state governments, dominating the other branches. But legislators were also typically subjected to annual elections, and towns often gave their representatives instructions on how to vote on key issues. The basic impulse was to keep government on a short leash and to afford politicians as little discretionary authority as possible.[13]

By the late 1770s, however, a reaction emerged against the initial preference for legislative supremacy. New constitutions in Massachusetts and New Hampshire called for stronger governors and courts, and the very method of writing constitutions underwent a profound change. Early efforts to set constitutions apart from ordinary legislation by proclaiming them to be fundamental or by requiring supermajorities for amendments did not effectively prevent legislatures from subsequently trespassing limits they themselves had set. The challenge was to find a constitution-making authority that legislatures would have to acknowledge as superior, and here the Americans put the old idea of a "convention" to a new purpose. Formerly assemblies called in the absence of royal authority—and therefore, in the British context, legally defective—conventions now became special representative bodies solely entrusted with the high responsibility of drafting or revising a constitution. Because they met only once for a single purpose, constitutional conventions were less susceptible than a legislature to suspicions of self-aggrandizement. An approved constitution also carried direct popular endorsement if, as in Massachusetts, a convention submitted its drafts to the voters for discussion and ratification. With this new method of constitution-making came a new concept of constitutionalism. Britain's unwritten constitution had evolved out of political experience, but at any moment Parliament could change it. In contrast, Americans spelled out their constitutions in print and came to view them as agreements of the people, prior to government, creating and regulating its power.

Nowhere was the initial, Revolutionary-era suspicion of power more evident than in the Articles of Confederation, which were approved by the Continental Congress in 1777 and served as the charter of the United States from their ratification by the states in 1781 until they were supplanted by the ratified federal Constitution in 1788. Rather than creating a single nation-state, the Articles left each of the states sovereign and independent. The United States, the Articles declared, was a "a firm league of friendship" of states established "for their common defence, the security of their liberties, and their mutual and general welfare." The Confederation had no direct relationship with individual citizens; it drew its power from the states, not from the people of those states, nor from the American people as a whole. Representatives to the Confederation's unicameral Congress were chosen by state legislatures and could be recalled by them at any time, and each state's delegation cast only a single vote. The Confederation had no distinct executive branch, though the Articles authorized a Committee of the States to exercise certain functions when Congress was not in session. There was no judiciary, except that Congress had authority to establish admiralty courts and to arbitrate disputes among the states. There was no authority to regulate commerce or to prevent the states from issuing their own paper money.

The chief powers of the Confederation were to manage foreign policy, make war and peace, borrow money, regulate coinage, establish a post office, and determine weights and measures. But even this list is an exaggeration. For while the Confederation had authority to wage war and control foreign affairs, the Articles did not provide it with adequate supporting powers. It could requisition soldiers and money from the states, but as experience showed during the Revolution, states could ignore the Confederation's demands, and it was unable to enforce them. As the Articles gave the Confederation no power over individuals except via the states, so they gave it no power to impose taxes of its own or to conscript soldiers. And although the Confederation could enter into treaties with foreign powers, it could not bind the individual states to comply with those agreements.

These problems were already of concern to a group of nationalists by 1780, even before the Articles were ratified. As a result of its fiscal incapacity, the government defaulted on its debt, and unpaid soldiers grew restive and even mutinous, yet the nationalists failed in their efforts to modify the Articles to authorize the Confederation to levy a tax on imports. After the war ended in 1783, the Confederation became severely debilitated; indeed, it was so broke that it could not pay to ship to England the ratified Treaty of 1783 guaranteeing American independence! (The French paid an English sea captain to carry it.) The Confederation was also unable to compel the states to fulfill American obligations under the peace treaty—for example, regarding the return of property expropriated from loyalists—and in response, Britain refused to give up territories and posts that it had agreed to surrender. The Confederation had the capacity neither to enforce the terms of the peace treaty nor to retaliate in 1784 when Spain closed the Mississippi to American trade. Once the Continental Army was disbanded, the government maintained only a few hundreds troops; at one point in 1783, the entire military force of the United States consisted of some eighty men.[14]

Political and military weakness had economic repercussions. By blocking critical routes for American exports from the trans-Appalachian region, Britain and Spain were deliberately encouraging settlers to switch their loyalties and imperiling American expansion. Along with the other mercantilist European powers, both countries also denied American ships access to their ports. Opening European markets to American goods was vital for the new nation's prosperity and development, but because the Confederation had no authority to regulate commerce, it could not retaliate against other nations economically any more than it could retaliate against them militarily. The economy had suffered during the Revolution, and recovery in the 1780s was slow. The per capita gross domestic product of the original thirteen states fell 46 percent between 1775 and 1790, according to the limited data available, and though these may exaggerate the contraction, there is little doubt that a substantial economic decline affected people at all levels.[15] During the 1780s, Americans also faced sharp tax increases from state governments that were trying to pay off debt from the war; an armed tax revolt by farmers in western Massachusetts led by Daniel Shays was a symptom of the accumulating pressures. In response to distressed farmers, politicians tried printing paper money, staying debt collection, and other measures that the propertied elite saw as evidence of popular irresponsibility and the need for a strong federal government that might be less susceptible to demagogic schemes. The idea that America was in a deep crisis, however, was not merely propaganda of an "aristocratic" party of federalists. The Confederation suffered from severe problems of governmental incapacity and was on a course that might well have ended with its bankruptcy and disintegration into competing states.

The framing of the Constitution in 1787 and its ratification the following year represented a second American revolution—this one in favor of making the United States into a single nation with a government at its center that had fiscal, military, judicial, and regulatory powers denied to the Confederation. The Constitution was not, as it is so often represented, chiefly concerned with limiting government; in the first instance, it was a plan to create power where there had been none. Indeed, seen in an international context, the Constitution was a state-building project akin to those undertaken in early modern Europe, though under distinctive American conditions.[16]

The Philadelphia convention in 1787 had been authorized only to propose revisions to the Articles of Confederation, which required the unanimous agreement of all the states for any changes. The delegates ignored these constraints and used the new ideas of constitutionalism and popular sovereignty that emerged during the Revolutionary era to overturn the weak government that the Revolution had initially produced. From the opening words, "We the people," to its method of ratification (through popularly elected conventions, separate from the state legislatures, and requiring only nine states to go into effect), the Constitution announced that it would draw its legitimacy from the people, not from existing law. A bicameral structure for Congress allowed the Framers to balance not only the interests of large and small states but also two different kinds of representation. Like the Confederation Congress, the Senate would represent the state governments equally (state legislatures originally chose senators), while the House of Representatives became the first national institution to be based on direct popular election (under the same qualifications as applied to voters for "the most numerous Branch of the State Legislature"). The creation of an executive branch under a president with a four-year term and no requirement for rotation in office would give the new government the "energy" missing in the Confederation. By making the choice of the president separate from Congress and dependent on popular election, albeit via the Electoral College, the Constitution reflected the new understanding that the entire government, not just the legislature, could draw its authority from the people. This sense was crucial in gaining acceptance of broad federal authority and a stronger executive. The states would retain power wherever the Constitution did not explicitly exclude it, but they would no longer mediate the federal government's revenue-raising or military powers or be able to impede domestic trade or refuse to abide by international treaties. The new government, unlike the Confederation, could impose its own taxes, raise an army, regulate interstate and foreign commerce, and make use of federal courts to obtain compliance with treaties and other laws.

But, as the federalists understood the science of politics, a government with such formidable powers would need even stronger structural barriers against their misuse. The Confederation had only a unicameral legislature, no independent judiciary, and no bill of rights; its powers were few, but so were its internal checks. The Constitution sought to discipline the power it created by dividing it among different branches and checking it through varying modes of representation and requirements of transparency. According to the theory James Madison expounded in Federalist No. 10, ambition would counter ambition, and the size of the country would make it more difficult for tyrannical majorities to gain control and more likely that the nation's leadership would attend to the common good. At the Constitutional Convention, the Framers originally held that because the government would exercise only its enumerated powers, a bill of rights was unnecessary. In fact, the Constitution did include guarantees of some rights; for example, it prohibited the use of any religious test for officeholders, guaranteed trial by jury in criminal cases, and banned bills of attainder. The antifederalist opposition during the ratification debate, though primarily opposed to the fiscal, regulatory, and judicial powers under the Constitution, showed the depth of support for additional guarantees of liberty. As a result, in the first Congress under the new government, the Federalists themselves—led by Madison—adopted the Bill of Rights and sent it to the states in the hope of averting a second constitutional convention that would overturn the work of the first. Together, the Constitution and the Bill of Rights raised the equilibrium of power and liberty to a higher level. They magnified the powers of the state, and they clarified and codified the limitations on those powers.

Like earlier state-building measures in Europe, the Constitution was singularly important for its enlargement of the government's fiscal and military powers. The antifederalists objected that these came without express limitations (other than those arising from the separation of powers); the Constitution did not confine the federal government to particular kinds of taxes, restrict the amount of taxation or borrowing, or impose any constraint on the establishment of a standing army. In Federalist No. 31, Alexander Hamilton was emphatic that no fixed limits could be set on these powers because it was impossible to foresee the dangers that the republic might face in the future. Like the Country forces in England, the antifederalists were reflexively suspicious of a central government with unrestricted taxing authority and troops to feed. But the United States had just been through a long and difficult war, and there is no way to understand the Constitution without appreciating that experience. The federalists who shaped the Constitution were, by and large, a group of relatively young men who had come of age during the Revolution. Many believed that the Confederation's weakness, particularly its dependence on the states for revenue, had caused them needless privation as soldiers, prolonged the fighting, and very nearly cost them victory. Of the fifty-five delegates who attended the Constitutional Convention, twenty-six had served in the Revolutionary War, eighteen of them as officers.[17] Nearly half the delegates in Philadelphia, in other words, were veterans, presided over by their former commanding general. Their bitter memories of an impotent Confederation may help explain why the Constitution so radically extended the federal government's revenue-raising and war-making powers.

The postwar fiscal crisis confirmed how grave the Confederation's debilities were. Not only was the Confederation broke; overhanging debt from the war had left many of the states in severe difficulty. The states' problem arose from a mismatch between their fiscal needs and capacities. Because manufacturing had yet to develop in America, states had little opportunity to generate revenue from an excise—the tax on domestic production that was a pillar of British finance. Although taxing imports was an option, states without major ports could not wring much revenue from that source. That left taxation levied directly on individuals, chiefly in the form of taxes on land. But because many farmers had little cash, states found that land taxes caused serious hardship and generated intense opposition. The federalist program was not, as the antifederalists suspected (and as some historians still argue), to use an undemocratic central government to force the people to part with their money. In the ratification debate, the federalists insisted that the least oppressive tax would also be the most productive and that this would be a tax on imports, which the federal government could collect more efficiently than the states, primarily on the waterfront in the Atlantic ports. And that is the policy the Federalist Party later followed. Under Hamilton's program, the federal government assumed the debt of the states as well as the Confederation and then converted those obligations into a long-term, "funded" debt (following the British example of paying only interest, not principal). These measures restored the credit of the United States in European money markets and enabled the federal government to sell public debt certificates in Amsterdam and Antwerp on favorable terms. The substantially reduced annual costs of servicing the debt were then defrayed largely through a tax on imports. In short, while the federalists wrote unlimited tax powers into the Constitution, they established a "waterfront" state where most Americans never saw a tax collector. The more affluent classes who were the primary market for imported commodities bore the brunt of taxation. And because the federal government assumed state debts from the Revolution, the states were able to cut direct taxes by 75 to 90 percent by 1795. So it was, writes the historian Roger H. Brown, that "the Constitution brought tax relief to rural America."[18]

In perhaps the most debated book about American history, *An Economic Interpretation of the Constitution* (1913), Charles Beard argues that many of the Framers had a financial interest in a strong federal government because it would sharply increase the value of the public securities they owned. The federalist program did have that effect, and recent statistical analysis indicates that delegates to both the Constitutional Convention and later state ratifying conventions who owned public securities were more likely to support a strong central government.[19] Such immediate concerns, like the experience that many of the Framers had as soldiers in the Revolution, may help explain who assumed initiative and leadership in the movement for a stronger national government.

But other considerations better explain why their leadership was accepted and their program proved successful. By strengthening the fiscal, military, and regulatory powers of the government, the federalists repaired the Confederation's weakness in the international state system, giving the new government the power, for example, to negotiate the opening of European markets to American exports. And by relying on what was virtually a luxury tax, the federalist program lifted the burden of taxation from cash-poor farmers and resolved the fiscal crisis that threatened internal political stability. Beard was right that the Constitution satisfied economic interests; he just had too limited a conception of what those interests were.

The constitutional and fiscal revolutions in the United States in the late 1780s and early 1790s repeated the pattern that England had followed almost exactly a century earlier. Despite fears of oppressive taxation, both revolutions resulted in enlarged fiscal powers, a transformation of public finance, and the creation of a long-term "funded" national debt. The stability and reliability of these systems provided a long-term payoff in low interest rates for government borrowing. Notwithstanding opposition to standing armies, both postrevolutionary governments created them; yet in both countries the military had a limited presence in everyday life. To be sure, there were major differences between the two. The

United States kept taxes much lower than in Britain and did not initially create a military on the same scale as Britain's; the strategic challenges facing the early republic, as well as its capacities, were smaller. But the Constitution's endowment of powers created an elastic state that could adjust to changing circumstances and proved capable of overcoming all obstacles to continental expansion and mobilizing overwhelming force when threatened internally or abroad.[20] Even in the nineteenth century, this was not a weak state, as southerners discovered when they tried to secede from it.

Also as in England, "Country" forces suspicious of power strengthened a liberal state that they would not have chosen to build on their own. While the federalists created an endowment of powers, the pressure of the antifederalists helped to create an endowment of rights—the Bill of Rights, which is now as important to Americans as the Constitution itself. This endowment of rights, like the endowment of powers, was not fully exploited in the early republic. Before the Civil War, the predominant view of the Bill of Rights was that it limited only the federal government, not the states. But on the basis of the amendments to the Constitution passed after the Civil War—particularly the Fourteenth Amendment's guarantee of the equal protection of the laws—the Supreme Court later extended the guarantees of the earlier amendments to the states and struck down state laws abridging individual rights. At the Constitutional Convention, Madison had failed to get a provision authorizing Congress to veto state laws; in the first Congress, when he sat in the House and was responsible for drafting the Bill of Rights, Madison had also failed to get adoption of an amendment that would have protected individual liberties against infringement by state governments. But eventually the Madisonian view prevailed that the Union ought to guarantee liberty *all the way down*—an extension, simultaneously, of both federal power and individual rights.

In 1794 Madison observed that whereas power had granted liberty in Europe, liberty had granted power in America. This was a different understanding from the original Whig belief that power and liberty are mortal enemies. Americans had quickly discovered that the two had to be reconciled—that liberty needed power, and that by protecting liberty, the nation could be made more powerful. Some historians portray the Constitution as the outcome of an antidemocratic movement to shift power from local majorities and upstart politicians in the states to a more elite, national leadership. This was doubtless the intention of many federalists, but it was not, in the end, what they accomplished. Compared to the Articles of Confederation, the Constitution was a more democratic national charter; it rested on the idea of popular sovereignty, called for the first national elections, and applied the principle of representation to a chief executive as well as the legislature. Moreover, by creating a powerful government, the Constitution gave Americans strong incentives to enter the public arena and compete for popular support. When governments are weak, they cannot sustain political commitment. Under the Articles of Confederation, Congress had difficulty even attracting a quorum and became a subject of ridicule and contempt. People will do the work of representative government—campaigning, voting, serving in office—only if they believe that the government has genuine power. Weak states are no basis for strong democracies. The Constitution laid the foundation for democracy *because* it created a powerful national government.

The late eighteenth century marks a decisive turning point in the history of constitutional liberalism. It is with the formation of the American republic that a state for the first time was deliberately built with liberal, constitutional principles. More countries have since adopted a parliamentary government on British lines than have adopted an American-style presidential system. But the American idea of a constitution as a written and popularly approved design of government has become the primary mode of establishing liberal states. With the American founding, constitutional liberalism became both a state-limiting and a state-building strategy, at once a method for creating power and building in checks against its misuse. This was the liberal revolution in statecraft, and we turn now to look more closely at its elements.

3

The Classical Discipline

CONSTITUTIONAL LIBERALISM, I HAVE BEEN ARGUING, NOT ONLY imposed limits on state power but also enabled states to become powerful within those limits. How to subject government to a discipline that would protect liberty and strengthen overall societal powers was a central challenge generally for classical liberalism—by which I mean now to include classical *economic* liberalism as well as constitutional doctrine.

Rulers have often followed a policy of "divide and conquer"—dividing their people the better to control them. Liberalism follows the reverse policy—dividing power the better to control it. Many of the liberal principles for the discipline of power call for drawing lines to partition spheres of action that were previously fused, closely connected, or poorly distinguished. A typical liberal strategy to avoid tyranny or monopoly is to set autonomous centers of power against each other—ambition against ambition—by creating boundaries and countervailing pressures between state and society, within the state, or in civil society and the private economy. The public-private distinction, the separation-of-powers and checks-and-balances doctrines in constitutional design, and the theories of economic competition, societal pluralism, and contested political elections are all applications of this strategy.

Organic theories of politics often claim wholeness and harmony as their virtues. Monarchical political theory, for example, often represented society as a family or as a body, in each case with the king as its head. Liberals rejected this vision because it assumed that monarchical rule and popular dependency were built into the natural order of things. Modern communitarian theories, from both left and right, have bemoaned the loss of social unity, blaming it on liberal individualism, and sought to restore a singleness of purpose in public life. From this perspective, divisions and disagreements are symptoms of a disease in need of cure. Liberalism's view is different. While seeking to tame violent and destructive forms of discord, liberalism accepts divergent values and opinions and views public disagreement as a constructive method of resolving conflict and discovering new ideas. Liberalism values various kinds of separation (separation of powers, of church and state, of knowledge and politics) as a means of protecting values specific to particular institutions and spheres of life. These separations and boundaries—as well as the rules about when the lines may be crossed—constitute the inner structure of liberalism and the basis of the classical discipline of power.[1]

PUBLIC VERSUS PRIVATE

Critics of liberalism often describe it as favoring the private over the public, and self-interest over civic virtue. Liberals have certainly upheld rights to private choice and argued that government ought to reflect a realistic appraisal of human motivation. But rather than single-mindedly preferring the private to the public, liberals have sought to establish a balance between the two, giving each one clearer definition and a stronger legal foundation.

The rise of liberalism in the eighteenth and nineteenth centuries brought about a redrawn and sharpened public-private distinction: on the one hand, the privatizing of religious belief and practice and of economic activity formerly regulated by the state; on the other, a commitment to public law, public political discussion, and public knowledge. Liberals called not only for making a person's life and property more securely private but also for making government and politics more thoroughly public. Strengthening the public character of the state is not a recent modification of liberal doctrine; it is a continuity in liberal thought from its classical to its contemporary phases. Classical liberals understood that representative government requires eliminating some kinds of markets, such as the buying and selling of votes. Like other modern state-builders, they sought to suppress private armies, private justice (revenge), and private ownership of governmental offices and instead to reserve such functions exclusively to the state itself. These extensions of government were vital to limiting the arbitrary and unauthorized use of its powers and ensuring civil peace. Liberals also sought to make government more public by subjecting its performance to public examination in the press and opening up politics to public discussion.

Here two meanings of the public-private distinction need to be distinguished. First, public may be to private as the whole is to the part: "public opinion," "public health," and the "public interest" each refer to something that pertains not to a specific individual or class but to all of society or to "any member or members of the community, without distinction."[2] "Public" in this sense may mean "governmental," but the two terms do not always coincide.

Second, public may be to private as the open is to the closed: A "public event," a "public meeting," or a "publication" all refer to something that is open and accessible and may therefore be available to any members of the community. Public and private here vary along a dimension of visibility: the transparent versus the secret, hidden, and confidential.

Liberalism called for making government and politics more public in both of these senses. Liberals held that government, rather than being the private domain of a ruler or venal officeholders, exists for the public's benefit and ought to serve its interests. And to ensure that government does so, liberals sought to make it more transparent—to publish laws, to open up trials and legislative proceedings, to require government officials to disclose their actions, and to allow the press to circulate political news and critical discussion that would enable citizens to form their own judgments.

At the same time, liberalism marked out a private sphere where individuals enjoyed strengthened rights against the state, such as rights to practice their own religion and control their own property. Here the presumptions were reversed. Unless reasonably suspected of violating the law, private individuals and associations were neither publicly answerable for their actions nor obligated to open up their churches, homes, or other property to government officials or the public at large. Indeed, liberals sought to guarantee individuals protections against such demands (for example, against unreasonable searches).

Yet while liberals supported contrary principles for the two spheres, the underlying purpose was the same. Liberalism provided—and still provides—a deeply resonant vocabulary for making claims against the state. On the one hand, because public officials in a liberal state are answerable for their performance, citizens believe they have a right to expect their government to be public not only in its ends but also in its processes. To claim that something is rightfully public is to invoke those expectations. The rules here are not absolute; some aspects of government, such as diplomatic communications, are still accepted as legitimately confidential. But the default expectation of a liberal state is for it to act in a fully public way. Exceptions need to be justified—and over time fewer exceptions have been accepted as legitimate.

On the other hand, when people say that their homes, businesses, churches, and other forms of association are private, they are claiming another set of limits to the state's power. These limits are also not absolute—the government, for example, can assert "eminent domain" and override private property rights for a public use if it provides compensation. But when crossing from public to private the presumptions shift, and any state intervention must meet tests of a compelling or rational public interest. Both sets of rules, in other words, are aimed at getting government to serve public purposes and those alone.

For just this reason, while "public" and "private" both constrain the state, they can also strengthen it. As the development of the English state in the late seventeenth century shows, a more public government may be a more powerful one. Eliminating the private ownership of government offices increases the state's unity of control, and making the government more transparent may reduce corruption and inefficiency and strengthen confidence and loyalty. Conversely, some kinds of privatization do not weaken the state; the privatization of rancorous religious differences promotes peaceful cooperation, and more secure guarantees of private property encourage people to make long-term investments that ultimately redound to the state's advantage.

Like other liberal antinomies, the public-private distinction can be complex and frustrating. What is public in one respect may be private in others. And some things may change over time. The modern distinction between the public and private sectors of the economy is the outcome of a historical process. Medieval Europe did not distinguish clearly between a public realm of sovereignty and a private realm of property; a feudal lord's rights over land included the power to administer justice on it. In early modern European states, chartered corporations included cities, monasteries, universities, guilds, and overseas trading companies; no clear line separated public from private corporations. Even in the United States, there was at first no clear public-private legal boundary separating cities and business enterprise. By the mid-1800s, however, the law classified cities as agencies of the state, while treating business corporations as if they were individuals. As public agencies, cities possessed only such powers as states delegated to them; as fictive individuals, private corporations enjoyed rights protected by the Constitution.[3] This bifurcation between powers and rights lies at the foundation of the modern legal distinction between the public and private sectors. So much came to hinge on the public-private dichotomy that every organization and relationship had to be classified and analyzed in its terms.

The dichotomy is critical to understanding liberal thinking about the public or common good. Classical liberals believed that, with certain limited exceptions, the individual pursuit of self-interest in the private economy yields a spontaneous harmony. That is not to say they celebrated "possessiveness" or the gratification of the self; they generally believed that competition leads not only to economic but also to moral exertion—to virtues such as frugality, thrift, perseverance, personal responsibility, and self-control. The pursuit of self-interest in the private economy was therefore a positive moral force as well as a rational basis of economic activity. But classical liberals had more complicated views of action in the public realm. Here what many of them feared was not so much calculating interest as the unruly passions, particularly the passions for glory and honor that led men to turn to violence and go to war, even over slight causes. By comparison, rational self-interest seemed to them a more trustworthy source of motivation, less likely to produce cruelty, fanaticism, and self-destructive conflict.[4] Moreover, education and public discussion could raise self-interest to a higher level—to enlightened self-interest—which could be a powerful force for progress. Some liberals, notably John Stuart Mill, believed that the very experience of participating in government would lead an individual "to weigh interests not his own; to be guided, in case of conflicting claims, by another rule than his private partialities: to apply, at every turn, principles and maxims which have for their reason of existence the common good." Like many other liberals, Mill believed that public action required different values from private life and that those in public office, as well as voters, had a responsibility to act on behalf of public interests rather than "private partialities."[5]

Earlier republicans also held that politics demands a devotion to the public good, but they conceived of civic virtue as a quality that only leisured gentlemen could be trusted to display. Skeptical of such claims, liberals looked to political institutions as a machinery for the public good that could work reliably with men as they really are, not as dreamers and dissemblers might wish them to be. This impulse lay behind their rationale for representative government and the deliberative procedures embodied in it. And nothing was more critical to this aspect of the classical political discipline than the idea of dividing power.

RULE OF LAW AND
THE DIVISION OF POWERS

Dividing power is a method not only for enabling the people to control their rulers but also for pursuing two ancient ideals, the rule of law and the public good. Law plainly never rules by itself, but the ideal calls for governing a society according to standing, general laws known to all rather than by diktats that are ad hoc, peculiar to particular classes, secret, retroactive, vague, contradictory, impossible to carry out, or

applied differently depending on the persons in authority or those subject to them. Constitutionalism is the rule of law over government
itself—the rule of law reinforced by a second tier of standing laws over
the lawmakers—but not all constitutions are liberal. Dividing power is
critical to the distinctive liberal strategy for ensuring a "government of
laws, not of men." Locke made the case concisely: "It may be too great
a temptation to humane frailty, apt to grasp at Power, for the same Persons who have the power of making Laws, to have also in their hands
the power to execute them, whereby they may exempt themselves from
Obedience to the Laws they make, and suite the Law, both in its making and execution, to their own private advantage."[6]

The liberal theory of divided power—consisting chiefly of two closely
related ideas, *separation of powers* and *checks and balances*—is easily confused with the earlier theory of "mixed government," which held that
the state's different branches ought to incorporate representatives of different strata of society. Each of the classical forms of government—
monarchy, aristocracy, and democracy; rule by the one, the few, and the
many—was supposed to have its virtues, and each its vices. But mixing
and balancing the three forms—vesting power, for example, in a
monarch, an aristocratic upper house of the legislature, and a popularly
elected lower house—could achieve the best of all possible worlds.
"Mixed government" was a system of checks and balances in which the
checks arose from the countervailing power of social classes and status
groups explicitly incorporated into different parts of the state. Once
hereditary political privilege was abolished, the theory collapsed, and
the doctrine of separation of powers emerged as an alternative—first
during the English Civil War in the mid-seventeenth century and then
again during the American Revolution.

The basic principle of separation of powers is that each of the state's
branches should be responsible for a specific function so as to minimize
the chance that any individuals or groups will be able to bend the law, as
Locke said, "to their own private advantage." Early versions of the theory
divided government into legislative and executive functions (with the
courts being conceived as part of the machinery for executing the laws);
by the eighteenth century, Montesquieu and other exponents of the

doctrine increasingly gave the judiciary a distinct and independent role. Fully developed, the doctrine calls for three kinds of separation: a separation of *agencies* (that is, relative autonomy of the branches of government); a separation of *functions* among these branches; and a separation of *persons* (no individual occupying positions in more than one branch). In its purest form, the doctrine calls for cleanly dividing all of these, with no overlap. But the rare attempts to put the pure doctrine into practice, such as American state constitutions of 1776, have been unsuccessful. Complete separation means that the different branches cannot effectively moderate each other, and the result may be either deadlock or the supremacy of one branch. A modified doctrine therefore calls for a partial separation of powers with stronger checks and balances—for example, giving the executive a veto over legislation, and the legislature the power to confirm executive appointments and to impeach officials guilty of grave misconduct. Through these checks, the powers of government, instead of being wholly separated, are actually shared—and it is this sharing that tempers their use.

There is nothing unusual about the separation of agencies; all large organizations develop specialized departments. The division of power, however, is more than a division of labor: it is a deliberate effort to prevent some kinds of coordination that might otherwise occur. The idea is to make government more permeable to the public's influence and to embody different values in the several branches by varying the degree of permeability, the procedures of decisionmaking, and the likely officeholders. Elections of varying frequency, for example, are aimed at making the legislature and executive more responsive to public opinion than the judiciary, and the lower house of the legislature more responsive than the upper. The structure of the more insulated branches (courts and senates) typically shows a residual influence of the old theory of "mixed government," but without an explicit assignment of representatives on the basis of social class. Rules requiring a deliberative process in the legislature and "due process" in the courts embody the ideal of a fair hearing for competing arguments and evidence. Combined with requirements for transparency, the separation of powers also creates a system of public communication among the branches and a public record not just of decisions taken but of the grounds and justifications for those actions. The separation of powers thereby amplifies the information available to the voters to enable them to assess how well their government is representing them.

The general liberal rationale for dividing power does not demand a particular constitutional design; parliamentary and presidential systems apply the principles in different ways. The American system is the extreme case, as it allows control of the executive and legislature to be in the hands of opposing parties, gives final constitutional authority to judges with lifetime tenure (the majority of whom are likely to have been appointed by earlier administrations), and leaves extensive powers to the states. Indeed, the system is so weighted with checks and balances that it has frequently been criticized as prone to deadlock; major shifts in policy usually require winning not just one election but several in succession. This is the continuing legacy of the early suspicion of power in America, but it is not the only example where the United States has divided power more radically than in other liberal societies. The separation of church and state is another instance.

RELIGIOUS LIBERTY AND THE SEPARATION OF CHURCH AND STATE

As Marxists have described it, liberalism is the ideology of the bourgeoisie and from its beginning was concerned, above all else, to uphold the rights of property. But while economic freedom was indeed important to early liberals, there was another kind of freedom at least of equal significance. This was "freedom of conscience," or religious liberty.

Liberalism emerged out of a world where religion was entangled with political power and where that entanglement was a principal source of war and civil strife. Nearly all seventeenth- and eighteenth-century European states tried to achieve religious uniformity by giving a single church a legal monopoly not just over faith but over important services and privileges, both sacred and profane. Under the law, only the clergy of the established church could preach, proselytize, and perform such sacraments as marriage; only its creed could be taught in schools; and typically only its members could attend universities or assume governmental and military offices. Even where dissenters were not actively persecuted, they were denied civil and political rights, and their religious organizations were forced to operate, if not underground, then without benefit of the right to own property, receive bequests, or seek legal recourse when threatened or harmed. The logic of religious uniformity seemed overwhelming. To those who believed that the established faith was the exclusive path to righteousness and salvation, it was obvious that other religions should be suppressed so as to save people from error and eternal damnation. And to those who cared more about the peace of *this* world, it seemed clear that an established church supported a strong and harmonious state by maintaining a shared faith and inculcating obedience and that any lessening of the church's monopoly would invite discord and rebellion.

Early liberals embraced a contrary logic, both religious and political. As it is the individual's duty to find salvation, Locke and later liberals argued, civil authorities must not use their power to try to impose religious beliefs. True faith must come from within. The efforts to impose it, far from producing strong and unified societies, had actually generated self-destructive violence. Religious toleration therefore represented a means not only of protecting individual conscience but also of achieving social cooperation and political order. No doubt liberal thought expressed tendencies toward greater individualism, but the wars of religion in continental Europe had shown that the passions excited by religion failed to produce social harmony. Liberals wanted to end the cycles of cruelty and persecution committed in religion's name. To the new generations of liberal revolutionaries in late seventeenth-century England and eighteenth-century America, the failure of England's own Puritan Revolution was also an important cautionary lesson about the dangers of religious fervor.

Broadly speaking, two currents in liberal political thought about religion emerged from the late seventeenth and eighteenth centuries, the age of the Enlightenment. One tendency, particularly strong in England and America, sought to develop a political framework of religious liberty that would accommodate diverse faiths. The second tendency, particularly strong in France, identified religion with superstition and unreason and attacked clerical power. The first was the spirit of Locke, the second that of Voltaire; the first, liberalism *toward* religion; the second, liberalism *against* religion. The first called for a shared public sphere, the second for a secular public sphere. The first sought to release minority faiths from the tyranny of the established faith; the second sought to release science, education, and the mind itself from all faith and dogma. The first culminated in the American Revolution, the second in the French Revolution.

The first line of liberal thought had religious toleration as its initial political aim. In seventeenth-century England, "toleration" referred to any relaxation of the penalties and disabilities suffered by dissenters from the established Church of England. The 1689 Toleration Act, as we have seen, brought only a partial relaxation, as it allowed some dissenting Protestants the right to worship but failed to repeal laws excluding them from government office and the universities and did not extend any rights to Catholics or non-Christians. Even where toleration was more comprehensive, it was conceptually only a limited step. Toleration is a grant of liberty by the state, not the recognition of an inalienable human right; it exemplifies Madison's dictum that in Europe power granted liberty rather than the reverse. Moreover, if we think of religious liberty as having two dimensions—free exercise of religious belief; and the state's neutrality, or the disestablishment of religion—the 1689 Toleration Act brought the first (at least to Protestant dissenters) but not the second: it did not disestablish the Anglican Church or eliminate the legal privileges that the church enjoyed.[7]

Two other liberal approaches to religious liberty sought to make the state neutral in religion, though they interpreted neutrality in almost opposite ways. One called for nonpreferential support of religion: government aid to a plurality of churches, proportionate to their support among the public. The other called for complete separation of church and state: no state aid to any religious activity. Nothing better illustrates the choice between these two options than the dispute that developed in Virginia during the Revolutionary era. In colonial Virginia, as in four other southern colonies, the Anglican (later the Episcopalian) Church had enjoyed a legal monopoly, while Baptists and other evangelicals had faced punishment, in some cases jail, for practicing their faith. Immediately after independence, in 1776, the Virginia legislature repealed many of the criminal penalties for religious dissent and suspended the taxes that all Virginians had been forced to pay to support the Anglican Church. But the legislature then deadlocked over the next steps to take. In 1784 Patrick Henry introduced a bill based on "the liberal principle" of treating all Christian denominations equally, which called for a tax that individuals could direct to the church of their choice. The alternative, a "Bill for Religious Freedom," drafted originally by Jefferson, though Madison led the fight for it in the legislature, called for separation of church and state: "No man shall be compelled to frequent or support any religious worship, place, or ministry whatsoever." Jefferson's bill passed in 1785 thanks largely to a deluge of petitions in its favor, primarily from evangelicals who after years of legal persecution wanted to keep the state entirely out of religion. It was this alliance of evangelicals and Enlightenment liberals that originally produced separation of church and state in the United States.[8]

Five years after his victory in Virginia, Madison played the central role in drafting the Bill of Rights in the new national government. The First Amendment's language—"Congress shall make no law respecting an establishment of religion, or prohibiting the free exercise thereof"— addressed both dimensions of religious liberty. (The Constitution itself had already declared that "no religious test shall ever be required as a qualification to any office or public trust under the United States.") But because the Bill of Rights was understood at first to apply only to the federal government, seven of the fourteen states in the early 1790s continued to maintain establishments of religion. None of these had established churches in the European sense—that is, an exclusive monopoly of a single church. Rather, as Henry had proposed for Virginia, they had general or multiple establishments under laws that permitted taxpayers, under varying procedures, to assign their assessment to a church of their choice. In one state after another, however, the politics of tax support of religion led to the same outcome as in Virginia. Massachusetts was the last state to abolish government financing of churches in 1833. The case for nonpreferential state aid to religious institutions would later be revived primarily in regard to education and social services, but there was no serious move to return to tax financing of churches themselves.

With the separation of church and state came the rise of a fully deregulated and unsubsidized religious economy in the United States. In contrast, liberal states in Europe either continued to recognize an established religion while providing rights of free religious exercise (as in England) or gave nonpreferential aid to churches (as in the Netherlands). Some opponents of church-state separation in America feared that eliminating state support of churches would lead to the eventual fading away of religion. It did not work out that way. In fact, a comparison of the European and American experiences suggests that government financing of religion reduces the level of religious participation in a society (as measured, for example, by the proportion attending church once a week). Inasmuch as churches in a free, pluralistic religious economy depend on voluntary contributions rather than government subsidies, they tend to be more innovative and entrepreneurial than tax-supported churches in developing and marketing services that attract and keep members. Like any competitive market, an unregulated religious economy also allows stronger "firms" to emerge; denominational change in the United States from the start favored the more rapid growth of the evangelical denominations. Where a single church has a monopoly, however, the incentives and opportunities for innovation are limited, and the proportion of the population attending church every week tends to be low.[9]

Two different logics were at work in the separation of church and state. As in the case of the separation of powers, the drawing of boundaries helps to preserve values specific to different institutions. In this case, separation helps to protect religious life from political control, and government from entanglement in religious passions. In addition, separation generates a competitive dynamic that would be dampened or eliminated if the state directly financed religious institutions. In this respect, the logic of separating church and state is not all that different from the logic of separating the private economy from the state.

ECONOMIC FREEDOM AND
PROPERTY RIGHTS

Private property and economic freedom were important to all of the classical liberals, but liberal thought about these matters underwent a profound change with Adam Smith (1723–90) and the rise of classical economics. Locke had based his analysis of labor, property, and capital accumulation on a theory of natural law and natural rights. In Locke's conception, God gave men the earth and the right to appropriate its fruits, which they had originally done, in a state of nature, by virtue of their labor. Government, Locke argued, then arose chiefly from men's interest in preserving their property, which, however, he defined as including not just their material goods but also their persons and liberties—all that was properly due them and that it would be an injustice to take away. At its foundations, the theory was teleological; it defended private property and individual enterprise as a fulfillment of God's purposes.[10]

Nearly a century later, when he published *The Wealth of Nations* (1776), Smith still used the language of natural rights, but his arguments were secular, empirical, and utilitarian. Jeremy Bentham (1748–1832), the founder of utilitarianism as a philosophical system, dismissed natural rights entirely, claiming that all law and policy ought to be based solely on the greatest happiness of the greatest number. Though they significantly amended Smith and Bentham, the classical economists who followed in their wake—David Ricardo (1772–1823), J. B. Say (1767–1832), James Mill (1773–1836), John Stuart Mill (1806–73), and others—also framed their analysis of economic institutions and policies entirely in terms of their effects on consumption and utility. It is with Smith, Bentham, and later classical economists that we reach "economic liberalism" in the generally understood sense: a belief in the spontaneous harmony of the market, bottomed on a system of law but with a minimum of government regulation. Economic liberalism shared the suspicion of concentrated power characteristic of constitutional liberalism. Preserving the independence of private property and commerce reflected the same overall commitment to maintaining spheres of autonomy from the state; opposition to monopoly was the economic counterpart to the separation-of-powers doctrine. Classical economics, however, gave liberalism a comprehensive, analytical basis not just for doubt about concentrated power but for positive confidence in what Smith called "the system of natural liberty."

Economic liberalism rested on the presumption that individual consumers and producers are best able to make decisions for themselves. As Smith put it, "Every individual, it is evident, can, in his local situation, judge much better than any statesman or lawgiver can do for him." And just as each of us can best determine what is in our own interest and act accordingly, so we expect others to act for their advantage in any exchange: "It is not from the benevolence of the butcher, the brewer, or the banker, that we expect our dinner, but from their regard to their own interest," Smith famously wrote. Here, he argued, lies the genius of liberty: from countless self-interested choices arise mutually beneficial bargains, the division of labor, and increased wealth. An individual "intends only his own gain" but is "led by an invisible hand to promote an end which was no part of his intention."[11]

Although Smith believed in a natural identity of interests in economic exchange, his earlier work, *The Theory of Moral Sentiments*, gave central importance to sympathy as an innate source of moral judgment and law, described justice as "the main pillar that upholds the whole edifice," and argued that the natural "consciousness of ill desert" and "terrors of merited punishment" serve "as the great safeguards of the association of mankind, to protect the weak, to curb the violent, and to chastise the guilty." Morality and law, in Smith's conception, provide the framework of an economy where individuals are best left free to make choices for themselves. This was the basis of "the liberal plan of equality, liberty, and justice."[12]

When Smith first set forth these ideas, they had a more radical and progressive thrust than is generally appreciated today. The basic premises contradicted the regnant paternalism in both philosophy and state policy, which assumed ordinary working people to be economically as well as politically incompetent. Emphasizing the contributions of labor and enterprise, liberalism downgraded the aristocratic and genteel values of honor and leisure. It was wholly opposed to the entire structure of archaic rules and customs that prevented individuals from exercising free choice, such as guild regulations of apprenticeship, laws of settlement restricting the mobility of the poor, and restrictions on the buying and selling of various commodities. Liberals wanted to remove the obstacles that stood in the way of effort, energy, and enterprise: They favored the career open to talent, unhindered by the privileges of rank. They sought freedom to buy and sell land, unlimited by feudal tenures. They approved of freedom to borrow and lend money at interest, unrestricted by laws against usury. And, of course, they agitated for free trade, unfettered by exclusive colonial empires, excessive tariffs, and other barriers.

All of this must be taken in its political context. The mercantilist states of Smith's era created monopolies, imposed barriers to trade, and otherwise intervened in the economy with the deliberate aim of supporting privileged interests. Limiting the reach of the state, as classical liberals knew it, seemed therefore to be a means of expanding both liberty and equality. Far from being an apologist for the capitalist class, Smith showed his sympathies for workers throughout *The Wealth of Nations*. In his chapter on "Profits of Stock," for example, he wrote, "Our merchants and master-manufacturers complain much of the bad effects of high wages in raising the price and thereby lessening the sale of their goods. . . . They say nothing concerning the bad effects of high profits. They are silent with regard to the pernicious effects of their own gains. They complain only of those of other people." High wages, he maintained, were a good thing:

> Servants, labourers and workmen of different kinds make up the far greater part of every great political society. But what improves the circumstances of the greater part can never be regarded as an inconveniency to the whole. No society can be flourishing and happy, of which the far greater part of the members are poor and miserable. It is but equity, besides, that they who feed, cloath and lodge the whole body of the people, should have such a share of the produce of their own labour as to be themselves tolerably well fed, cloathed and lodged.[13]

Smith's opposition to government regulation partly reflected his view of whose interests government was likely to serve. "Whenever the legislature attempts to regulate the differences between masters and their workmen, its counsellors are always the masters," he declared. "When the regulation, therefore, is in favour of the workmen it is always just and equitable; but it is sometimes otherwise when in favour of the masters." In another passage that might be mistaken as coming from Karl Marx, Smith declared, "Civil government, so far as it is instituted for the security of property, is in reality instituted for the defence of the rich against the poor, or of those who have some property against those who have none at all." While Smith did not want government to tell businessmen what to do, he was just as unenthusiastic about businessmen telling government what to do. "Any new law or regulation of commerce" proposed by merchants, Smith wrote, ought to receive "the most suspicious attention," as it "comes from an order of men whose interest is never exactly the same with that of the public, who have generally an interest to deceive and even to oppress the public, and who accordingly have, upon many occasions, both deceived and oppressed it." When he died in 1790, revolutionary France celebrated his achievement, while England snubbed him. It was only after his death that Smith was converted into a political conservative.[14]

Smith saw government as necessary chiefly for three purposes: defense against external enemies, protection against oppression and fraud (the administration of justice), and the creation of "certain public works and certain public institutions, which it can never be for the interest of any individual, or small number of individuals, to erect and maintain . . . though it may frequently do much more than repay [the expense] to a great society." In addition to these provisions, Smith indicated his approval for various other interventions, such as regulation of the price of bread when a monopoly controlled the supply. Smith also favored the establishment of local schools that would have masters "partly but not wholly paid by the public" and charge a fee low enough that even common laborers could afford to educate their children. In the context of its time—Britain would not adopt public financing of education for another century—Smith's position implied a significant

expansion of government's role. Other classical economists also supported publicly financed education and, in general, took a more flexible
view of government policy than is commonly thought, even as they upheld non-interference as a presumptive ideal and advocated free trade
and other measures to liberalize the economy.[15]

In politics and public life, however, economic liberalism took on a
more dogmatic character. Calling for a wholly self-regulating market
economy, the publicists of laissez-faire interpreted nearly all state intervention as incompatible with property rights, free trade, and freedom of
contract. In early nineteenth-century Britain, the Manchester School—
liberals campaigning for free trade—successfully fought against all taxes
and restrictions on imports and exports. Perhaps their greatest achievement was the 1846 repeal of the Corn Laws (tariffs on foreign grain),
which opened the way to cheap food for British workers, a major factor
in their improved standard of living in later decades. The laissez-faire
liberals, however, also opposed a minimum wage or any regulation of
working conditions for adult men, and this view prevailed for a long
time. Laissez-faire came to stand for free trade in labor and land as well
as goods. Yet whether there was ever an "age of laissez-faire" in Britain
or the United States is a point disputed by historians because state intervention in the economy, far from disappearing during the mid-1800s,
took new forms, such as growing public health regulation.[16] Only
Britain consistently upheld free trade; the United States, Germany, and
France (after 1870) remained protectionist. Ideologically, laissez-faire
prevailed in its strongest form in Britain during the middle decades of
the nineteenth century, when it exercised a predominant role in shaping social and economic policy. After the steep rise in taxes during
the French Wars, Britain saw public spending grow more slowly than
the economy; the government never adopted any sort of economic
strategy or plan for growth other than letting the market take its course,
and it did little to control depressions or to soften their impact. But
laissez-faire was not applied consistently, and both the classical economists and liberal governments made an increasing number of exceptions
to the non-interference principle in the face of rising social problems
from industrialization and the growth of cities.

Laissez-faire in practice never meant the government entirely abstained from shaping the structure of economic institutions. The state continued to set the basic "rules of the game" in the economy, and in this respect its role was more than that of a neutral umpire. In labor disputes, for example, the law was heavily weighted on the side of employers. Where property rights conflicted, economic liberals also generally favored the property interests associated with industrialization and economic growth. Property rights are not fixed and absolute, and in cases of conflicting rights there is no way to avoid essentially political decisions about which interests to recognize or to prefer over others. Consider a typical nineteenth-century conflict between an industrialist who wanted to build a mill on a river and landowners nearby or downstream whose property might be diminished in value by the mill. Although the common law in England and America had traditionally given priority to the neighbors' rights in line with the maxim "first in time is first in right," the courts shifted toward rules favoring industrial expansion and freeing industrialists of strict liability.[17]

The most striking development along these lines—that is, toward reducing commercial liability in order to spur growth—was the rise of the limited-liability, or joint-stock, corporation. Though feared as an invitation to reckless commercial behavior, the corporation was nonetheless needed for development so that capital could be raised from investors who were not active partners in an enterprise. Early business corporations, which had required special charters from the state, were few in number and often condemned by liberals as privileged monopolies. But rather than eliminate such corporations altogether, economic liberals favored opening up rights of incorporation through laws that made it necessary only to satisfy minimal administrative requirements, not to receive a special legislative charter. The United States and Britain both introduced general incorporation laws in the mid-nineteenth century.

Liberal policy therefore did not merely support the rights of individual property owners; it supported rights of a particular kind, and it populated the economy with new types of organizations. Liberal policy toward civil society and political life had a similar effect, not merely recognizing the rights of individuals but giving rise to new forms of association. And because the new organizations—economic enterprises, civil associations, and political parties—enjoyed the protection of liberal rights, they provided an institutional base outside the state for the classical liberal discipline of power.

CIVIL SOCIETY AND
REPRESENTATIVE GOVERNMENT

Besides religious and economic freedom, classical liberalism upheld other aspects of individual liberty that affected the structure of society and government. These were no longer framed as the liberties of particular social groups or localities, but rather as the rights of citizens, or even more broadly, as universal human rights. In language echoing the American Declaration of Independence, the French National Assembly's Declaration of the Rights of Man and of Citizens, adopted in 1789, proclaimed that men are "free and equal in respect of their rights" and that the purpose of "all political association" is the preservation of those rights, which it described as "liberty, property, security, and resistance to oppression." How far did those rights extend? "The exercise of the natural rights of every man," the Declaration said, "has no other limits than those which are necessary to secure to every other man the free exercise of the same rights; and these limits are determinable only by the law." Immanuel Kant, writing in 1797, made the coexistence of one individual's freedom with another's, under a law applicable to all, the central criterion of what he called "the universal principle of right." In an earlier essay, Kant had written, "The highest purpose of man—i.e., the development of all natural capacities—can be fulfilled . . . only in a society which has not only the greatest freedom, and therefore a continual antagonism among its members, but also the most precise specification and preservation of the limits of this freedom in order that it can co-exist with the freedom of others."[18]

Some classical liberals distinguished between two kinds of liberty, political and civil. Political liberty consists in the power of filling "public offices, or, at least, of having votes in the nomination of those who fill them," whereas civil liberty is simply "that power over their own actions, which the members of the State reserve to themselves, and which their officers must not infringe," the clergyman and scientist Joseph Priestley, later famous for his discovery of oxygen, wrote in 1768.[19] The plural form "civil liberties" did not enter general use until the twentieth century and now typically covers voting rights and other aspects of political liberty. "Civil liberty," as Priestley and others understood the idea, referred to all rights to freedom of private action, whether religious, economic, or otherwise.

But could a society that protected civil liberty, prized private pursuits, and rewarded economic self-interest also sustain political liberty, social harmony, and the public good? Some doubted that it could. In *An Essay on the History of Civil Society* (1767), for example, the Scottish philosopher Adam Ferguson described civil society as having progressively evolved from a "rude" to more "polished" stages of development. Like his contemporary Adam Smith, Ferguson believed that individuals have an innate moral sense that civil society helps to cultivate. But, reflecting the anxiety of classical republicanism, Ferguson worried that as civil society advanced, self-interest and the division of labor would undermine civic virtue: "Society is made to consist of parts, of which none is animated with the spirit of society itself."[20]

The French liberal Benjamin Constant posed the problem in particularly acute fashion in a famous lecture on "ancient" and "modern" liberty in 1819. In the ancient republics, Constant argued, liberty was the "active and constant participation in collective power," whereas in the modern world, liberty consists of "peaceful enjoyment and private independence." The ancient republics completely subjected the individual to the collective power: "No importance was given to individual independence, neither in relation to opinions, nor to labor, nor, above all, to religion." But the busy citizens of the modern world's great commercial nations relish their independence, and they rely on a representative government to take care of public affairs. For them, Constant maintained, there is no going back to the ancient world's little warrior republics, where slaveholding citizens had the leisure to devote themselves to the polis, and he upbraided Jean-Jacques Rousseau for trying to resurrect the ancient republican ideals, as these had served, during and after the Revolution, only as "deadly pretexts for more than one kind of tyranny." But Constant's point was not to idealize the modern absorption in private life. For if people neglected politics—if they failed to monitor their representatives and hold them accountable—they would surely lose their individual independence as well as their political liberty. The task, he concluded, was to "learn how to combine the two."[21]

A little more than a decade later, in 1831–32, another French liberal, Alexis de Tocqueville, visited the United States and came back with an answer to the problem that Constant had posed. Tocqueville used a new word, "individualism," to describe a tendency he had observed in America. While egoism, according to Tocqueville, is "a passionate and exaggerated love of self" disposing men to prefer themselves to others, individualism is "a mature and calm feeling, which disposes each member of the community to sever himself from the mass of his fellows and to draw apart with his family and his friends, so that after he has thus formed a little circle of his own, he willingly leaves society at large to itself." The danger to society, as Tocqueville saw it, arises from the growing number of people who, while not necessarily rich, have acquired enough to satisfy their own wants: "They owe nothing to any man, they expect nothing from any man; they acquire the habit of always considering themselves as standing alone, and they are apt to imagine that their whole destiny is in their own hands."

But in America, Tocqueville found, countervailing forces kept individualism in check. Political liberty itself, particularly at the local level, drew people into public life. The problems of their own communities, far more than the great and distant concerns of the world, interested citizens in the public good and convinced them "that they constantly stand in need of one another in order to provide for it." "Local freedom"—epitomized by the New England town meeting—was therefore crucial in bringing people together to see their common needs. "Civil associations" serving causes of all kinds, building churches, schools, and hospitals or providing entertainment and sociability, also linked individuals to wider public concerns. "Wherever at the head of some new undertaking you see the government in France, or a man of rank in England, in the United States you will be sure to find an association." Public communication was critical in generating new voluntary organizations. Because Americans were not united by "firm and lasting ties," only persuasion could obtain their joint effort, and nothing was so useful to that end as the press: "Nothing but a newspaper can drop the same thought into a thousand minds at the same moment." Newspapers were vital therefore, not just in protecting individual freedom but even more in overcoming individualism and maintaining the common life: "Newspapers make associations, and associations make newspapers."[22]

Freedom of association and freedom of the press were critical aspects of civil liberty that, as of 1830, were both more securely established in the United States than in Europe. Tocqueville showed that a new structure of civil society was being built in America on the basis of those rights. The French Revolution had swept away local privileges and autonomy and, in the interest of promoting loyalty to the nation alone, suppressed all independent associations. The state maintained this posture under Napoleon and even after his ouster, severely restricting associations and the press and keeping governmental power centralized in Paris. In its reaction against the French Revolution, Britain had also cracked down on popular assemblies and associations, though it later relaxed its controls. But as Tocqueville suggested, deference to men of rank in Britain inhibited the growth of associations. In both Europe and America, churches served as a template for other organizations, and Europe's established churches provided little room for popular participation. All these conditions were reversed in the early American republic. America's more democratic, congregational churches, often organized in new settlements without any formally trained minister, provided large numbers of people with experience in creating and running associations. The United States did not require a license or any other form of official permission to start an association, hold a meeting, or found a publication. American policy also positively promoted the proliferation of newspapers. Fearing a popular press that could stir unrest, European states censored newspapers, restricted their access to the post office, and imposed onerous taxes on them so as to make them more expensive and limit their circulation. In contrast, the United States left the press untaxed, gave all newspapers access to the Post Office, subsidized them through cheap postal rates, and thereby deliberately facilitated their establishment and distribution throughout the country, even in small towns on the frontier. The federal government, in other words, did not just guarantee the press non-interference; it also created the positive conditions for its decentralized expansion.[23]

The American developments pointed the way toward a new understanding of civil society and its relation to the state. Edmund Burke, perhaps more than anyone else the founder of modern conservatism, had attacked the French Revolution's stripping away of traditional social distinctions as a catastrophic loss of the cumulative wisdom of civil society. Tocqueville believed that the Burkean conservative impulse was futile because equality was an inexorable tide and that civil society could be reconstituted in a free society as long as that society controlled the tendencies toward individualism, on one side, and the expansion of the state, on the other. Other nineteenth-century theorists, notably Hegel and Marx, conceived of civil society as resting entirely on self-interest. Marx wrote that the only bonds holding men together in civil society are egoistic and that the "so-called rights of man" fail to go "beyond man as a member of civil society, that is, an individual drawn into himself, into the confines of his private interests and private caprice, and separated from the community."[24] For Marx and others, there was only a twofold distinction between the state and a privatized civil society, whereas Tocqueville suggested a conception of civil society as a third sphere that functions as a counterweight to both the state and the private economy. In this view, civil society has the twin virtue of diverting responsibilities from the state and of educating citizens about the broader public welfare; it keeps government within limits but heightens civic participation. "A government can no more be competent to keep alive and to renew the circulation of opinions and feelings among a great people than to manage all the speculations of productive industry."[25] The value of both civil associations and the press consists, then, not merely in their role as watchdogs over government, but as an animating source of public energy, capable of focusing and mobilizing autonomous effort in society. And, in this way, civil society contributes to the overall power of the society—it strengthens the connections and mutual trust that are the basis of what is now called "social capital."

As religious liberty implied a plurality of churches, so civil liberty— as liberals understood it—implied a plurality of other associations to serve and represent their members' joint concerns and public purposes. These freely created associations, unlicensed and uncontrolled by the state, may even compete with each other for support of the same constituency. This pluralist model of civil society differs from a "corporatist" system in which the state authorizes a single organization to serve as the official, compulsory association for each of a series of important interest groups in society. Just as classical liberalism conceived of the economy as a sphere of free choice and competition, so a parallel liberal conception of (non-economic) civil society emerged as a sphere of free choice and competition.

Competition for the right to represent the public was also at the heart of the liberal theory of representative government. The liberal conception of the public—the political nation—still encompassed only a limited fraction of society, and even within these limits, classical liberals were not simple majoritarians; their emphasis on checks and balances reflected a suspicion of majorities, especially ephemeral ones. Constitutions and courts were expected to provide ballast against sudden swings in public opinion. The classical liberals also did not expect the people's representatives merely to transmit the wishes of their constituents but rather to reason their way to a higher ground through discussion and mutual accommodation. Representative government, Constant argued, is the logical correlate of modern liberty: "The representative system is a proxy given to a certain number of men by the mass of the people who wish their interests to be defended and who nevertheless do not have the time to defend them themselves."[26] Rousseau had written of the English that they were free only when they voted but were slaves the rest of the time. Classical liberalism upheld the contrary view that the people can maintain their liberty by periodically holding their representatives accountable and by using the press, separation of powers, and other mechanisms as safeguards during the intervals between elections. Bentham in his later years and other "philosophic radicals" took the position that universal suffrage, by forcing governments to register their citizens' equal interest in happiness, would be more likely to serve the happiness of the greatest number. By and large, however, the classical liberals were not democrats, at least not as we understand democracy today. But by broadening rights to public knowledge, expanding and entrenching the representative principle, creating systems of political competition, and furthering the growth of an independent civil society, the liberal revolutions in America and France helped to furnish institutions that would later allow democracy to succeed.

THE LIMITS OF
CLASSICAL LIBERALISM

By the mid-nineteenth century, classical liberalism was both a highly developed system of ideas expounded by philosophers, economists, and political thinkers and a set of principles expressed in constitutions, laws, and government policies. Of course, even where liberal thought influenced politics and institutions, as it did in Britain and the United States, it was never the sole influence, and some failings of those societies—such as the persistence of slavery in antebellum America—reflected not liberalism itself, but the inability to put it into practice. In other respects, however, the injustices and shortcomings of liberal societies were directly related to the limitations of contemporary liberal thought. With one hand, classical liberalism extended the promise of universal human rights, but with the other, it withheld those rights from the greater part of humanity. Classical liberalism proposed a powerful abstract model for understanding a market economy and releasing its energies, but the model failed to anticipate the damage that the market could do to society, the natural environment, or the stability of the economy itself.

The limits of liberal universalism were particularly evident in relation to the conquered and colonized peoples who belonged to civilizations that Europeans and their descendants considered strange and inferior. Some of the leading advocates of free trade, such as the Manchester liberal Richard Cobden (1804–65), envisioned a world without empires in which nations were peacefully bound together through commercial ties. But most liberals were not anti-imperialist. Indeed, far from impeding the rise of imperialism in the eighteenth and nineteenth centuries, classical liberalism generally helped to rationalize it. Following Locke, liberals held that all men are naturally free, equal, and rational, but the same liberals viewed uncivilized peoples as given to superstition and irrationality and therefore as incapable, at least for the time being, of exercising their natural rights. A key element here was a progressive vision of history, which arranged civilizations in a hierarchy and provided a warrant for the advanced to dominate the backward. According to John Stuart Mill, who worked for the East India Company for thirty-five years and wrote more than thirty official reports on British colonial policy, the principles of liberty applied only in societies where "mankind have become capable of being improved by free and equal discussion." Mill distinguished between colonies "of similar civilization to the ruling country," such as British possessions in North America and Australia, which, he believed, ought to enjoy representative government, and colonies with barbarous peoples, such as India, for whom sadly there was only a "choice of despotisms." Colonial rule, according to Mill, was "as legitimate as any other" if it best facilitated the transition of the subject people to "a higher stage of improvement."[27]

At home, Mill was a radical, a rare and eloquent advocate of equal rights for women. Although Locke rejected earlier patriarchal theories of politics that conceived of the state as the family writ large, he posited a social contract as the basis of government that was an agreement only of male property owners. For Locke and other early liberals, women did not figure in the public realm; the appropriate locus for the expression of female virtue was the private sphere of the family. The liberal revolutions and later liberal government, however, did extend women's rights before the law (for example, in regard to inheritance) and resulted in more widespread female education and literacy, often justified, according to the ideals of "republican motherhood," on the grounds that women needed to take proper care of the household and educate their sons to be good citizens, not that they would be better equipped themselves for the public arena. In the excitement stirred by the American and French Revolutions, a few works, notably Mary Wollstonecraft's *Vindication of the Rights of Woman* (1793), claimed civil and political liberty as women's equal birthright, and during the nineteenth century liberal arguments about individual rights became central to the movement for women's suffrage. But most liberal theorists throughout this period defended the exclusion of women from political participation.[28]

There was more dissension among liberals about the political exclusion of men without property. The traditional view among classical republicans and early liberals was that only men with sufficient property could make genuinely independent political choices—choices, moreover, that would reflect the stake they had in a well-ordered society. But by the late eighteenth century, liberal revolutionaries such as Thomas Paine favored universal manhood suffrage; Vermont imposed no property requirements for voting when it was admitted to the Union in 1790, and by the 1830s most states had swept away such requirements. In England and the rest of Europe, the extension of political rights to working-class men came later, and the denial of those rights during the nineteenth century contributed to the rise of socialist movements that rejected liberalism altogether. Despite moves toward a wider franchise, classical liberalism had a hierarchy of liberties as well as a hierarchy of peoples, and civil liberty (understood as embracing religious and economic freedom) generally came before political liberty.

The conflict between the promise of universal rights and the practices of political and social exclusion was a continuing source of tension within liberalism as well as opposition to it. The other great unresolved liberal tension concerned the role of the state and the problem of inequality. Smith had argued for minimal government intervention partly on the grounds that government usually intervened on behalf of monopoly and privilege and that ordinary people, as producers and consumers, would do better in the marketplace. But if reform addressed the first of these problems—the undemocratic distribution of political power—by extending the franchise, could government intervention then be used more fairly as a means of protecting popular interests and achieving equality? The classical economists' support for publicly financed education suggested how it might. As the industrial revolution unfolded, measures to protect workers came to seem more urgent, even to those who believed in free trade and other liberal economic policies. Yet the tenets of classical liberalism often pointed in contrary directions. For example, the principle of freedom of association supported the right of workers to form unions, while the belief in free competition suggested that any combination in restraint of trade, even by workers, was illegitimate.

In the face of such questions, two lines of thought emerged from liberalism's classical beginnings. On the one side was the liberalism of laissez-faire, increasingly embraced by political conservatives. Laissez-faire liberals opposed government regulation of working hours and conditions, workers' rights to organize unions, and other similar measures on the grounds of freedom of contract: individual workers and employers knew their interest best and had a right to enter into whatever bargains they struck with each other. Drawing on the work of the classical economist Thomas Malthus, laissez-faire liberals also argued that the relief of poverty, unless carefully restricted, was likely to have perverse effects because it would lead the poor to reproduce faster, creating more mouths to feed than society could support. Later, particularly through the influence of Herbert Spencer, who coined the phrase "survival of the fittest," laissez-faire became joined with social Darwinism in an attack on virtually all forms of government intervention on behalf of public health and welfare.

The other line of thought from classical liberalism favored greater equality and a state that was more democratic and more competent. As liberalism called for equal rights before the law, so these liberals insisted on equal rights in the making of the law—equal political liberty, not just equal civil liberty. In their view, an equal chance in life implied public education and a variety of measures to rationalize law and administration so as to improve government's capacities to improve public health and well-being. As Tocqueville predicted, democracy was a swelling tide, and liberalism itself was subject to it. The rising power of radical and socialist movements forced liberals to revisit their founding principles, reinterpret their conflicting commitments, and adapt to a new political environment. Liberalism invited democracy. Then democracy changed liberalism.

II

MODERN
DEMOCRATIC LIBERALISM

————

4

Lineages of Democratic Liberalism

———

Modern liberalism emerged from, not one, but a series of changes in liberal ideas and institutions during the late nineteenth and early twentieth centuries. The tension in classical liberalism between the language of universal rights and entrenched practices of political exclusion was resolved, as a matter of principle, in favor of democracy: an equal right to freedom came to include political liberty. In economic and social policy, liberals embraced stronger rights for labor and new forms of government intervention to achieve prosperity, control private corporate power, and protect individual dignity and independence in the face of adversity. While favoring greater regulation of the economy, liberalism came to stand for the deregulation of private life, stronger protection of civil liberties and individual self-expression, and respect for cultural diversity. At the international level, liberalism called for resistance to authoritarian and totalitarian regimes and the creation of an institutional framework aimed at deterring aggression, ensuring national self-determination, and advancing democracy and human rights.

Each of these developments—the democratization of liberalism, the rejection of laissez-faire in favor of positive government, the growth of civil libertarianism, and the rise of liberal internationalism—had a somewhat different lineage, in some cases originating in movements that liberals themselves, especially laissez-faire liberals, resisted. But by

the early twentieth century, the various elements formed a unified out-
look and began to influence policy, as in Britain's Liberal governments
before World War I and the reforms of the Progressive era and New
Deal in the United States.

Two stories—one of betrayal, the other of progress—are commonly
told about the shift to modern liberalism. In the story of betrayal, favored by free-market conservatives, liberals abandoned the earlier
commitment to individual freedom when they began advocating a
stronger role for government. Modern liberals, however, are no less
committed to individual liberty than their predecessors—indeed, in
some respects they are more committed, as they no longer put the
rights of white men above those of everyone else. They have changed
their ranking of liberties, however, elevating rights to civil and political
liberty and basic requirements of human development above the rights
of property. Modern liberalism continues to rest on the principles of
constitutional government that earlier liberals upheld. The elements
of the classical discipline of power described in the previous chapter—
the public-private distinction, division of powers, separation of law and
religion, a market economy, an independent civil society, and representative government—remain the foundations of modern democratic liberalism. The constitutional liberalism of the eighteenth century, as I
have tried to show, already provided for the creation as well as the control of state power, and even the classical liberal economists called for
government to finance education and public goods. Where modern liberalism has called for government to take on new roles, it has done so
in the face of growing agglomerations of private power and on the basis
of distinctly liberal principles to safeguard individual freedom and guarantee equal protection of the law.

But if the shift from classical to modern liberalism is not a case of betrayal, neither is it simply the result of "progress," if by that we mean an
inexorable trend toward modernization or moral improvement. The
trouble with a progressive, evolutionary story of modern liberalism is
that it makes it appear as if only a liberal and democratic outcome
is possible in the modern world: it falsely equates liberalism and modernity. It leaves out the historical uncertainties, moral ambiguities, social
conflicts, internal tensions, and reversals that accompanied the emer-

gence of a more democratic liberalism, and it is too complacent about the inevitability and permanence of changes that have occurred. It is entirely possible to believe that liberalism has brought moral and economic progress without believing in the teleological proposition that progress has brought liberalism.

Modern liberalism offers a distinct vision of what an equal right to freedom requires. Formal guarantees of civil and political rights, liberals have come to believe, are an insufficient basis for a free and just society unless government also acknowledges rights to minimum conditions of security and human development. Broader interpretations of other earlier liberal commitments also follow from the effort to put equal freedom into practice. Just as the state must treat people of different religious faiths equally, so it must show equal respect for people of diverse ethnic and cultural groups. In the international arena, that same equality of respect requires a rejection of colonialism and imperialism in favor of support for the aspirations of diverse peoples for national independence and democracy.

Although the change from classical to modern liberalism may be described as an intellectual or philosophical development, it did not take place only on the plane of thought. Modern liberalism was the response to a long struggle for power within and among nations; liberalism had to adapt to compete in an era of wrenching social change, recurrent economic crises, and war on a previously unimaginable scale. Although the elements of modern liberalism were already in evidence by the early 1900s, the almost continuous crisis of the twentieth century—World War I, the Great Depression, World War II, and the Cold War—was critical in the consolidation of modern liberalism. In the darkest years of that crisis, many people doubted that liberal societies and liberal leaders were made of strong enough stuff to endure. But liberalism didn't just endure; the long crisis helped to clarify what was truly important in a liberal world, and worth fighting for.

DEMOCRACY, EDUCATION, AND CITIZENSHIP

The phrase "liberal democracy" is so familiar that it no longer seems to denote a compound concept. The two elements, however, are not just theoretically separable—liberalism and democracy were historically distinct developments. The liberal revolutions of the eighteenth century called for government that rested on the consent of the governed and assured their inalienable rights. But through various strategies of evasion—by claiming, for example, that socially subordinate groups were irrational, had too dangerous a will, or lacked any independent will at all—classical liberalism sanctioned the denial of rights to women, men without property, and people of color. By the early to mid-twentieth century, modern liberalism had repudiated these exclusions and the excuses supporting them and become committed to making true citizens of all who had been merely subjects of the state. The project of liberal citizenship that the American and French Revolutions began, modern liberalism has sought to complete.

From the eighteenth century, liberal citizenship has developed in a reciprocal relationship with the nation-state. It is to the nation-state that citizens must chiefly look for the guarantee of their liberties as well as for protection from force and fraud; it is the nation-state that provides the primary site of political life and the boundaries of the public to which government is accountable; and it is to the nation-state that citizens owe their political allegiance. (The growth of a global civil society and international institutions has not fundamentally changed these realities, though someday it may.) Critics of liberalism often say that it is solely about rights, not obligations, but the fundamental obligations of liberal citizenship ought never to be in doubt. These include loyalty to the nation, payment of taxes, and possibly service in the military that may lead to the ultimate sacrifice of one's own life. It is precisely because of the awesome claims of the state that the rights against it are so vital and receive so much emphasis in liberal thought.

Beyond these fundamentals, citizenship in a liberal democracy implies further responsibilities, though these cannot, as a general matter, be enforced by law. Here we require a distinction. In a minimal sense, citizenship means nationality—a status imprinted, for example, on a passport, carrying with it a legally defined bundle of rights and obligations. But a good citizen, a true citizen, voluntarily fulfills civic responsibilities that may range from staying informed to voting, to serving the community or nation and devoting effort to public purposes. How to cultivate citizenship in this active, normative sense has never been obvious. A socially exclusive ideal is one alternative. Classical republicanism revered the active citizen, but according to its criteria of manliness and independence, only property-owning white men could fulfill the role. These assumptions were embedded in early liberalism and challenged only by the most radical of eighteenth-century liberals. With the extension of the franchise and other rights, modern liberalism has had to develop a different understanding of how all people, regardless of means or identity, could become good citizens and do the work of popular self-government.

Liberal democracy operates on the premise that individuals, no matter who they are, know their best interests as voters. When they speak at the polls, their word is final, and no one has the right to set aside an election on the grounds that they know what the people need better than the people themselves. All the same, elected leaders are not bound afterward to carry out the voters' will as if it consisted of a list of fixed instructions. Legislators and other officials must be open to each other's arguments and new information, even as they attempt to sway public opinion to their side. Liberal democracy also presupposes that over a longer period citizens and leaders are capable of improved judgment, not only through exposure to robust debate but also through education and experience. In the nineteenth and early twentieth centuries, as the franchise was extended—and, in the United States, as large numbers of immigrants arrived—liberals who supported a more democratic society saw the expansion of public schools and other forms of education as a vital requirement for the making of good citizens. This was one of several reasons that the expansion of democracy and education occurred together.

The extension of the right to vote in the United States and Europe was originally a struggle over the relationship of political liberty and property, one facet of the broader tension between citizenship and class. Eighteenth-century liberals saw liberty as upholding property, and property as upholding liberty. When America declared its independence, most states retained property qualifications for voting. But because landownership was widely diffused, the franchise was also widely distributed, at least for that time. As of 1790, 60 to 70 percent of white men were eligible to vote, compared to only about 15 percent of men in England. In the early American republic, the proportion continued to climb, particularly in the 1820s and '30s, as the older states reduced and then eliminated pecuniary qualifications, and the states entering the Union after 1800 did not include them in their constitutions. Britain moved far more slowly to reduce economic barriers to voting through parliamentary reform bills in 1832, 1867, and 1884. In 1831, before the First Reform Bill, the electorate in England numbered only 440,000 out of a total population of 14 million; in Scotland, only 5,000 out of a population of 2.7 million could vote. Yet even after the Third Reform Bill, the registration lists carried only 59 percent of men; it was not until 1918 that Britain achieved universal manhood suffrage. France, less stable during the nineteenth century, adopted manhood suffrage in 1830 and 1848, only to see it overturned each time, until it became more firmly established after the advent of the Third Republic in 1870. Other European countries also moved toward parliamentary governments and manhood suffrage in the late nineteenth and early twentieth centuries—Belgium in 1894, Italy in 1911. Nineteen countries, including Britain and the United States, gave women the right to vote between 1915 and 1920.[1]

There is no single, generally accepted explanation for democratization in all the many contexts in which it has occurred. Under a representative government, democratization takes place only when a majority of the existing electorate, or a dominant party or coalition, finds it in its interest to share power with the disenfranchised or at least is no longer able to defend their exclusion. But it may reach that decision for more than one reason. During the nineteenth century, changes in social structure—notably the rise of urban working and middle classes and, perhaps even more important in Europe, the relative decline of the landed aristocracy and the peasantry—altered the landscape on which political competition occurred. Popular movements demanding the franchise put the issue on the public agenda, and the established parties often decided under pressure that incorporating those movements into the existing political system was preferable to the risk of violence and revolution and to the alternative of repressive, authoritarian rule.[2]

The most popularly oriented liberals supported universal suffrage on principle, but even the parties to which they belonged were more likely to act on those principles when they coincided with their political interest. The Democrats in the United States and the Liberals in Britain, for example, favored reduced economic barriers to voting that stood to benefit them politically by adding more of their supporters. In some cases, however, a party that was expected to lose from an expanded franchise concluded that some change was inevitable and, rather than antagonize future voters, championed reform of its own making. So it was that Britain passed the Second Reform Bill in 1867 under the Conservative Party leader Benjamin Disraeli, who, it was said, could discern potential conservatives in the working class as Michelangelo could see angels in marble.[3] In still other cases, a political consensus supported a broad franchise. In nineteenth-century America, for example, the western states had such a strong interest in attracting settlers that they allowed immigrants to vote if they merely declared their intention to become citizens.

War has repeatedly created this kind of consensus in favor of a wider suffrage. In the United States, the franchise was extended after both the Revolutionary War and the War of 1812 (through reduced property qualifications); after the Civil War (to African Americans, through the Fifteenth Amendment); after World War I (to women, through the Nineteenth Amendment); and during the Vietnam War (to eighteen-year-olds, through the Twenty-sixth Amendment). In Europe war also led to expanded rights of citizenship. But war per se does not necessarily have that impact; the effects seem to depend on the form of warfare and the level of mobilization, especially the "military participation ratio" (the proportion of the population under arms). The higher the ratio, the sociologist Stanislav Andreski has argued, the more likely war will have a socially leveling impact. Governments in need of popular enlistment and mobilization are especially likely to expand citizenship rights as a means of securing loyalty and commitment. The experience of wartime mobilization may also promote social solidarity, especially a sense of obligation to soldiers. Calling for African Americans to be given the franchise, General William Tecumseh Sherman declared toward the end of the Civil War that "when the fight is over, the hand that drops the musket cannot be denied the ballot."[4] After members of a group, even a stigmatized one, have risked their lives for their country, it becomes extremely difficult to deny that they can be responsible citizens.

Black enfranchisement after the Civil War, however, also underlines another point: change has not necessarily been permanent or linear. Despite the Fifteenth Amendment, whites reestablished exclusive political domination in the South, denying blacks the vote through terrorism by the Ku Klux Klan and such legal measures as poll taxes and literacy tests. Laws restricting the right to vote of immigrants, ex-felons, and other stigmatized groups also contributed to a contraction of the American electorate in the late nineteenth and early twentieth centuries. Democracy came early to America if we think of it only in terms of eliminating class barriers to voting. But because of the failure to guarantee voting rights to African Americans until the 1960s, the United States was actually one of the last Western democracies to achieve universal suffrage.

In nineteenth-century Europe and America, the enfranchisement of (white) workingmen created a dynamic in favor of other rights as well, including a right to primary and later secondary education. Political parties now had to compete for the support of voters who couldn't otherwise afford to send their children to school. That's not to say, however, that the rise of schooling was solely a matter of politics or, insofar as it was political, that it was solely liberal in inspiration. In the Protestant world— notably in Sweden, Britain, New England, and parts of Germany—the concern that individuals be able to read the Bible had been an early factor in the extension of schooling. In continental Europe, "enlightened despots" in Denmark and Prussia during the late eighteenth century had been the first to create national systems of primary education. Laws requiring school attendance, from ages six to ten or twelve, made education a duty as well as a right, and education appealed to some regimes as a way of inculcating habits of obedience and piety. Yet universal schooling, conservatives also feared, might raise expectations and encourage discontent and insolence among those who were destined to be servants and laborers; as Bernard Mandeville, the author of *The Fable of the Bees* (1714), put it, "Should a Horse know as much as a Man, I should not like to be his Rider."[5] This was long the view of much of the English political elite.

In contrast, American politics even in the early republic favored the democratization of competence in the free states and territories (slavery inhibited the growth of public education, even for whites, in the slave-holding areas of the South). The federal government primed the pump of educational finance with land grants for public schools as early as 1785, and communities in the North, which were still overwhelmingly rural, voted to tax themselves to pay for primary education. As urban artisans and mechanics, shopkeepers, and ordinary laborers gained the right to vote in the early 1800s, they also demanded schools for their children. Like universal manhood suffrage, public education as a right of citizenship emerged sooner in the United States than in Britain; the major steps toward the creation of public school systems occurred in the 1830s and '40s in America, but not until 1870 and later in Britain.

Lack of education among the mass of the people had once counted as a reason against their enfranchisement; enfranchisement now counted as a reason in favor of their education. Schooling was the social entitlement most clearly endorsed by liberal ideals. While nineteenth-century liberals saw poor relief as undermining incentives for work and favored making it available only with severe restrictions, they saw education as wholly compatible with individual enterprise and equal opportunity as well as responsible citizenship. Education fit into the liberal vision in more ways than one: it could provide the means of individual self-development and self-discipline, economic growth, and the transmission of a national culture. Whatever the rationale, education was at the center of liberal state-building in the nineteenth and early twentieth centuries.

Liberal interests in equal political rights, the making of good citizens, and the fostering of good government did not, however, always work in the same direction. Concern about corrupt influences on both voters and politicians in late nineteenth-century America led to measures that indirectly reduced lower-class voting participation. Civil service reformers, for example, sought to remove government jobs from the benefits that political leaders could bestow on their followers and thereby aimed to cleanse the public realm of self-enrichment. As necessary as such reforms were for the integrity and efficiency of government, they undermined the ability of political leaders to mobilize voter turnout. Tighter voter registration laws had the same effect of shrinking the electorate. Progressives in the early 1900s supported democratic innovations such as political primaries and referenda and sought to inspire greater participation through a variety of civic organizations. But they also favored greater reliance on professional expertise, which in some respects restricted the scope for popular decisionmaking. Even as liberals came to agree on universal suffrage and a right to basic education, they were divided over how thorough a democracy—how active a public—is realistically possible.

Different conceptions of democratic possibilities also affected liberal concerns about the character of education. In the nineteenth century, as the fear of lower-class political power ran deep, so middle-class liberals hoped that schools and other means of popular education would promote sobriety, respect for the law, and other habits and beliefs that would lead workers to spurn revolution and join in the patient work of reform. But a liberal conception of citizenship could also encourage a more radical view of education in a democracy. By the beginning of the twentieth century, John Dewey and other advocates of what came to be called "progressive education" repudiated the traditional, didactic methods of instruction and called for a greater emphasis on developing students' initiative, critical habits of mind, and ability to relate education to the practical world. This view of education corresponded to a view of citizenship as active, critical, and participatory.

Although struggles over the right to vote and the extent and purpose of education hardly came to an end in the early twentieth century, the fundamental philosophical question of political equality was resolved on liberal and democratic terms. Conservatives and liberals no longer fought over the principles of universal suffrage and a universal right to primary (and later secondary) education. The opposition between them began to be drawn more sharply on other grounds.

EQUALITY, LABOR, AND
POSITIVE GOVERNMENT

If there is one change usually held to mark the difference between classical and modern liberalism, it is the embrace of an enlarged role for the state in economic and social life. Though the change was immense, the usual shorthand description of it as the "end of laissez-faire" lends itself to misunderstanding because liberal governments in the nineteenth century never practiced laissez-faire consistently. In the very decades when laissez-faire ideas were at their height in Britain, the state expanded into new areas. It began inspecting and regulating factories in the 1830s and adopted landmark public health legislation in 1848. An administrative revolution, including the creation of the civil service, strengthened both the state's capacities and public confidence in employing them, as when Parliament in 1870 nationalized the telegraph industry and put it under the Post Office.

In the United States, Alexander Hamilton and other Federalists in the 1790s, and later Henry Clay and the Whigs in the 1830s and '40s, had ambitious plans for using the federal government to promote economic development. What held back their efforts was chiefly a preference for leaving such measures to the states, which were heavily involved in building canals and railroads as well as regulating business generally. Indeed, the $200 million in debt that the states piled up by 1840, largely to invest in canal and railroad companies, exceeded all federal borrowing up to that point. The federal government did play a key role in economic development through grants of public land, particularly to railroads, which received 210,000 square miles, or one-twelfth of the continental United States. Unlike Britain, America in the nineteenth century did not opt for free trade; it maintained a high tariff, justified as protection for domestic industry. The United States also refused to recognize the intellectual property rights of foreign authors and inventors. In short, it behaved in some ways that its own government today would regard as highly reprehensible, shortsighted, and inconsistent with free-market principles.[6]

But in a relative sense, laissez-faire was not a myth in Britain or America. The liberal state in the nineteenth century was less actively involved in directing or coordinating the economy than either its mercantilist precursor or its modern liberal successor. The state assumed no macroeconomic responsibility. Political leaders did not expect, and were not expected, to control sharp swings in the economy or to use positive governmental action as part of an overall strategy for economic growth. Nor did they regard the distribution of income as a proper concern of government. The state did not attempt to relieve the consequences of unemployment or such other sources of adversity as sickness, workplace accidents, and old age, except for minimal, subsistence provision for the poor given under punitive conditions. In Britain both taxes and expenditures were at lower levels during the nineteenth century after the end of the Napoleonic Wars than they had been in the eighteenth century or would be in the twentieth, and taxes were generally even lower in the United States. (Britain had an income tax throughout the 1800s; the United States had one only during the Civil War.) Laissez-faire liberalism reached its height in Britain from 1820 to 1870; the peak years of laissez-faire in the United States came later, in the final three decades of the century. Although both countries adopted some labor and public health statutes, regulation remained limited, and in the United States the Supreme Court struck down some of the state laws regulating working hours and conditions on the grounds that they interfered with the rights of property and freedom of contract guaranteed— as the Court then saw it—by the Fourteenth Amendment.

In each of these areas, modern liberalism would eventually endorse a legitimate role for the state, but it is not as though liberals first conceived an alternative model of political economy and then applied it systematically. On the contrary, modern liberal policy developed mostly in fits and starts through what seemed at the time to be ad hoc responses to particular problems, often at moments of crisis or public outrage. Theory lagged behind practice. The ad hoc character of new governmental measures was true throughout the 1800s and as late as the New Deal. In nineteenth-century Britain, the Conservatives had, if anything, fewer reservations than the Liberals about using the power of the state for social and moral purposes. But governments under both parties enlarged the state's role, and some of the early steps expanding the state could readily be justified within the framework of classical liberalism. The first labor regulations, for example, were adopted to protect children and adult women, who, unlike adult men, were thought incapable of defending their interests through freedom of contract and were therefore an acknowledged exception to the principle of non-interference in the market. Sanitary and public health concerns created another widely acknowledged set of exceptions. Education was an exception for all the reasons mentioned earlier. The helter-skelter growth of cities and the rise of slums created further demands for new forms of regulation and public service.

And so it went: historical experience repeatedly showed the limitations of laissez-faire. The classical economists had predicted great benefits from the free play of markets, and some of those benefits had materialized in the form of greater prosperity. But unregulated markets also led to morally and politically unacceptable consequences such as child labor in factories and mines, epidemic disease in cities, destitution in the midst of plenty, despoliation of the environment, and periodic panics and depressions with mass unemployment. It was out of the trial-and-error responses to these problems, typically coming in waves of scandal, crisis, and reform, that a new "progressive" or "reform" liberalism began to take shape.

The early impetus for public remedy came chiefly from middle-class humanitarian reformers and philanthropists, acting out of moral conviction, sympathy with the "deserving" poor, and often a belief in new scientific and administrative methods to relieve social distress and combat disorder. During the second half of the nineteenth century, however, the rise of labor unions and the expansion of the working-class electorate created a second source of pressure for social reform and economic regulation. In both Britain and the United States, the labor movement benefited from increasing liberal acceptance, and labor's influence and growing strength led liberals to reexamine their attitudes and policies.

Classical liberalism regarded unions with, at best, a deep ambivalence. While acknowledging that workers had a right to freedom of association, classical liberals were suspicious of any combination in restraint of trade and held that unions should have no power over individual workers. Nineteenth-century labor law gave expression to this position. After a ban on "combinations" in 1799–1800, Britain legalized unions in 1824 but for decades thereafter barred them from negotiating a "closed shop" (requiring all workers to belong to a union) or from using any tactics, including picketing, that could be construed as intimidation. Strikes opened unions to suits for damages by employers; any worker who violated a contract of employment was also subject to criminal prosecution, whereas an employer who violated an employment contract could be sued only for civil damages. Parliament finally eliminated this disparity in 1867 by decriminalizing work stoppages and gradually lifted most of the limitations on unions. By 1906 Parliament had freed unions of any liability for damages from calling a strike and expanded their right to picket, though the law still prohibited any use of coercion.[7]

In the United States, the liberalization of labor law took longer and faced especially deep and protracted opposition from the judiciary. As in Britain, workers by the mid-1800s generally had a right of association but were denied legal means of exerting economic power. Employers were able to go to court to secure broad injunctions against strikes, picketing, and boycotts, and even when legislatures passed laws seemingly in defense of unions, judges struck them down as unconstitutional. In 1898, for example, Congress prohibited interstate railroads from discriminating against workers on the basis of union membership, and some states passed analogous laws protecting union members in other industries. But the Supreme Court overturned such statutes on the grounds that employers had a constitutional right to employ, or not to employ, whomever they wished. The decisive legislative and judicial shift in favor of unions and collective bargaining did not come until the New Deal in the 1930s.[8]

The liberal acceptance of organized labor reflected a fundamental reassessment of the meaning of equality. Increasingly, liberals acknowledged that there was no real equality of bargaining between individual workers, often living at the edge of subsistence, and employers, who could readily replace them. Individual freedom of contract therefore did not reflect free and equal consent to wages and working conditions. Especially as firms grew in scale and combined into larger corporations, unions seemed a legitimate way to enable workers to stand on a more equal footing with their employers. Yet liberals continued to be wary of some unions' strong-arm tactics and to regard both business and labor as special interests that needed to be balanced, conciliated, and harmonized in a higher, public interest.

The late nineteenth and early twentieth centuries, particularly the years from 1900 to World War I, saw the shift in liberal understanding of the state, labor, and equality translated into public policy and political theory. In Britain a group of intellectuals and political leaders developed what became known as the "New Liberalism," while the analogous movements and tendencies in the United States went under the banner of "Progressivism." Though there were differences between them, the New Liberals and Progressives reflected the same intellectual currents and advocated many of the same policies. Politically, however, things worked out differently in the two countries.

The immediate context for the development of the New Liberalism was a crisis in Britain's Liberal Party. In 1886, after dominating British politics for a half-century, the Liberals suffered a devastating split precipitated by their longtime leader William Gladstone's endorsement of Irish home rule. One-third of the party's members of Parliament, including a group of Radicals (Liberal Unionists) led by Joseph Chamberlain, defected to the opposition. Chamberlain was both an ardent imperialist and an advocate of a wider government role in social policy, including workers' compensation (for industrial accidents) and old-age pensions; as mayor of Birmingham, he had expanded public services and municipal ownership of utilities. Except for Gladstone's final, weak government of 1892–94, the Conservatives in coalition with Chamberlain's Liberal Unionists ruled Britain from 1886 to 1906. It was this Conservative government that introduced workers' compensation, the first element in what would become the modern welfare state. And it was during these two decades in the political wilderness—when the Liberal Party was besieged not only from the right but also from labor union leaders to their left who were no longer content with Liberal leadership and began building a party of their own—that the New Liberalism took shape.[9]

The New Liberals sought to reconcile principles of individual liberty and responsibility with an expanded program of social reform to address the problems of poverty, economic insecurity, inequality, and urban squalor that beset Britain in the industrial age. Rejecting a conception of society as composed of isolated individuals, they stressed the central importance of mutual interdependence and the moral priority of the "common good." This "organic" view of society, according to Leonard Hobhouse, one of the leading New Liberals, did not postulate a natural harmony of interests (as in classical economics), but "only that there is a possible ethical harmony" attainable "partly by discipline, partly by the improvement of the conditions of life" and "that in such attainment lies the social ideal."

Central to this ideal was a broadened conception of liberty—for women as well as men—involving not just civil and personal freedom but also social liberty, that is, freedom from "restraints on the individual which flow from the hierarchic organization of society," as Hobhouse put it. The struggle for liberty was necessarily a struggle for equality: "Full liberty implies full equality." That did not imply an absolute economic equality, for equality too was subject to considerations of the common good: "If it is really just that A should be superior to B in wealth or power or position, it is only because when the good of all concerned is considered, among whom B is one, it turns out that there is a net gain in the arrangement as compared with any alternative that we can devise." At the same time, like earlier Victorian liberals, Hobhouse insisted that a liberal society also requires the creation of character and individual responsibility. An individual may be kept in line "by arbitrary control and harsh punishment," he wrote, but this "is doing less than nothing for the character of the man himself," whereas teaching "the same man to discipline himself . . . is to foster the development of will, of personality, of self control or whatever we please to call that central harmonizing power which makes us capable of directing our own lives. Liberalism is the belief that society can safely be founded on this self-directing power of personality, that it is only on this foundation that a true community can be built."

The New Liberals found justification for economic regulation and redistribution within the framework of liberal principles. They did not deny that property has its rights but insisted that it also has its obligations. All rights, as Mill had taught, are limited by the "harm" principle: just as an individual has no right to injure others by force or fraud, so the owner of a factory has no right to maintain unsafe and unsanitary conditions or to exploit child labor. "May we not say," Hobhouse wrote, "that to impose twelve hours' daily labor on a child was to inflict a greater injury than the theft of a purse for which a century ago a man might be hanged?" Classical liberalism had opposed privilege and supported equality of opportunity. Taking those commitments seriously, the New Liberals favored a shift in taxes from the poor to the rich and from "earned" to "unearned" income (including inheritances), as well as an increase in spending on behalf of working people and their children to expand their economic and educational opportunities. Did not the principle of "equality of sacrifice" in taxation imply that rates should be higher at higher incomes? The New Liberals insisted, moreover, that redistributive measures were ultimately justified, not by the "sectional" interest of workers and the poor, but by the common good. Britain as a whole would be stronger and more prosperous if it enabled all of its people to reach a higher standard of life. During the Boer War (1899–1902), the abysmal physical condition of many recruits became a focus of public discussion and seemed to confirm earlier sociological findings that roughly one-third of Britain's people were too poor to maintain adequate nutrition and health. As liberals had long defended free trade on the grounds that it made the economy more productive, so the New Liberals advocated redistributive reforms and other measures on the grounds that they would reduce the squandering of human and natural resources and thereby increase "national efficiency." The economist J. A. Hobson, another of the New Liberals, argued that periodic economic depressions left millions of workers unemployed—their productive power wasted—because of inadequate demand. The poor were unable to sustain a decent life, while the rich could find no outlet for their savings in productive investment at home. The solution was to put purchasing power in the pockets of workers who would spend it. The New Liberals did not transform a classical doctrine concerned with "wealth" into a modern doctrine concerned with "welfare." They held a different view of the relation of welfare to wealth, and of distribution to production, arguing that a more equal society can be a more productive and prosperous society all around. To paraphrase Hobhouse, it is just to tax B to help A because when the good of all concerned is considered, among whom B is one, there will be a net gain in the arrangement as compared with any alternative.[10]

These ideas were in wide circulation among Liberals in 1906 when the party won a landslide victory and returned to power. Although they at first moved hesitantly, the Liberals introduced old-age pensions the following year, and in 1908 a reshuffled cabinet brought the two leaders of the party's progressive wing—David Lloyd George and the young Winston Churchill—into key economic posts. Lloyd George's "people's budget" of 1909 raised taxes on high incomes and inheritances. National health insurance and unemployment insurance, along with "labor exchanges" aimed at helping the unemployed find jobs, came in 1911 after the Liberals had won two more elections. (This was also a key moment of constitutional change: as a result of their repeated electoral victories, the Liberals were able to force the House of Lords to give up its power to obstruct legislation.) Originally limited in coverage, the Liberals' social programs were early steps in the development of the welfare state. But they had little to do with "welfare" in the sense that Americans understand it—that is, aid to the nonworking poor. Rather, the programs introduced by the New Liberals were aimed at preventing workers from falling into poverty. Although the old-age pensions were financed out of general taxes, both health and unemployment insurance were paid for jointly by employers and workers. The key intellectual innovation here was conceiving poverty as the result not of individual failings but of exposure to "risks," such as sickness, whose economic impact "insurance" could mitigate. To be sure, many workers had previously participated in various forms of voluntary mutual insurance, but these often failed because they were actuarially unsound. Government-mandated insurance programs required employers as well as workers to share in the cost, made participation compulsory for certain groups, and thereby put "workingmen's insurance," as it was originally called, on a more stable and lasting foundation.

No doubt there was a loss of individual liberty in making such programs compulsory. But this was not a simple trade-off of liberty for welfare. By enabling workers to avoid the loss of personal independence that comes with destitution, these programs preserved their liberty and self-respect at the most vulnerable moments in their lives. Because workers helped to pay for contributory insurance, they had every reason to regard it as their right and not as a demeaning form of charity. Thus, the state-mandated insurance programs avoided creating the psychology of dependency that conservatives (and earlier liberals) had warned would follow from a larger government role in social welfare.

While the New Liberalism emerged from a relatively small circle of intellectuals and politicians, American Progressivism was a more diffuse movement, reflecting broad currents in thought and politics at the opening of the twentieth century. Like their British cousins, the Progressives repudiated laissez-faire, insisting that property carries obligations as well as rights and calling for government to regulate working hours and conditions, child labor, housing, and the supply of food, drugs, and other products and activities affecting the public health. They were also instrumental in bringing about a more progressive tax system, with the ratification of a constitutional amendment allowing a federal income tax in 1913 and the introduction of the federal estate tax in 1916. And, like the New Liberals, they supported increased spending on public goods and services, from national parks to the supply of clean water.

In support of these measures, Progressive intellectuals also drew on many of the same arguments about social interdependence and the common good, and they too framed social reform as a means of reducing waste of resources and increasing social efficiency. If anything, the latter theme was more pronounced in the United States: the idea of employing scientific method and systematic organization to reform desultory and irrational social practices was central to Progressive thought. Yet while emphasizing the value of science, the Progressives also conceived of politics in deeply moral terms, inveighed against corruption, and viewed their mission as restoring integrity to public life. They were great believers in strengthening the role of the professions as a means of combining scientific knowledge and high moral principles to improve the performance of institutions, public and private alike.

Though the Progressives favored more scientific and professional management, they were troubled by the growing corporate concentrations of economic power. Opposition to monopoly was an old American theme, going back to the Jacksonian Democrats in the early nineteenth century, and it had been central to the Populism of the 1880s and '90s. A rural movement that rose in opposition to the power of the railroads, banks, and other big corporations, the Populists had called for more government regulation and public ownership of vital industries. But they had come to focus their efforts on fighting the gold standard and increasing the money supply—a cause that held little appeal for labor or the urban middle class—and never succeeded in building a broad enough coalition to win national elections. Progressivism, in contrast, was more of a middle-class movement, with both urban and small-town support, and it left a deep impact on American society and politics, so much so that the period from 1900 to 1918 is known as the Progressive era. Though sharing some of the Populist antagonism to the trusts, the Progressives differed among themselves about the objectives of reform. Some wanted to break up big corporations and restore an earlier world of small-business competition, while others accepted big business and aimed only to check predatory behavior and other abuses through antitrust and regulatory legislation. It was the latter conception that prevailed. The growth of antitrust enforcement and government regulation, particularly under the presidencies of Theodore Roosevelt and Woodrow Wilson, was a singular American development. Despite the long influence of laissez-faire, the United States developed a far more extensive system of corporate regulation in the early twentieth century than Britain or, for that matter, Germany and France.[11]

In the early republic, Hamilton had called for the national government to intervene in the economy to promote industry and commerce, while Jefferson had opposed such measures on behalf of agricultural interests and a vision of America as a rural republic of independent and equal freeholders. To call for federal intervention in the economy to achieve a more equal society still went against the Jeffersonian grain in the American tradition. But new conditions, Progressives such as the writer Herbert Croly concluded, required Americans to pursue Jeffersonian ends by Hamiltonian means. "I feel confident," Wilson said in his 1912 campaign, "that if Jefferson were living in our day he would see what we see. . . . Without the watchful interference, the resolute interference of the government, there can be no fair play between individuals and such powerful institutions as the trusts." As business operated on the national level, so government regulation had to move to that level to be effective. "Centralization has already come in business," Theodore Roosevelt declared. "If this irresponsible outside power is to be controlled in the interest of the general public, it can be controlled in only one way—by giving adequate power of control to the one sovereignty capable of exercising such power—the National Government."[12]

Many of the innovations of the Progressive era, such as the establishment of the Federal Reserve Bank, the Department of Labor, and the Federal Trade Commission, were state-building reforms aimed, as the Constitution itself had been, at bringing the federal government's capacities into line with the real conditions and urgent demands of the time. But the Progressives were unable to carry out the full program favored by many of their leaders or to match the achievements of Britain's New Liberals. Because the Supreme Court continued to interpret the Constitution as limiting the federal role in social welfare, most initiatives in social policy still had to come at the state level. The one social insurance program to pass in the states before World War I was workers' compensation, which had strong support from employers because it introduced fixed compensation for industrial accidents in place of jury awards in a period when juries were increasingly sympathetic to accident victims. But a Progressive campaign to pass compulsory health insurance in several states ended in defeat, and no headway was made on unemployment insurance or old-age pensions. The entry of the United States into World War I in 1917 diverted energies from domestic reform as the Progressives turned to the war against Germany with the same fervor that had characterized their attack on commercial abuses and municipal corruption at home.

Although Progressivism may seem only a prelude to the more extensive reforms of the New Deal, it also served as a cautionary experience. The Progressives were moral as much as social reformers, little concerned about free expression or other individual rights, as became all too apparent during World War I and its immediate aftermath.

CIVIL LIBERTIES AND THE
LIBERALIZATION OF CULTURE

The coming of modern liberalism, it is often said, enlarged the role of government, and so it did—in regulating the economy. But it also diminished the role of government in regulating moral behavior, culture, and political dissent as liberals in the twentieth century came to favor— and eventually to win—stronger constitutional guarantees of freedom of expression and other civil liberties. These constraints on government have not only safeguarded individuals in the exercise of their rights but also shielded entire institutional fields from state supervision, thereby contributing to the autonomy of the arts and sciences, the free flow of public discussion, and democracy itself.[13]

Liberal governments in Victorian Britain and America were much less protective of intellectual and personal freedom than of property rights. To be sure, classical liberalism celebrated freedom of thought, and some nineteenth-century liberals were committed to a broad view of personal liberty. John Stuart Mill, for example, argued that as long as individuals do no harm to others, they must be allowed the right to think freely and to pursue their own good in their own way. Ultimately, according to Mill, liberty serves a useful public purpose: a society that affords its members freedom to experiment stands to gain from creative genius and from the varied contributions that ordinary people with diverse tastes and dispositions can make if allowed to cultivate their faculties to the highest degree.[14] But Mill's radicalism was not the ruling philosophy of the time. Indeed, in some respects, state policy became more restrictive of cultural nonconformity in the second half of the nineteenth century, when first Britain (in 1857) and then the United States (in 1873) enacted laws against indecency and obscenity that became the basis for government regulation of literature, the arts, and moral life. In both countries, claims of free expression from radical political dissenters as well as writers and artists met with little sympathy from the courts. In the United States, federal authority to prosecute publishers and writers for obscenity, legally defined as including any information about birth control, was vested for forty-two years in the hands of a single official, the postal inspector Anthony Comstock, whose salary was paid by a private Christian association. The Supreme Court did not call upon the First Amendment to protect free speech before the 1920s.

The reform movements of the late nineteenth and early twentieth centuries generally sought, not to limit, but to extend the regulation of culture and private life. Many of those who agitated against child labor or squalid housing also agitated for temperance laws and censorship of literature, movies, and other forms of entertainment. Invoking a sanitary rationale, these reformers saw the prohibition of "dirt" in books and movies as analogous to the control of impure food and drugs and the attack on urban filth. They sought a "clean" moral as well as physical environment, and individual freedom could not be allowed to stand in the way of so important a social good. The Progressives' interest in eugenics, including forced sterilization of the mentally deficient, reflected the same indifference to the rights of individuals. Accustomed to battling the laissez-faire view of property rights, Progressive intellectuals were little inclined to acknowledge any individual rights as trumping collective interests. Some bohemian artists and intellectuals, anarchists, and radicals in the early 1900s did make free speech into a cause, but their protests had little impact on law or the main political currents of the day. The two great Progressive presidents, Roosevelt and Wilson, both reappointed Comstock to the position of postal inspector and moral arbiter of American culture.

World War I brought the repressive zealotry of the preceding years to a culmination. For models of preparedness and mobilization, American Progressives looked to Europe, where all the major belligerents used state-directed propaganda and censorship to shape and control public opinion in the efforts to marshal their entire societies for total war. Though a late entrant to the fighting, the United States also established a formidable machinery for drumming up hatred of the enemy and suppressing wartime opposition. Through the Espionage Act of 1917, Congress prohibited any statements interfering with military recruitment, a provision interpreted by the Wilson administration and the courts as criminalizing any criticism of the government and the war that might discourage enlistment. The Sedition Act of 1918 went further, banning all expressions of disloyalty regardless of whether they had any influence. Used chiefly against socialists and radicals, these laws had a generally chilling effect on the press and public discussion. In addition, quasi-public vigilante organizations kept dissenters and foreign-born groups under surveillance, and in some cases mobs beat and murdered people they believed to be disloyal. The end of the war did not bring an end to the wave of repression. Alarmed by the Soviet Revolution, the government refocused its attention on Russian immigrants and the leftists among them. In violent raids ordered by Attorney General A. Mitchell Palmer in late 1919 and early 1920, federal officials rounded up hundreds of people thought to be affiliated with subversive organizations, wrecked their offices, and tried to deport them en masse. Although Britain did not experience the same repressive hysteria, its government passed emergency legislation suspending ordinary legal protections and created an unprecedented propaganda effort, centered in a new Ministry of Information.

"If the war didn't happen to kill you," George Orwell later wrote, "it was bound to start you thinking." In the United States, Progressives who had enthusiastically backed the expansion of governmental powers, including wartime censorship, now became more leery of the state. Frederick L. Howe, Wilson's commissioner of immigration, who resigned in 1919, wrote afterward, "The war had changed an abiding faith in the state into questionings of it. I hated the new state that had

arisen, hated its brutalities, its ignorance, its unpatriotic patriotism."
During the war, a small pacifist organization called the National Civil
Liberties Bureau had tried without much success to defend the free
speech rights of the war's critics; at the end of 1919 the group broadened the membership of its board and adopted a new name, the American Civil Liberties Union.

That same year several appeals of convictions under the Espionage
and Sedition Acts reached the Supreme Court. In previous free speech
cases, the Court had held that the government, under its "police powers," could lawfully restrict any speech that tended to produce a result
the government had authority to prevent (the "bad tendency" doctrine).
In a 1915 case, for example, the Court upheld the conviction of a writer
who had published an article in support of nude bathing, which was illegal in his state. Writing for the Court, Justice Oliver Wendell Holmes Jr.
declared that "by indirection but unmistakably the article encourages
and incites a persistence in what we must assume would be a breach of
the state laws against indecent exposure." According to the same logic,
the Court in March 1919 upheld the conviction and imprisonment of
Eugene Debs, who had been the previous candidate for president of the
Socialist Party, for telling an audience of workers during the war that
they were "fit for something better than slavery and cannon fodder."
These words, in the Court's view, tended to interfere with military recruitment. But in another opinion released the same day also upholding
the conviction of an opponent of the war, Justice Holmes used new language to describe the Court's understanding of free speech rights. "The
question in every case is whether the words used are used in such circumstances and are of such a nature as to create a *clear and present danger*
that they will bring about the substantive evils that Congress has a right
to prevent. It is a question of proximity and degree."

Advocates of free speech seized on the phrase "clear and present danger" as enunciating a more stringent criterion for punishable words than
a mere "bad tendency," and Holmes himself soon came to the same conclusion, broke with the Court's majority, and produced the first of a
string of dissenting opinions, with Justice Louis Brandeis, in favor of
stronger First Amendment protections. "When men have realized that

time has upset many fighting faiths," Justice Holmes wrote, "they may come to believe even more than they believe the very foundations of their own conduct that the ultimate good desired is better reached by free trade in ideas—that the best test of truth is the power of the thought to get itself accepted in the competition of the market, and that truth is the only ground upon which their wishes safely can be carried out." That, Holmes said, was "the theory of the Constitution," which was "an experiment, as all life is an experiment," and as long as Americans live by that experiment, "we should be eternally vigilant against attempts to check the expression of opinions that we loathe and believe to be fraught with death, unless they so imminently threaten immediate interference with the lawful and pressing purposes of the law that an immediate check is required to save the country."

The Holmes-Brandeis dissents presaged a broader shift on free speech, and not just on the Court. The conventional view of the 1920s as a conservative period, at best a pause between the Progressive era and the New Deal, misses the fundamental cultural and institutional changes during the decade that were critical in the formation of modern liberalism. The Twenties saw a rebellion against Victorian standards in everyday fashions and manners as well as literature and art. From changes in women's dress to popular ideas about psychology and health, there was a turn toward a more open sexuality. The novelists and social critics of the time rejected the traditional culture of gentility and reticence and demanded that their readers face up to unseemly realities. These currents in the arts and popular culture now found support in the law. Turning against literary censorship, state courts during the 1920s began to reject prosecutions of writers and publishers for passages about sex or other taboo subjects in books regarded as having literary, scientific, or other value. Comstock's successors lobbied for more stringent "clean books" laws but for the first time met organized opposition and were defeated. Nothing so epitomized the changing sensibility of the era as the failure of Prohibition. Passed by Congress during the war and ratified just after the armistice, Prohibition reflected the same moral impulse as censorship laws, and the two causes drew their support from much the same Protestant base. But when Prohibition boomeranged and gave rise to speakeasies, bootlegging, and general disregard of the law, it confirmed popular skepticism about other kinds of moral reform. Conservative forces still held political power, but the ground was shifting under their feet.

It was just in this period that the language of American politics registered a subtle shift in thinking: by 1920 some people who had called themselves "Progressives" were beginning to refer to themselves as "liberals." As early as the 1916 presidential campaign, amid the collapse of the Progressive Party (which had backed Teddy Roosevelt as its candidate four years earlier), editors at *The New Republic* needed a term to distinguish their viewpoint and began using the word "liberal." The success of Britain's New Liberals over the preceding decade in redefining their party's ideas, winning elections, and introducing major social reforms had given liberalism new cachet. After World War I, as many erstwhile Progressives grew wary of excessive state power, "liberal" had the additional merit of highlighting a connection to a long philosophical tradition that gave central importance to individual liberty. Liberalism was more than Progressivism renamed; it reflected a sense that the earlier movement was blind to the dangers of excessive state power.

Coincidentally, just as "liberal" entered the American political lexicon, the Liberal Party in Britain was imploding. In 1916 the Liberal prime minister Lloyd George formed a coalition government with the Tories, which he maintained for six years, even after the war was over, splitting his own party in two. During the war, Lloyd George had promised social reforms for a land "fit for heroes," but as the economy fell into a severe postwar recession and tax revenues dropped, the government cut spending sharply, intensifying the downturn. The Liberals never recovered from their internal schism and failure to deliver on postwar promises. Before the war, they had been unable to resolve their differences with the union leaders who had formed the Labor Party; the 1918 expansion of the franchise then added to Labor's support, and during the 1920s Labor climbed decisively ahead of the Liberals and took their place as the leading alternative to the Tories. In contrast, no independent labor party ever came close to assuming a central role in American politics. From the early 1900s, the American Federation of Labor backed the Democrats rather than the Socialists, and by the time Franklin Roosevelt won the presidency in 1932, liberals and labor had formed a lasting alliance.

As a result of these cultural, legal, and political developments, American liberalism had crossed an ideological divide by the time of the New Deal. Both the Progressives of the early 1900s and the liberals of the New Deal supported state regulation of the economy—indeed, the latter were prepared to go further than the Progressives in extending the power of the federal government. But the New Deal had much less of the moralism of the Progressives; it ended Prohibition, and the judges whom Roosevelt appointed to the Supreme Court confirmed the movement toward stronger protections of free speech and a liberalized culture. The New Deal liberals also transformed the legacy of Progressivism in another respect. They gave liberal internationalism a new life and more durable institutional forms.

LIBERAL NATIONALISM
AND INTERNATIONALISM

Except for their commitment to free trade, liberals during the eighteenth and nineteenth centuries had far less consensus or clarity about international relations than about the design of the nation-state. Enlightenment philosophers offered principles and plans for justice and peace among nations, but no institutional means were available to carry out their ideas. In practice, the international views of liberal political leaders ranged across a wide spectrum of positions, from imperialist, on one side, to pacifist and isolationist, on the other. Among these diverse lines of thought and policy were the precursors of a liberal internationalism that rejected both imperialism and pacifism and sought to protect human rights, support free trade, promote liberal governments, and aid in their mutual defense. Britain's efforts to suppress the international slave trade and its intervention on behalf of republican forces in Greece in the early nineteenth century belonged to the early history of this tradition. So did the U.S. policy expressed in the Monroe Doctrine, opposing the reestablishment of European colonial rule in Latin America. But it was only in the twentieth century, notably with Woodrow Wilson, that liberal internationalist ideas were fully articulated and began to weigh heavily in the world's affairs.

Two obstacles long stood in the way of applying liberalism to international relations. The first was international anarchy: liberal democratic theory assumes a state, and the international system itself has none. The second was that, however universal its vision, liberalism was married to the nation. In Britain and the United States, liberal constitutional doctrine and political economy served as a basis for both regulating the nation-state's power internally and promoting its interests in the world. Elsewhere, liberal ideas rode to power on the back of nationalism. In Latin America, southern and eastern Europe, Africa, and Asia, the early diffusion of liberal ideas and institutions was closely tied to movements for national unification and national independence. Constitutional liberalism and democracy could not have advanced otherwise; nationalism gave emotional power to liberal ideals. Liberal democracy requires a political community, and the nation supplied it; even today no one has yet figured out how to organize democratic participation at the international level. Nationalism fostered the common identity and loyalty necessary for sustaining democratic citizenship and a sense of mutual obligation. But the marriage of liberalism and nationalism was not untroubled. If liberalism rode on the back of nationalism, it was sometimes consumed by the beast. Nationalist passions undercut ideals of human equality, and even where those passions were subdued, liberals often faced a tension between their commitment to national interests and their desires for the peace and progress of the world.

According to one strain of classical liberal thought, the advance of capitalism could be counted on to dissipate this tension. Trade would have a softening influence on men's warlike impulses, nations would find their interests so intertwined as to make war obsolete, and humanity would consequently evolve from a "military" to a "commercial" stage of civilization. This happy vision—subscribed to in one form or another by liberals of the Enlightenment and later by Richard Cobden, Herbert Spencer, and Joseph Schumpeter—seemed especially plausible during the century from 1815 to 1914. But it was destined to collapse under the repeated shock of world war.

Broadly speaking, there have been two other principal ways of interpreting the implications of international anarchy for liberal democracy. The key dividing question is whether liberalism is strictly to be practiced at home or can become the basis of international order. "Realists" hold that the international system is inherently lawless and Hobbesian and that the task of foreign policy is accordingly to protect one's own nation from the power of others through alliances and diplomacy if possible and military force if necessary. Seeing only a world of power politics and doubting that democracies act any differently from other states, realists are not just skeptical but often downright contemptuous of "moralistic" crusades for human rights and democracy around the world. That does not necessarily mean they are any less committed to liberal democracy where it has already taken root; they are merely doubtful that liberal institutions can be the basis of international security or exported elsewhere. The central concern of realists has been to maintain or control the balance of power so as to prevent any other state or alliance from dominating their own. But realists themselves have divided into different camps according to historical circumstances and their understanding of national interests. Some have favored an expansive projection of national power (for example, through increases in military capacities, colonization, or efforts to open foreign markets to trade). Other realists have supported more cautious policies aimed at maintaining a balance of power, without overreaching one's own resources, by matching commitments with capacities. And still others have called for a policy of isolation, the better to insulate a republic from entanglements in power politics that might not only jeopardize its survival but lead to the militarization of its internal political life.

On the other side of the conceptual divide have been those who believe that it is possible to subject the anarchy of international relations to the equivalent of a constitutional discipline, carried out through international law and institutions and alliances of the liberal democracies. Liberal internationalists, unlike realists, assume that the ideology and internal structure of states influence their conduct toward the world: as authoritarian regimes rule by force, so they are likely to resort to force in their relations with other states. Persuaded that liberal democracies are more likely to be peaceful (at least toward each other), liberal internationalists argue that policies supporting the spread of free institutions are a matter not of altruism but of self-interest. By expanding the zone of peace among liberal states, the citizens of liberal democracies reduce their own risk of war. While the realists conceive of a world where war is a perpetual possibility and one nation's advantage is another's jeopardy, liberal internationalists conceive of a world at least potentially at peace, where one nation's security and economic development benefit others as well. In its visionary, global form, the liberal project takes on breathtaking proportions: the establishment of liberal democracy as the prevailing pattern of government in the world and of liberal norms of human rights, self-determination, non-aggression, and free trade as the basic framework of international order and security.

It was Wilson, more than anyone else, who first formulated liberal internationalism as a coherent alternative to balance-of-power realism. In a message to the Senate in January 1917, he declared: "The question upon which the whole future peace and policy of the world depends is this: is the present war a struggle for a just and secure peace, or only for a new balance of power?" No one, Wilson maintained, could guarantee the stability of any new equilibrium: "There must be, not a balance of power, but a community of power; not organized rivalries, but an organized common peace."

Wilson's plan for the postwar world attempted to bring that "community of power" into being. At the foundation of his plan, Wilson proposed not to fight nationalism, but to enlist it in the pursuit of international security. National self-determination would be the system's first principle: "No nation should seek to extend its polity over any other nation or people, but every people should be left free to determine its own polity, its own way of development, unhindered, unthreatened, unafraid, the little along with the great and powerful." These self-determining nations would preferably be democratic, linked together through a nondiscriminatory trading system; like many earlier liberals, Wilson believed that capitalism, trade, and democracy reinforce each other and discourage war. Finally, the nations of the world would agree to join in a system of collective security, carried out through a League of Nations, and the United States would take on a role of disinterested moral leadership and assure the League's success. This final element— together with a proposed treaty committing the United States and

Britain to defend France if it was attacked by Germany—implied an element of traditional realism in Wilson's thinking: an American commitment to the League and to its wartime allies would plainly have affected the balance of power in Europe.

But Wilson's efforts utterly failed—and not only because he was unable to convince the U.S. Senate to approve membership in the League or the maintenance of the wartime alliance with Britain and France. Wilson's conception of the League suffered from inherent constitutional debilities. There are essentially four options for the organized enforcement of international liberal norms: a broadly representative international institution such as the League; a council of the Great Powers, in which liberal states have at least a veto; an alliance only of liberal democracies; and a single liberal superpower (or "hegemon") capable of policing the system. Wilson relied chiefly on the first of these: the League was the heart and soul of his scheme. Yet, because it was a broadly representative body without a strong executive council, the League had no capacity to thwart aggression. It seems extremely doubtful that any such organization, even with U.S. participation, could have kept the peace during the ensuing years when the communist revolution in Russia and the Nazi rise to power in Germany raised fundamental ideological and strategic challenges to liberal democracy. Wilson had called on Americans to wage a war to make the world safe for democracy, and the Versailles treaty ending World War I had in fact established new democratic states in eastern Europe. But it was not long before they were overturned by military coups and fascist aggression.

The program that Wilson first formulated, however, was separable from the institutional means he proposed for carrying it out. The lesson drawn by the generation of internationalists that followed Wilson was that it was possible to join a realist's grasp of power politics to a liberal vision of international order. If liberal internationalism was not to be a politically impractical and irrelevant set of ideals, it had to be adapted to cope with the realities of power. That was the lesson of constitutional liberalism from its beginnings. And it was the challenge that democratic liberalism faced in dire tests of strength through most of the remainder of the twentieth century.

5

Liberalism and the
Long Crisis, 1914–1991

———

TOTAL WAR, GLOBAL DEPRESSION, AND A PROTRACTED CONFRONTATION between nuclear-armed alliances provided the context for the development of liberal states for nearly the entire period from the beginning of World War I through the end of the Cold War. On the basis of the relatively benign conditions of world politics from 1815 to 1914, many people in the early twentieth century had concluded that like a plant that grows only in bright sunshine, liberalism flourishes only in peace. Reflecting on the decline of his own party after World War I, David Lloyd George, the Liberal Party's last prime minister, later wrote, "War has always been fatal to Liberalism."[1] But if this had been true of liberalism generally, it could never have survived, much less have emerged in the first place, given the frequency of war throughout modern history. In late seventeenth- and eighteenth-century Britain and America, constitutional liberalism took shape partly in response to the imperatives created by the military revolution of the early modern world. And democratic liberalism in the twentieth century also came to maturity not just as the result of domestic political movements but in response to new international realities, including an increase in the scale and destructiveness of war and weaponry to previously inconceivable dimensions.

Although the central ideas of modern democratic liberalism were already clearly formulated by the early 1920s, much of that project was far from being carried out on either side of the Atlantic. The Progressive movement foundered in the United States without securing the unemployment and health insurance programs, old-age pensions, or protections for labor that Britain's Liberals had won, and even in Britain most of the social reforms of the New Liberalism did not extend to all citizens. The aims and assumptions of laissez-faire still constrained economic policies, and liberals had no consensus about alternatives. Fundamental civil and political rights continued to be denied to blacks and other minorities in the United States and to colonial populations under European rule. Conservative forces resisted pressures for broader freedom of expression and cultural experimentation, and Wilson's efforts to establish a new liberal democratic framework for international relations failed. If World War I had been followed by an extended era of prosperity and peace, perhaps old ideas and political alignments would have survived longer, but the repeated episodes and persistent pressures of the twentieth century's long crisis allowed democratic liberalism to find new political openings and more effective leadership.

Crises, especially wars, are well known for begetting state expansion. So it is not surprising that the liberal embrace of positive government at the turn of the century would grow stronger in the following decades. Nor is it surprising that wars requiring mass conscription and popular mobilization would break down social hierarchies. Rather, the puzzle is why individual liberty and limits on state power survived at all during a century of global wars, hot and cold. What is even more surprising is that on the whole, despite bouts of collective anxiety and hysteria, the liberal democracies grew more liberal as well as more democratic over the course of the twentieth century. Instead of collapsing in the face of crisis, the institutions and ideas of constitutional liberalism shaped and limited policies adopted in the Anglo-American world to cope with depression and war. And just when they mattered most, those choices proved successful, reinforcing the commitment to liberal democracy and validating confidence in its principles as a basis of security as well as justice.

The explanation for the deepening of liberalism also lies in the particular adversaries that liberal states faced. Fascism and communism posed threats to liberal democracy that were simultaneously ideological and strategic.[2] In opposing and fighting totalitarian regimes, the liberal democracies appealed for both domestic and international support on the basis of ideals of freedom and equality and in the process were forced to confront such contradictions as racial injustice at home and their own role as colonial powers. The global struggle for dominance ended not only with the defeat of the Nazis and Soviets, but also with the discrediting and repudiation of anti-Semitism, racism, colonialism, and other ideologies denying human equality that had long enjoyed respectability in Europe and America.

It is a commonplace that the modern state is the product of war, but it is nonetheless an error to suppose that bigger wars would make ever bigger states. Wars force states to create power, but they do not simply leave them one way to do it. Like other crises, wars often lead to the scrutiny and testing of different options, and the ultimate impact on the size and scope of the state may depend on actual experience, or at least the lessons that people draw from it. During the long crisis, the fascist and communist states mobilized resources in different ways from the liberal democracies. Lacking accountability to voters, internal checks and balances, a free press, and independent power centers in civil society, the totalitarian regimes had a relatively free hand in conscripting, taxing, and otherwise extracting resources from their societies and therefore seemed to hold advantages in the sheer force they could generate. This was certainly the fear in the liberal democracies, and some people were prepared to sacrifice freedom to meet the threat. But by virtue of their structure, the totalitarian states also suppressed initiative, lagged in critical technological innovations, and lacked means of self-correction. These deficiencies had fateful consequences. As it turned out, the modern forms of despotism were not a winning national strategy in the twentieth century. As before, governments with constitutionally limited powers proved to be more powerful than governments with unlimited powers.

But during the nightmare years from 1930s to the 1950s, when the Depression, World War II, and the advent of nuclear weapons and the Cold War followed each other in uninterrupted succession, no one could be certain of the outcome. Indeed, many intellectuals, liberal and conservative, were deeply pessimistic about the prospects of freedom, not only because of the totalitarian challenge but also because of the tendencies within capitalism toward growing bureaucratization in the private as well as public sector. The "managerial revolution," James Burnham warned, would lead to the rise of a suffocating managerial state. The bureaucratized corporation, the economist Joseph Schumpeter feared, would undermine entrepreneurship, innovation, and commitment to private property and ultimately pave the way for a socialist state. From George Orwell on the left to the economist Friedrich Hayek on the right, there was a widespread anxiety about ominous tendencies in the world toward oppressive centralized power. Liberals such as the Protestant theologian Reinhold Niebuhr and the historian Arthur M. Schlesinger Jr. shared the same concerns. But unlike Hayek and other conservatives, these liberals saw the possibility of finding a path for politics that would preserve freedom and the dynamism of a market economy while using the power of government to provide for security, achieve economic stability and growth, and limit inequality. This path—the strategy of the "vital center," as Schlesinger called it—was the source of liberalism's great achievement in the twentieth century's most dangerous decades.[3]

LIBERAL STATECRAFT UNDER PRESSURE

The development of economic policy during the New Deal proved to be critical for the formation of liberalism's expanded yet still limited view of the state's role. The Depression was worldwide, but it hit the United States harder than most other countries. Between the election of Roosevelt in November 1932 and his inauguration in March the next year, there were widespread calls for him to assume dictatorial powers. On the left, many saw the economic collapse as proof of the need for state planning and management of the economy, and some members of Roosevelt's administration shared that view. But this was not the outcome. Rather, by trial and error the New Deal arrived at policies that the historian Alan Brinkley has described as ways to "manage the economy without managing the institutions of the economy."[4]

During the early years of his presidency, Roosevelt's economic policies did not follow a unifying principle or plan but were rather a jumble of efforts that reflected the conflicting impulses, ideas, and groups joined together in his administration. The first one hundred days alone brought a torrent of legislation and executive actions, including measures to restore confidence in the banking system, support agricultural prices, and finance public works and other emergency jobs and relief programs. In 1935 Congress passed the National Labor Relations Act guaranteeing labor unions the right to organize, increased taxes on the wealthy and corporations, and enacted Social Security, including both unemployment insurance and old-age pensions. Political observers as well as Roosevelt himself saw clear affinities with the program that British Liberals had introduced between 1909 and 1911. Under fire for the pace of change, Roosevelt responded, "Lloyd George a quarter of a century ago put through in two years a greater body of radical reforms than the New Deal has attempted in five." FDR's use of the term "liberal" to describe his program and politics definitively established the modern American meaning of liberalism over the protests of some on the right who still identified liberalism with laissez-faire and claimed the word as their own.[5]

Until near the end of Roosevelt's presidency, however, the New Deal lacked a unified theory of economic policy. If there was any dominant idea at the beginning, it was the attempt to create a "concert of interests," bringing together business and labor through the National Recovery Administration (NRA) to design codes for running the economy, industry by industry. But even before the NRA was declared unconstitutional in 1935, this corporatist vision of economic coordination and planning was clearly failing to resolve the Depression and generating widespread political dissatisfaction on the grounds that it was fostering cartels. Roosevelt's second administration then veered in the opposite direction, intensifying antitrust prosecutions, but that impulse died with the onset of World War II. Both corporatist industrial planning and the breakup of monopolies represented attempts at structural change of the economy. The alternative idea of boosting aggregate demand through high levels of deficit spending had its advocates during the 1930s, but Roosevelt was not initially among them. Campaigning for president in 1932, he called for a balanced budget, and though he ran deficits in his first term, he did not see them as a constructive policy. After being reelected, he agreed to follow his Treasury secretary's advice to balance the budget by cutting expenditures, whereupon the economy plunged into a severe downturn in 1937. Meanwhile, an increasing number of his advisers were coming under the influence of the leading economist of Britain's Liberal Party, John Maynard Keynes, who argued for a deliberate compensatory fiscal policy to revive demand. Roosevelt finally came around to support large-scale deficit spending in 1939, yet it was not until World War II blew the lid off expenditures that Congress raised spending and borrowing to a level that could bring the economy back to full employment.

The extraordinary recovery of the war years put to rest the idea that a "mature" industrial economy was incapable of high growth. In the minds of most liberal economists, the New Deal and wartime experience also showed that fiscal policy could achieve the growth and stability that structural reforms did not deliver. Liberals did not entirely dismiss planning (for example, at an urban or regional level) or antitrust enforcement; each of these could have a limited function within the overall framework of a market economy. Moreover, the New Deal and the war had brought higher levels of taxation and spending, and though the immediate postwar years saw cutbacks, liberals did not want—nor did conservatives seriously try—to return to the pre-1933 size and role of the federal government. In 1929 federal outlays totaled $2.9 billion, or less than 3 percent of gross national product; in 1948, at their lowest point after the war, they were $36.5 billion, or 14 percent of GNP, and a decade later they doubled in dollars and represented 17 percent of the overall economy.[6] It was precisely the larger scale of federal expenditures that made fiscal policy a plausible countercyclical device. Liberals were divided, however, between the advocates of "growthmanship," who wanted to use fiscal policy aggressively to maintain economic expansion and full employment, and others who favored more limited Keynesian policies aimed only at counteracting recessions. Divisions also emerged over the relative importance of fiscal and monetary policy. But especially by the 1960s, when Keynesian ideas had become a matter of consensus, the differences were no longer about the old ideological question of "plan versus market" but about the "fine-tuning" of a market economy.

The Cold War, following so closely after World War II, had the effect of sustaining the government's economic and social role. Concerns about defense capabilities provided a justification for a broad array of policies that probably could not have passed Congress in the absence of an external threat. Even before the alarm generated by the Soviet launching of its Sputnik space satellite, rivalry with the Russians was a major impetus to education spending. Federal support for science, health care, and even the interstate highway system was justified as contributing to defense and national security. Under the umbrella of defense programs, the federal government not only financed basic research but also helped to coordinate technical development (for example, by setting common technical standards) for the aerospace, computer, electronics, and other high-technology industries.

Like the Depression and World War II, however, the Cold War might have resulted in a far greater enlargement of state power than it did. In the early years of the Cold War, many people worried that the United States would become a "garrison state," as the political scientist Harold Lasswell had called it. The McCarthy era seemed to confirm those anxieties. But just as the "red scare" after World War I had provoked a civil-libertarian backlash, so did McCarthyism, and by the 1960s the Supreme Court upheld free speech and other rights more strongly than at any earlier time. In other respects as well, though for different reasons, the Cold War era saw less of an expansion of state power than would have been called for if the U.S. government had followed alternative policies that some advocated at the time. For example, rather than try to match Soviet and Chinese conventional forces, the United States substituted technology for manpower in defense strategy, relying ultimately on nuclear deterrence. Both the size and cost of the military were smaller as a result. And to develop new technology, the U.S. government primarily financed research in universities and other independent organizations instead of building up government-run laboratories. To be sure, the "military-industrial complex," as Dwight D. Eisenhower called it, was immense, but it was more decentralized and absorbed a smaller share of national income than its Soviet counterpart. The institutions that historically had fragmented and diffused power in the United States continued to do so even in one of its main phases of state expansion, and the resulting choices—by helping to maintain high levels of innovation and economic growth—contributed to the outcome of the Cold War.[7]

Some of the limits of government intervention, however, were counterproductive. By deferring excessively to private interest groups, Congress made some programs more costly and less effective—a style of "passive intervention" that was characteristic, for example, of federal policies in health care and housing.[8] But, in general, the circumscribed expansion of federal powers during the long crisis exemplified that inner tension I earlier described as the creative reluctance of liberal statecraft. The United States found ways of providing for both national and economic security within an institutional framework that fit the liberal uneasiness about expanded state power.

The long crisis had a somewhat different impact in Western Europe, though ultimately the similarities among the liberal democracies mattered more than the contrasts. In Great Britain and France, the world wars resulted in a much greater enlargement of the state's size and economic role than in the United States. Government expenditures soared during wartime and, even after dropping back afterward, stabilized at sharply higher levels than before. Government control of the economy showed the same kind of "ratchet" effect. The shift toward regulation and state ownership in Britain had special significance in light of its earlier role as the champion of laissez-faire. Though the British government was initially slow to institute economic controls in 1914, the regulation and planning it eventually established during World War I provided a model for more interventionist policies during the next two decades. With the outbreak of World War II, the state quickly took all but complete control of the economy, preparing the way for a Labour Party government elected in 1945 to nationalize the coal and steel industries, railways and airlines, utilities, and the Bank of England—the so-called "commanding heights" of the economy, representing about one-fifth of the gross domestic product and employing more than two million workers. Likewise, postwar France moved toward greater state control, instituting an economic planning system.[9]

The world wars also had a democratizing impact on the relationship of Western European governments to their citizens. In many countries, including Britain and Germany, World War I led to the final steps in achieving universal suffrage. Nearly all the major European countries gave women the right to vote within two years of the armistice; the two major holdouts, France and Italy, extended the franchise to women with the arrival of the liberation forces at the end of World War II. The wars, moreover, destroyed the last remnants of aristocratic power and gave moral force to the political claims of ordinary working people, as Churchill recognized when he said of the workers of Britain in 1945: "They have saved this country; they have the right to rule it." For much the same reason, the world wars were also associated with growing social rights as governments universalized the earlier fragmentary programs of workingmen's insurance. Britain extended its unemployment insurance program to all workers just after World War I. During World War II, a British government commission chaired by one of the leading figures of the Liberal Party, William Beveridge, assured the people of Britain that they could look forward to a "better world" after the war and in two reports set forth the design of a comprehensive social-insurance system and full-employment policy. These proposals were the basis for the National Health Service and other elements of the British welfare state established in the late 1940s.

The postwar contrast between European social democracy and American liberalism reflected differences in the ideology and power of the leading parties of the left. On the one hand, Labour's nationalization of industry in Britain and similar expansions of state-owned enterprise elsewhere in Western Europe had no parallel in the United States. America's liberal Democrats simply did not share the socialist commitment to state ownership of the means of production. On the other hand, many American liberals did support a broader welfare state; in 1943 Roosevelt's National Resources Planning Board released two reports suggesting comprehensive social-insurance and full-employment policies along the lines Beveridge proposed. In 1944 FDR called for an "Economic Bill of Rights," and later in the decade President Harry Truman waged a campaign for national health insurance. Even in regard to social rights, however, the American proposals had a more traditionally liberal character. For example, while Britain nationalized its hospitals in creating the NHS, Truman's plan would have left health care facilities (though not insurance) in private hands. Nonetheless, a conservative coalition of Republicans and southern Democrats defeated universal health coverage and the general movement to establish social rights of citizenship. In the same period, however, Congress enacted an enormous social program in the form of the GI Bill, giving the generation coming home from the war aid for higher education, vocational training, access to health care, and loans for buying homes and starting businesses. In addition, after the surge in labor union membership during the New Deal, the nation's largest companies accepted collective bargaining and negotiated an accord with labor for growing wages and fringe benefits that amounted to a private welfare state. To be sure, these social protections were far from universal, and labor's power in America was significantly restricted by legislation adopted in the late 1940s. But on both sides of the Atlantic the trend was to soften the workings of capitalism and reduce the extent of economic inequality through Keynesian and welfare-state policies and a partnership between business and labor.

World War II and the Cold War also created pressure to ameliorate another aspect of inequality in the United States. Preoccupied with economic concerns and determined to hold on to the South, FDR and the Democratic Party had largely ignored racism and the plight of African Americans. Indeed, because of concessions to powerful southerners in Congress, many of the New Deal programs, including Social Security, provided little benefit to blacks. During World War II, however, even as the federal government maintained segregation in the armed forces and white domination continued in the South, the president and other American leaders denounced the ideology of racial supremacy espoused by the Nazis. "Our very proclamations of what we are fighting for have rendered our own inequities self-evident," said Wendell Willkie, who had run as the Republican candidate for president in 1940. In his classic

1944 study, *An American Dilemma*, the Swedish sociologist Gunnar Myrdal highlighted the contradiction between racism and the principles of individual dignity, human equality, and rights to freedom, justice, and opportunity that the United States claimed to represent. "In fighting fascism and racism," Myrdal wrote, "America had to stand before the whole world in favor of racial tolerance and cooperation and of racial equality." The tensions between America's claims abroad and its practices at home were heightened by the Cold War, when racial segregation and violence became a major liability of the United States in its competition with the Soviets for influence, especially in the Third World. As civil rights protests received attention around the world, federal policymakers pressed for reform partly on the ground that it would improve the standing and influence of the United States abroad. This is not to minimize the achievement of the civil rights movement. The international conditions, however, changed the calculations of those who held power, making them more susceptible to pressures for equality.[10]

In yet another respect, the long crisis had a democratizing effect on American society. Voter turnout and other aspects of civic participation were at low ebb during the 1920s. But the New Deal, World War II, and the Cold War swept up millions of Americans into public life. Long after the 1940s, the generation that came of age during that time continued to show higher levels of voting and civic engagement than their predecessors. The "long civic generation," as Robert Putnam calls it, was the linchpin of the overall high levels of civic participation that peaked in the 1960s and declined afterward.[11] Liberals during the Cold War were preoccupied with the repressive aspects of the anticommunist fervor in America. But taken as a whole, the long crisis unexpectedly served as a catalyst for liberalism—internationally as well as domestically.

THE UNEXPECTED WORLD REVOLUTION

Underlying the long crisis was a struggle over the foundations and control not just of individual states and societies but of the international system. Indeed, it was the thrust of both fascism and communism for total domination that put the fate of civilization itself in the balance. The fascists foresaw a world based on militarism and racial supremacy, carved into spheres of influence for the aggrandizement of the ruling powers. The communists anticipated a world revolution that would replace capitalism and "bourgeois democracy" with an international alliance of proletarian dictatorships (guided, as the Soviets conceived it, by Moscow's hand). The twentieth century did bring about a world revolution, but the international order that emerged was a comparatively liberal one. The means by which that order was established, however, did not always follow high principles of Wilsonian internationalism.

To many liberals of the 1940s and after, the failure of Wilson to prevail at Versailles and the inability of the League of Nations to prevent aggression were lessons in the dangers of moralism in foreign policy and the need to face the realities of power without sentimental delusions. During World War II, the leaders of the liberal democracies had no doubt that it was imperative to make common cause with the Soviet Union. In a conversation with Churchill in 1942, Roosevelt quoted a Balkan proverb, "My children, it is permitted to you in times of grave danger to walk with the devil until you have crossed the bridge," and when the war was over and the Cold War began, the liberal democracies faced another dangerous walk to a bridge even farther away. Again they formed alliances with illiberal and undemocratic governments, this time in the interests of stopping Soviet expansion. And again, balance-of-power considerations took precedence over support for democracy and human rights. "He's a son of a bitch," but he's "our son of a bitch," Secretary of State Dean Acheson famously said of Yugoslavia's communist dictator, Josip Tito, after Tito's split with Stalin.[12]

During World War II and the postwar era, however, the United States and its allies did not simply turn to a realist foreign policy to defend their national interests. They continued to uphold a liberal internationalist vision in defining their long-term interests and postwar plans. In August 1941, after Congress had approved aid to Britain but before the United States entered the war, Roosevelt and Churchill negotiated a statement of Anglo-American aims known as the Atlantic Charter, setting out the principles of a liberal world order. Their first principles were Wilsonian. The two leaders proclaimed their nations' intentions to "seek no aggrandizement, territorial or other," their respect for "the right of all peoples to choose the form of government under which they will live," and their wish "to see sovereign rights and self government restored to those who have been forcibly deprived of them." (While Roosevelt viewed the Charter's language as a commitment to decolonization, Churchill rejected that interpretation.) Echoing the language of the New Deal, they also declared that they sought international collaboration "in the economic field with the object of securing, for all, improved labor standards, economic advancement and social security" and that "after the final destruction of the Nazi tyranny" they envisioned "a peace which will afford to all nations the means of dwelling in safety within their own boundaries, and which will afford assurance that all the men in all the lands may live out their lives in freedom from fear and want." In January 1942, with the United States now in the war, the Allies signed a Declaration of the United Nations that recognized the Atlantic Charter as a "common program of purposes."[13]

During the Cold War, the Western powers sometimes violated these ideals with disastrous effects, as in Indochina. But liberal internationalism was not merely a hypocritical rationale intended to manipulate public opinion at home and abroad. It had a profound influence in shaping critical decisions about the international order that emerged first from World War II and later from the Cold War. The democratization and demilitarization of Germany and Japan, the end of European colonialism, the beginning of European economic integration, and the establishment of a network of international institutions, agreements, and alliances aimed at containing communism, peacefully resolving conflicts so as to avoid World War III, and promoting international trade and economic growth—these achievements of the post–World War II era all stemmed from a more mature and sophisticated effort than Wilson's to put liberal internationalist ideas into practice.

Postwar security arrangements exemplified the liberal accommodation with realism in international relations. During the war isolationist sentiment in the United States had declined sharply, but the future shape of U.S. involvement in international affairs remained uncertain.

Ever since Congress had rejected membership in the League of Nations, American internationalists had cherished the hope that the United States would join the League or participate in a new parliamentary-style international institution. More attuned to power politics, Roosevelt privately favored an effort to maintain peace based on cooperation among what he called the "Four Policemen" (the United States, Britain, the Soviet Union, and China), while another influential approach envisioned the Atlantic powers as the core of a new international organization.[14] The General Assembly of the United Nations, established in 1945, corresponded to the first of these conceptions (an international parliament); the UN Security Council, with the addition of France as a permanent member, to the second (a concert of the great powers); and the North Atlantic Treaty Organization, established in 1949, to the third (an alliance of the liberal democracies). A variety of other alliances and organizations were created for regional and specialized purposes. In short, rather than focusing, as Wilson had, on a single, internationally representative body with predictable constitutional defects, the postwar settlement created a plurality of institutions, with varying degrees of inclusiveness and rules for authorizing the use of force.

Moreover, through the Truman Doctrine, the Marshall Plan, and other policies, the United States took over Britain's earlier role as the liberal state willing and able to use its own resources to maintain the balance of power and to prevent another state from dominating continental Europe or other strategic areas. One overwhelming change distinguished 1945 from 1918. The United States emerged from World War II vastly more powerful and therefore more capable of acting on its interests and values than at any earlier time. To be sure, the emergence of the Soviet Union created a new bipolar world. But the defeat of the Axis powers and the exhaustion of Britain and France gave the United States a unique opportunity to transform the relationships of those states to the wider international system. The results turned the liberal project into a world revolution.

The transformation of Germany and Japan from war-making into trading states was central to the new liberal international order. Two of the great centers of war-making power in the world, they had been the primary sources of aggression and instability in Europe and Asia. Instead of attempting to cripple them permanently (as some seriously recommended at the end of World War II), postwar policy sought to democratize and demilitarize their political institutions, to rebuild their economies (weakening the social bases of fascist power in the process), and to integrate both countries into a wider liberal international trading system. The conversion of West Germany and Japan into liberal states not only reduced the danger of a fascist resurgence but also strengthened the West in relation to the Soviet Union. And, in the long run, because they prospered through liberalization more than they had under the militarist and mercantilist regimes that had led them to catastrophic defeat, the people of Germany and Japan were confirmed in the choices made under duress during the early postwar years and have ever since served as an example for the entire world of the advantages of liberal democracy over fascism and military aggression.[15]

The other transformative change in old power centers came with the end of European colonialism. In this respect as in several others, the long crisis served as a catalyst for political liberalization, at least in the sense of promoting national self-government. Just as the world wars destabilized traditional social hierarchies at home, so they created a social upheaval in Europe's African and Asian colonies. Britain and France recruited large numbers of soldiers and laborers from their colonial populations, uprooting them from their traditions and transforming their political consciousness. In both wars, the British and French also kept the support of indigenous leaders such as Gandhi by offering political concessions, in some cases including promises of political rights. Nonetheless, the colonial powers rejected demands for independence for the two decades after World War I, despite the hopes excited by Wilson's call for national self-determination. The Second World War, however, had an even greater effect than the first in disrupting colonial rule, depleting the powers of the British and French states, and undermining the willingness of their voters to bear the costs of empire.[16]

Under these circumstances, American opposition to European colonialism mattered far more than it had before. Although Roosevelt did not insist on decolonization immediately, he wanted the long-run aim to be clear and called for the British and French to set "timetables" for independence. In the eyes of Churchill and Charles de Gaulle, FDR's anti-imperialism was merely a rationalization for the extension of American influence. And, indeed, beginning with the Monroe Doctrine in 1823, the United States had long opposed European colonization partly because it threatened to close off foreign markets to American interests. The new elements in the postwar situation, however, were the shift of power to the United States and the quick onset of the Cold War. The American position on colonialism during the late 1940s reflected a belief that it was urgent to align the West with national aspirations in the developing world, rather than allow the communists to become their champion. Like racism in the American South, colonialism came into conflict with a strategic interest in cultivating international support, particularly in the nonwhite societies where much of the struggle with the communists was taking place. Although the United States later opposed anticolonial movements that it feared would lead to communist governments, the predominant American view at the end of World War II was that the European empires were doomed, nationalism was on the rise, and it was foolhardy to try to thwart national aspirations.[17] In fact, the most disastrous American error of the Cold War would come when the United States got on the wrong side of nationalism in Vietnam.

In Europe itself, the impact of World War II on liberal democratic change was mixed. The Second World War, like the First, led to a wave of transitions to democracy. These came not just in West Germany but in Italy, Austria, and—albeit in an unstable form—Greece and Turkey. In the East the outcome was obviously different. Britain had gone to war in 1939 on the immediate grounds of preserving Poland's independence from Germany, but in 1945 Poland lost its independence again when the Soviet Union betrayed its promise to hold free elections and installed a puppet government. Soon other Eastern European countries also lost their freedom. Convinced there was no choice short of another world war, the Western powers accepted the de facto partition of the continent and sought to hold the line. But the aftermath of World War II was altogether different from the democratic collapse that followed World War I. The Bretton Woods Agreements, negotiated in 1944, created the basis for monetary stability and room for individual countries to pursue Keynesian policies domestically. Three years later the United States adopted the Marshall Plan to aid Western European countries even under socialist governments as they developed mixed economies and broad social-welfare protections. By also encouraging the first steps toward European economic integration and turning West Germany into a democratic trading state, American-led policies promoted a new and lasting basis for a mixed system of liberalism and social democracy in Western Europe that in time would affect the entire continent.

The advent of the Cold War completely changed political alignments over foreign policy in the United States from the earlier divisions between isolationists and internationalists. The mainstream of New Deal liberalism joined in the bipartisan support for the twin policies of Soviet containment and European reconstruction represented by the Truman Doctrine, on the one hand, and Bretton Woods and the Marshall Plan, on the other (the latter were a direct extension of the New Deal into foreign policy). Accepting the need to deal realistically with Soviet power, these liberals saw themselves as upholding the center against the more ideologically driven extremes. To the right, in contrast, were conservatives who believed that containment was too weak a response, that liberal cowards in the State Department had "lost" Eastern Europe and later China, and that the West should try to "roll back" communism. And to the left were communists and socialists as well as liberals blind to the realities of Soviet rule, who held the United States primarily responsible for the Cold War and favored accommodating Stalin. In 1948 many in this latter camp backed the third-party campaign of former vice president Henry Wallace's Progressive Party. By this time, the term "progressive" implied a position to the left of liberalism, typically calling for an alliance of all groups left of center, not excluding communists, in the tradition of the "popular front" of the late 1930s. Most liberals, however, rightly rejected that plea as failing to recognize that communism was utterly incompatible with liberalism as to both means and ends. Even as the New Deal had convinced them of the promise of public remedy, the historical shock of totalitarianism and the Holocaust had given liberals a darker assessment of human nature and a determination to draw as sharp a line against the illiberal left as against the illiberal right. "The Soviet experience, on top of the rise of fascism, reminded my generation rather forcibly that man was, indeed, imperfect, and that the corruptions of power could unleash great evil in the world," Schlesinger later recalled. This recognition implied that Americans had to be uneasy about their own power and needed to exercise a degree of restraint that the right-wing believers in the pure goodness of American power saw as wholly unnecessary.[18]

Although containment sought to avert war through stable spheres of influence, George F. Kennan Jr. and others who formulated the strategy believed that patience would reward the West. Support for communism, Kennan argued, was greatest among those who had no direct experience of it; unhappiness and opposition were certain to grow under Soviet rule, and as some countries resisted Moscow's demands, fissures would develop within the communist bloc that the West could exploit. In the long run, as a result of its recovery and reconstruction, Western Europe would create a "gravitational" force that would pull Eastern European countries out of the Russian orbit and lead the Soviet Union itself to change from within.[19] Although for years these may have seemed like vain hopes, they were ultimately vindicated. Both the Soviet "outer empire" (in Eastern Europe) and its "inner empire" (within the USSR) disintegrated, and the world was spared a cataclysmic military confrontation. If, instead, the right-wing advocates of rolling back communism had shaped policy, they might well have brought on World War III at several junctures—as in Korea in 1950, when many on the right supported General Douglas MacArthur's desire to attack China instead of retreating to the thirty-eighth parallel and reestablishing the earlier partition of the peninsula.

To say that containment was vindicated, however, is not to say that all the policies associated with it were justified. Putting anticommunism ahead of all other concerns, the United States at the height of the Cold War lent its support indiscriminately to authoritarian regimes. After the high expectations for democracy in the early postwar years, there was a marked shift toward authoritarianism throughout the developing world from 1958 to 1974—the period running from the Cuban Revolution roughly through the end of the Vietnam War. In these years military coups overthrew democratic governments across Latin America, from Brazil and Argentina to Chile and Uruguay, while dictators took control in many newly independent African and Asian states. Altogether, between 1962 and 1975, the number of governments in the world that were the result of a coup d'état increased from thirteen to thirty-eight.[20] For fear of left-wing influence, the United States actively conspired in the overthrow of some democratically elected governments as American policy evolved from accepting "sons of bitches" as an unfortunate fact to welcoming them as more likely than democracies to develop effective states.

In the early postwar period, most American liberals had supported a bipartisan foreign policy that included the democratization of Germany and Japan and the decolonization of Africa and Asia as well as containment of Soviet expansion. American policy in the early Cold War had liberal purposes at its core. By the 1960s and '70s, however, in the name of containing communism, the United States was supporting authoritarian regimes throughout the world, and its claims to be defending freedom and democracy seemed hollow and hypocritical, especially to younger liberals. The Vietnam War was the primary source and focus of their discontent, but not its only cause. Many liberals felt that U.S. foreign policy had lost its moorings in democratic values, and it was this growing sense of alienation from the central thrust of American power in the world that led to a shift from the liberalism of the "vital center" circa 1950 to the left liberalism of the 1960s. Once again, political alignments changed. Turning against a Democratic president, Lyndon Johnson, left liberals joined in the opposition to the war and related policies with a New Left that was searching for an appealing model of socialism and instead fell prey to romantic delusions about Cuba, China, and Third World revolutionary movements. Trying to shake off the errors of an earlier generation of progressives about Soviet Russia, the New Left shifted its sympathies but repeated the old mistakes. Its fantasies about Third World revolutions might have had less appeal, however, if U.S. foreign policy had more consistently and convincingly upheld democracy and human rights.

And then, in the mid-1970s, the winds shifted, and a new wave of democratization began around the world, though its significance could hardly be grasped at the time. The change began in southern Europe with the revolution in Portugal in 1974, the overthrow of the Greek colonels, and the transition to democracy in Spain precipitated by General Francisco Franco's death in 1975. Later in the decade, in one country after another across Latin America, the military withdrew from politics, allowing democratic elections first in Peru, then in Argentina, Brazil, and Uruguay. The wave of democratization hit Asia as well with the revolution in the Philippines in 1986 and movements toward free elections in South Korea and other countries. The climax came at the end of the 1980s, with the openings in Hungary and Poland, the overthrow of communist regimes across Eastern Europe, and the collapse of the Soviet Union. There were disappointments, as in China's suppression of dissent in Tiananmen Square in 1989. From 1974 to 1990, however, some thirty countries moved from authoritarianism to democracy.[21]

While there is no single explanation for all these changes, the underlying economic circumstances were crucial. In the three decades after World War II, economic growth lifted many countries into the range where transitions to democracy were more likely to create durable governments.[22] Economic growth alone, however, is not an adequate explanation for all the changes in the late twentieth century; otherwise there wouldn't have been a shift toward authoritarianism from 1958 to 1975. In the mid-1970s, the oil shock and ensuing economic problems shook up governments all around the world. In democratic countries many parties in office lost elections, and in authoritarian countries governments were overturned. But as one dictator might have merely given way to another, this too is an insufficient explanation for transitions to democracy, though it helps explain why many transitions happened when they did.

The factors affecting the origin and success of democratic transitions varied in southern Europe, Latin America, and the European and Asian communist countries. Nonetheless, two world-historical developments seem to have been crucial to the political transformation of the last quarter of the twentieth century. A flourishing Western Europe had in fact exercised the "gravitational" pull that the strategists of containment originally predicted it would, first on southern and then on Eastern Europe. Indeed, the very idea of "Europe" became a factor in its own right. As Western Europe became increasingly prosperous, it established a new standard not just of political legitimacy but of political normality. Rather than being inspired by utopian visions, the revolutions of Eastern Europe reflected a desire to live in "normal" countries where ordinary citizens could travel, enjoy a decent standard of living, and express their opinions without fear of the secret police. The shift of the Catholic Church after Vatican II from support of authoritarian rule to championing democratic reform reflected and intensified the European transformation; the Church was a factor not just in Spain and Poland but in some Latin American countries as well. And second, the United States began sending new signals: beginning with President Jimmy Carter, American foreign policy returned to a Wilsonian emphasis on human rights and the promotion of democracy. Even though conservatives mocked Carter's efforts at the time, Ronald Reagan and George Bush Sr. continued to emphasize the same ideals.

By the late twentieth century, these complementary trends on both sides of the Atlantic had created a new ideological convergence in favor of liberal internationalism. At Versailles in 1919, the leaders of Europe may have regarded Wilson as naive, but by 1990 the leaders of those same countries not only upheld Wilsonian principles but often reproached the United States for not following them.[23] There is no small historical irony here. Liberal internationalism was long dismissed as mere utopianism and indeed in its original form was unable to reconcile high principles and power politics. But by the end of the long crisis, much of what had seemed hopelessly naive had gained a firmer foundation. To be sure, the liberal international order that emerged from the Cold War has its own serious problems, notably failed states and international terrorism. In much of the former Soviet world, the fall of communism led to an era of economic depression and political authoritarianism, not to prosperity and democracy. And, in the advanced capitalist democracies, it is not yet clear whether a fully developed international liberal economic regime is compatible with the domestic liberal commitments to broad guarantees of social and economic security. But before we deal with liberalism's current troubles, we need to look more closely at why liberalism has worked as well as it has.

6

Why Democratic Liberalism Works

ANY COHERENT FRAMEWORK OF POLITICS CONSISTS OF PRINCIPLES THAT define its values and of derivative policies and strategies, adjustable as knowledge and circumstances change, for putting the principles into effect. The shift from classical to modern liberalism involved an extension of the principle of an equal right to freedom and a continuing, pragmatic reconstruction of derivative policies in both domestic and international affairs. In the liberal reinterpretation, an equal right to freedom came to apply universally, without regard to property, race, or sex. And freedom came to include not only the right to be equal before the law, but also the rights to participate in political life and to enjoy access to such basic requirements of human development and security as are necessary to ensure equal opportunity and what Franklin Delano Roosevelt called "freedom from fear." The recognition of these rights entailed corresponding civic responsibilities and mutual obligations and, under the pressure of both domestic and international conflict, led to a series of political changes, notably including the rise of mass democratic citizenship and public education; a turn toward positive government, that is, an enlarged though still circumscribed social and economic role for the state; a countervailing expansion of civil liberties and deregulation of culture; and the creation of new international institutions and alliances aimed at deterring war and defending democracy and human rights. Although the liberal project remains incomplete (and new challenges have emerged), many of the changes in policy called for by modern liberalism are well established, even as conservatives have attempted, with varying degrees of success, to roll some of them back.

During the great political conflicts of the nineteenth and twentieth centuries, conservatives predicted that liberal reforms would be morally destructive, economically ruinous, and politically suicidal, while socialist critics maintained that the socioeconomic changes were merely cosmetic and would make no difference at all. Modern liberalism's historical record has turned out to be better than either of these camps anticipated. The world's rich nations, it will be observed, are liberal democracies that devote a large share of their national income to social expenditures without destroying freedom or moral responsibility. These countries have dominated their authoritarian adversaries in international conflict, though both conservatives and liberals claim credit for these successes. The rival heirs to classical liberalism, as I have emphasized throughout, differ not only in their conceptions of liberty and equality but also in their theories of power. Modern liberalism claims that the expanded meaning of equal liberty and associated derivative policies—including greater public spending on education and social welfare as well as economic regulation aimed at counteracting market failures—contribute to economic growth and societal power, whereas conservatism has long contested those claims and, in critical respects, continues to deny them.

Some of the objections to liberal reforms in the nineteenth and twentieth centuries were entirely plausible before the fact. For example, Thomas Malthus argued in his *Essay on Population* (1798) that any relief of poverty would be self-defeating because it would enable the poor to have more children. (The good reverend later revised his position to say that moral suasion could have some effect.) At the time he had no way of knowing that birth rates would decline in the course of economic development—as a result of urbanization, the education of women, and new means of contraception—and that smaller family size and higher per capita income would lead to rising parental investment per child and long-term gains in health and well-being. These changes have overwhelmed whatever effect, if any, social-welfare expenditures have on birth rates. The Malthusian case proved to be alarmist, in short, because of empirical relationships that became clear only with time.

Similarly, conservatives who made dire predictions about the economic consequences of the welfare state did not anticipate that unemployment insurance and other benefits would function as "automatic stabilizers"—that is, government outlays on benefits would rise whenever the economy sagged, helping to blunt recessions and prevent a self-reinforcing spiral of decline. The introduction of workers' compensation gave employers new incentives to invest in safer working conditions and led to reductions in workplace injuries. By no means were the indirect and unanticipated effects of reform always so positive; many policies failed for reasons their sponsors did not foresee, and conservatives seized upon such instances as proof of their own belief in the general futility of "social engineering." But rather than formulating policy from speculative axioms, liberal reformers beginning in the mid-nineteenth century increasingly devoted themselves to the systematic gathering and analysis of socioeconomic data. And partly through better knowledge, partly by trial and error, liberal governments discovered that certain forms of limited state intervention could help bring the promise of a free and just society closer to fulfillment while reducing the waste of human and physical resources and improving economic performance.

Modern liberalism has worked out far better than its critics expected, in other words, not because liberals were right about every policy and strategy from the start, but because they were able to assimilate new experiences and information and to adjust the design of institutions and policies accordingly. This flexibility has distinguished liberalism from competing viewpoints in political economy that have confused derivative policies with core principles. Marxian socialists and conservative advocates of laissez-faire have often resembled students who even before a question is asked have their hands in the air and are ready with an answer. For the socialists, that answer has been, "Socialize the means of production"; for defenders of laissez-faire, it is still, "Rely on the free market." Lacking an equally comprehensive remedy, liberals have been more willing to mix state and market, improvising and testing out different hybrid approaches. Gradually, more abstract theories have emerged from liberal political philosophy and the social sciences about the appropriate roles of the state, market, and civil society. But democratic liberalism has never been ruled by a theory in the way that Marxism and free-market conservatism have been. The same is true in liberal thinking about international relations, with its mixture of Wilsonian and realist elements. A pragmatic emphasis on experience and evidence—on how things work in practice—has been critical in making liberalism work.

SHARED PROSPERITY

The turn toward positive government in the liberal democracies brought two changes in public expectations. The first was an expectation that government would manage the overall performance of the economy. During the nineteenth century and up through the 1930s, the capitalist economies had been ravaged by periodic panics and depressions, which were generally understood as misfortunes akin to natural disasters that the state could do little to prevent or even to mitigate. The most important shift in economic thinking by the mid-twentieth century was the acceptance, not of Keynesianism in particular, but of the general idea that the public could properly hold the government accountable for the stability of the economy, its rate of growth, and the distribution of its rewards. Disagreements have persisted, of course, about how to achieve prosperity and about the legitimacy, efficacy, and cost of redistributive measures. But the idea that government is accountable for economic conditions has become a settled fact of political life.

The second change was an increasingly firm expectation that citizens would have access to education at least through secondary school and perhaps through college and to economic security in hard times, old age, disability, and other adverse conditions beyond their control. By plain implication, there was a corresponding public obligation—resting on taxpayers in particular—to support policies making it possible to meet those expectations. How far these expectations and obligations ought to go has continued to provoke the sharpest ideological conflict.

Of these changes, the role of government in economic stabilization has probably become the least controversial. What once seemed wholly beyond the capacity of the liberal state now seems clearly within it, thanks to the automatic stabilizers that maintain consumption during recessions and to the role of central banks such as the Federal Reserve in regulating the money supply. The old, blanket opposition to deficit spending during recessions has virtually disappeared, though public works and other programs adopted specifically to stimulate the economy have assumed less importance, at least in short downturns, because of the usual delay between legislative enactment and the disbursal of funds (the economic stimulus may simply come too late). One virtue of the automatic stabilizers and monetary policy is that they typically do not require any new political agreement; indeed, the comparative evidence indicates that economic performance is better when central banks are removed from immediate political pressures. Bad policies can surely still wreck an economy and sometimes do, but the structural capacities and knowledge now exist to enable governments in modern liberal states to minimize the volatility that was a recurring and destructive aspect of capitalism in its earlier phases. A more stable economy has obvious benefits to investors. No group, however, benefits from greater economic stability more than the poor, who typically get hit harder than anyone else by hard times. When an economy catches cold, they get pneumonia (and their kids get asthma). Of course, the primary purpose of unemployment insurance and other programs shoring up the incomes of low-wage workers is to protect them against the risk of impoverishment. Here stabilization and redistribution go together—the redistribution generally being aimed, not at equality per se, but at maintenance of a stable standard of living.

The relationship of democratic liberalism to economic growth is more controversial. Two separate questions need to be distinguished.

First, has liberal democracy in general, compared to authoritarian government, been a burden or an advantage in economic development?

And, second, among liberal democracies, has the rise of positive government—in particular, redistributive social spending—come at the cost of growth?

Democracy and national wealth are strongly correlated: overwhelmingly, the rich nations of the world have democratic rather than authoritarian governments. But the source of that relationship has been much debated. Does democracy lead to economic growth or the reverse—or are both of these true in some degree? A careful analysis of economic data on all the world's independent countries from 1950 to 1990 by Adam Przeworski and his colleagues finds that transitions from dictatorship to democracy occurred randomly at all levels of per capita income. But the higher the level of income, the greater was the persistence of democracy. Poor democracies often collapsed. Rich democracies never did during this period (and rarely ever have). Democracies and dictatorships had about the same record in promoting *total* economic output, but except for the poorest countries, there was a marked difference in economic growth per capita. In the democracies, both mortality rates and birth rates fell faster, population grew more slowly, and per capita income and other measures of well-being rose more rapidly than in dictatorships. Labor's share of national income was also larger in the democracies: "Dictatorships repress workers, exploit them, and use them carelessly," Przeworski writes. "Democracies allow workers to fight for their interests, pay them better, and employ them better." In the democracies, in other words, the benefits of growth are more widely shared, and individual workers become more productive.[1]

These and other findings contradict the theory of authoritarian advantage proposed in the late 1950s by some analysts who predicted that democracy in the developing world would hinder economic growth by generating demands for income redistribution and immediate consumption at the expense of investment. To be sure, some authoritarian regimes have produced rapid economic expansion, particularly over short periods, but it is not clear whether, as a general rule, they can do so over the long term in the face of the social changes that growth itself unleashes and the instability that authoritarian regimes often face in leadership transitions.[2]

Like the modern theorists of authoritarian advantage, the propertied classes in Europe and North America during the eighteenth and nineteenth centuries also feared that democracy would undermine economic progress. Conservatives as well as many of the classical liberals believed that if the lower classes received the vote, they would use that power to confiscate wealth and redistribute income to themselves. In fact, the rise of the New Liberalism, Progressivism, and social democracy did realize some of these fears. Labor law and other forms of regulation limited property rights, the adoption of progressive taxation increased the fiscal burden on the rich, and new social-welfare programs disproportionately benefited the working class and the poor. But the dire forecast of economic decline proved mistaken. As social expenditures grew during the twentieth century, the liberal capitalist democracies became more productive, mortality as well as birth rates fell, per capita income rose, and the circle of prosperity expanded. Rather than destroying private wealth, the modern liberal state made it more secure, economically and politically. The conventional wisdom suggests that rising taxes and expenditures should have impaired growth. But the economic history of Europe and the United States during the past two centuries does not show that the growth of public spending had a deleterious effect on overall performance.[3] Among the liberal democracies, the states with higher levels of social spending actually grew faster than those with lower expenditures for the period from 1960 to 1980, while the reverse was true for the years from 1980 to 2000. Even in the more recent period, however, the relationship of social spending to growth depended on the specific design of taxes, transfers, and other policies.[4]

Part of the explanation for continued economic expansion during the long rise of public expenditure in the capitalist democracies is that a significant proportion of spending has represented investment that otherwise would not have been made. The underlying principle is no different from the one that Adam Smith enunciated in writing of the legitimate role of the state in financing public works and institutions, "which it can never be for the interest of any individual, or small number of individuals, to erect and maintain . . . though it may frequently do much more than repay [the expense] to a great society."[5] What Smith and others originally failed to anticipate, however, was how broadly this principle would apply. The development of an urbanized, industrial economy and, more recently, the increased centrality of knowledge and innovation require investments in public goods and services that only government is in a position to make. These are typically complementary to private investment, rather than competitive with it, and involve not just tangible capital assets, such as roads, ports, and other aspects of physical infrastructure, but intangible assets as well. Unable to capture all the potential economic value from scientific research, for example, private individuals and firms rationally underinvest in new knowledge; public financing of research, especially in basic science, has the now generally accepted function of closing the gap between private and social gains. The same is true of government spending on education insofar as it contributes to a society's human capital, that is, the wealth represented by its people's knowledge and skills. Public financing of education, like research, compensates for a type of underinvestment—in this case, the underinvestment in children and young adults by families that would otherwise lack the resources or willingness to pay for schooling. A portion of government spending on public health and health care also generates a return to society by enabling the young to develop their capabilities, raising the productivity of the working population, and reducing the burdens of illness and disability within the family as well as in the economy at large.

The general point here is that much of what democratic liberalism calls for on grounds of equal rights to opportunities for human development and political participation also provides a return in economic productivity. In both the United States and Britain, as well as in many other countries, universal primary schooling came on the heels of an expanded franchise. This historical connection between democracy and public education was one of the main reasons why rising taxes and public expenditures did not have the negative effects on growth that the propertied classes anticipated from democratization. The redistributive state turned out also to be, in critical respects, a productive, developmental state, generating wealth as well as power. Equal opportunity policies have contributed to long-term growth just as social insurance measures have contributed to stabilization. If we want to know why modern liberalism has worked out economically as well as it has, this is a large part of the answer. Moreover, the policies that have softened the hard edges of capitalism have created a margin of security and confidence enabling workers to cope with the uncertainties and risks of technological change and free trade. Protecting workers against sharp declines in their standard of living makes it less likely that they will turn to Luddite and protectionist responses. This too is part of the economic logic of liberal social policy.

Not all social spending, however, represents a means of achieving economic stability and growth or a way of ensuring equality of economic opportunity. Some of it simply transfers resources from one group to another. There have been three principled grounds for support of such policies.

The first and most basic of these is properly described as "humanitarian" and involves the relief of immediate suffering—the help we would extend to drowning men without knowing anything about them. Liberalism is not unique in recognizing humanitarian obligations. From the Enlightenment, however, liberals have sought to reduce cruelty and harshness in human relations, as, for example, in the methods of raising children and forms of punishment for crime. Liberal opposition to torture reflects this tradition. Humanitarian obligations do not arise from the particular obligations of the liberal state to its own citizens; indeed, they extend across national borders to unknown strangers. And though they arise out of recognition of a common human condition, they are aimed, not at achieving economic equality, but at preserving life, reducing the reign of fear in the world, and enlarging the possibilities of reason and mutual aid and respect.[6]

The two other grounds for redistributive policies are related to equality, though in different ways. The first is a correlate of the extension of an equal right to political participation. Where wealth is overwhelmingly concentrated in a small oligarchy, political power is sure to follow. Popular self-government requires not that wealth be equally distributed, but that it be widely dispersed. In the eighteenth century, Jefferson's support for a wide diffusion of landownership among yeoman farmers, though only extending so far as whites, reflected a recognition of the need to anchor popular government in a broad base of stakeholders. In the twentieth century, the United States imposed land reform in Japan after World War II to break the power of the traditional landowner class and anchor a new liberal democracy in a restructured society. The commitment of democratic liberalism to equal political rights—to a "fair equality" of political opportunity—also implies support for a broad distribution of civic competence. If a people are to share in their own government, they require an education that equips them for civic life, not just for a job. A liberal democracy cannot be indifferent to the social basis of its own survival. The organization of society and politics therefore should not just allow citizens a right to participate but also prepare them to make active use of that right. For in the very process of doing so they will likely encounter alternative perspectives and unfamiliar problems, need to justify their particular concerns by virtue of a wider public interest, and in time perhaps come to take a broader view of what their own interest calls for.

The final justification for redistributive policies is that the liberal state has an obligation to afford its own citizens the equal protection of the law and to treat them with equal respect and concern. To treat people as equals does not necessarily mean recognizing their claims as identical; a disabled child, for example, may require special resources to acquire an education equal to what others receive. The same logic applies to minorities who have suffered persistent social exclusion: more public effort may be required to redress past injustices. Any effort to correct injustices to groups, however, risks contradicting the principle of equal treatment of individuals (that is, through reverse discrimination); the corrective action therefore ought to be narrowly tailored and limited in duration. But where membership in a group has been the basis of deep and prolonged disadvantage, the state cannot treat its citizens equally if it is blind to the legacies of inequality.

Against all these reasons for redistribution, the liberal project has to weigh other values. Liberalism is egalitarian in the sense of seeking to achieve a more equal distribution of income and well-being than would otherwise be generated in the marketplace. But it is not committed to erasing all economic inequalities or to achieving a perfect equality in the distribution of goods. Equity requires that those who work harder, take greater risks, or develop their talents to a higher degree be able to recoup a return from their efforts. This incentive is critical to innovation and prosperity, which redound to wider benefit. Liberalism regards the well-being of the least well-off as a central criterion for a just society, and it seeks to provide individuals with some degree of protection against risks beyond their control, but it accepts inequalities insofar as they are to everyone's long-run advantage and therefore aims for sustainable growth with widely shared gains.[7]

Moreover, rather than simply provide all redistributive benefits as an unearned entitlement, a liberal government may legitimately insist on conditioning some assistance on contributions or reciprocal actions by the beneficiaries. Social Security, veterans' programs, and work-related antipoverty policies are based on this principle; humanitarian relief is not. By rooting ordinary aid to the poor in a norm of reciprocity, a liberal state may help to preserve the dignity of beneficiaries and their sense that other people do not regard the assistance they receive as shameful because they are getting "something for nothing."

The pragmatic disposition of liberalism also implies that policies cannot be derived from moral principles alone, without regard to empirical realities. Experience shows that governments can bring about some results more readily than others. For example, social security systems can be run on an automated and highly efficient basis, with payroll deductions and benefits calculated according to formula, whereas programs that try to modify social behavior inevitably confront greater overhead costs and uncertainties about effectiveness. Public budgeting for such purposes has to take into account the limits of knowledge and the relative costs and probabilities of success. Finally, in a democracy, redistributive policies cannot be sustained without majority support. The same concern to make policy work in practice requires that it work in politics.

These considerations tend to lead democratic liberalism in the direction of policies that are dual-purpose: justifiable because they serve both the macroeconomic aims of economic growth and stability and the egalitarian aims of social inclusion—the goal of a shared prosperity. Growth that is widely shared not only raises the standard of living of the middle class and the poor but also strengthens other liberal values. Among the good things that broadly based prosperity buys are tolerance and generosity. "Before we can feel much for others, we must in some measure be at ease ourselves," Adam Smith writes in *The Theory of Moral Sentiments*. The economist Benjamin M. Friedman argues that growth itself has a moral dividend. Individuals evaluate their own situation in two ways, by comparison with how well they have done in the past and with how well others are doing at present. If they are doing better than they did in earlier years, they are more likely to take a generous view of policies that widen opportunity for others. The historical and statistical evidence also shows a strong association between economic growth, on the one hand, and democratization and liberalization, on the other.[8] In light of that relationship, the interest in economic growth ought to be considered, not as crass materialism, but rather as a means of achieving a good society in part through secondary effects on public attitudes and politics. As liberal democracy has been good for growth, so too growth has been good for democracy and liberalism. One of the central challenges of politics is to enter that virtuous cycle—and to avoid its opposite, the spiral of an illiberal and antidemocratic decline.

THE MODERN DISCIPLINE:
PLURALISM IN FULL

The growth of the liberal state and the rise of the modern business corporation have changed the landscape of power and the problem of freedom. Conservatives who identify business with freedom and government with power see the expansion of government as intrinsically harmful. In contrast, liberals generally believe that both corporations and the state are phenomena of power that may put freedom as well as other values in jeopardy and that conservatives aggravate the potential for domination and injustice by turning the state over to business. If the threat of overweening power came only from the state, the conservative preoccupation with shrinking government might be more justified. And if that threat of overweening power came only from the market, socialism would have a stronger case. But dangers lie in either direction, and modern liberalism has consequently tried to keep corporate as well as state power in check and to strengthen spheres of relative autonomy from both. Science and the professions, nonprofit institutions, elements of the communications media, and to some extent the law itself have the twin character of limiting the reach of politics and the rule of commercialism—and by doing so, creating greater freedom, energy, and power in society as a whole.

These aspects of liberal modernity do not overturn what I described earlier as the "classical discipline of power"—they extend it. Classical liberalism seeks to divide power the better to control it. Such devices as the public-private distinction, checks and balances within government, separation of church and state, economic competition, and pluralism in civil society all flow from the central animating idea of disciplining power by both separating and sharing it. Any discipline aims not only to set limits but also to cultivate strength—so too the modern discipline of power. By according formerly marginalized groups equal dignity and a share in government, democratic liberalism widens the base of citizenship and patriotism. It also puts more emphasis than its classical counterpart on checking the state through public accountability. But constitutional limitations, far from disappearing, become more precious as barriers against intolerant and overreaching majorities. More vigilant protections of freedom of expression and other civil liberties follow directly from the eighteenth-century constitutional idea that a state endowed with strengthened powers requires equally robust guarantees of individual rights.

These guarantees enable democracy and liberty to coexist, and they are charters of freedom for such institutions as the sciences and professions, the arts, and communications media. The protections against politicized control of knowledge and judgment extend into the modern liberal state itself. For while expanding government's social and economic role and concentrating more functions at the national level, liberalism has also called for building autonomous professional authority into scientific bureaus and independent regulatory agencies, dividing the performance of public tasks between governmental and private institutions, and requiring increased public disclosure through freedom-of-information laws—instances once again of the uneasiness about concentrated power and the commitment to corrective mechanisms that have been characteristic of liberal state-building from the eighteenth century.

This entire structure of countervailing forces must figure into any assessment of how liberal pluralism works as a basis for democratic politics. There is more to pluralism than the raw competition of interest groups; the struggle for influence in a democracy typically demands that groups publicly justify their positions with facts and reasons, and a variety of institutions in civil society play a role in evaluating those arguments. Science is not merely another interest group; neither are professions such as journalism, nor churches and civic associations. However imperfectly, pluralism is also a system for testing from different perspectives the validity and reasonableness of the claims made by all those interested in public influence.

Science and the professions occupy a particularly critical position in the modern liberal system of checks and balances in and outside of government. Since the Enlightenment, the liberal commitment to freedom of thought has included a defense of the autonomy of science from the dictates of political and religious authorities. That commitment has taken on new significance in a world where both governments and private corporations appropriate technical knowledge and the reputation of science for their own purposes. Although the independence of science and the professions is no guarantee of truth, their subservience to power and money is a sure path to their own corruption and a corrosive cynicism throughout society about both knowledge and politics.

Liberal support for the autonomy of science rests neither on a technocratic belief in experts nor on the naive idea that science is immaculately conceived without social influence, but rather on scientific methods and norms that create mechanisms of self-correction. Scientific claims to truth must be falsifiable—perpetually at risk of being disproved through experiments or other systematic logical or empirical tests. The norms of the scientific community also demand a mix of competition and cooperation (or "coopetition," as it is sometimes called). Scientists compete with each other for priority of discovery internationally and sometimes even across the disciplinary lines, and the intensity and scope of that rivalry reduce the likelihood that local blockages, blinders, and monopolies will obstruct the flow of new knowledge. All this takes place, moreover, under expectations of skeptical cooperation, notably a norm of transparency that obligates scientists to disclose all methods, data, and results when publishing their work so as to permit independent assessment of its validity. Science is obviously not democratic in the sense of being decided by popular majorities; rather, it is geared toward self-regulation, judgment by peers. But the structure of science, with its internal checks, is congruent with the larger liberal vision, and precisely because the sciences and scientifically grounded professions are largely self-regulating, they can serve as platforms for independent and critical judgment of the claims made by commerce and government. And in so doing, they perform a vital public function in a democratic society.

A great deal can go wrong, we know, with this system. Research may be falsified; legitimate work that challenges a reigning paradigm may be wrongly dismissed; the rights of research subjects may be abused; and the scientific enterprise may be subordinated to short-term commercial or political interests. The autonomy of science does not exempt it from obligations of truthfulness, law, or ethics; a society that demands respect for human rights can demand no less of its scientists. And just as a liberal democracy has an interest in ensuring that both markets and elections are contestable, so it has an interest in ensuring the contestability of scientific disciplines by preventing any group or organization from monopolizing the means of financing, publishing, or evaluating research. Liberal policy has shown that government can support science without stifling it—indeed, that government can strengthen science institutionally as well as materially—by developing strong traditions of professionalism in scientific agencies, relying on independent peer review of research proposals to minimize the dangers of politicized decisionmaking, and fostering multiple avenues for financing and conducting research in both government and the wider society. The central role of nonprofit institutions in science is vital for sustaining basic science against the pressures for applied work with an immediate commercial payoff. That science can help to create wealth and power, no one doubts. But with well-designed policies and institutions, science can also contribute to the control of wealth and power—and to an experimental and innovative approach to policy—that a liberal democracy also requires.

The use of scientific and professional authority in independent gov-ernment agencies is only one example of a more general strategy of the modern liberal discipline of power that might be described as depoliti-cization without privatization. The general purpose of the strategy is to limit discretionary political power while maintaining legitimate public purposes. For example, legislatures can allocate government funds to lo-calities or individuals according to fixed statistical formulas and other rules that minimize the opportunities for pork and corruption. Agencies with direct revenue, such as postal services and highway and port authorities, can be set up as public corporations and operated under relatively independent boards with long-term appointments. Private nonprofit institutions perform much the same function: preserving a public-service orientation as their primary responsibility (rather than a fiduciary obligation to shareholders), while limiting the reach of poli-tics. The public-service orientation of the professions, whether their members are working in a public or private setting, is similarly aimed at maintaining a sense of higher obligations than profit or political advan-tage. Each of these means is imperfect; taken together, however, they help to create an internal compass in society pointing to the common good without overloading political institutions with more decisions than they can intelligently make and with more power than they can be safely trusted to exercise.

Like science, the communications media create a knowledge-power dilemma for states of all kinds. Widely diffused social capacities for knowledge and communications (high rates of literacy, extensive com-munications networks, broadly distributed facilities for media produc-tion) promise economic growth, military strength, and other gains, but their development may also destabilize the social and political order.[9] Authoritarian governments often so fear free thought and free commu-nications that they constrict their development, ultimately possibly jeopardizing their own survival in international competition and con-flict. Liberalism accepts the risks to stability out of a principled commit-ment to freedom and in the conviction that the extension of knowledge and communications is a source of innovation and strength rather than weakness. The communications media have an analogous role to that of science in the liberal discipline of power. They can be a means of controlling power and of creating it. As classical liberals defended the autonomy of science, so they stood for the freedom of the press, expecting that the press would act as a guardian of the people's interest by providing an independent source of public information and discussion and a check on governmental abuses of power. The leaders of the early American republic, fearing for its survival, also hoped that the press could help sustain the connection between the people and their government and strengthen the new nation's unity by putting distant communities in closer communication with each other and national politics. The rowdy, partisan, and often vituperative press of the nineteenth century was the outcome of decisions from early in the nation's history to promote free communications, not only by establishing a negative right in the First Amendment against government control, but also by using postal subsidies as a positive stimulus to the proliferation of newspapers throughout the country.

In time, that decentralized press grew into a formidable media industry dominated by corporations that came to exercise power of their own. The classical liberal ideal called for government by public discussion; in all the liberal democracies today, the corporate media now govern that discussion, or at least a great deal of it. Within this system, the development of journalism as a profession has given it a distinctive role as a source of reliable information and as a check against commercial and political deception. Journalism itself, however, is perennially at risk. A free and flourishing press requires not only a bar against censorship and manipulation by government, but also the preservation of a hospitable private environment for inquiry and debate, with a diversity of voices and forms of media ownership, nonprofit as well as for-profit. As much as ever the public needs a journalism capable of defying both commercial and political pressures. As Walter Lippmann once wrote, "There can be no liberty for a community which lacks the information by which to detect lies."[10]

In the control of corporate and political power, however, only so much may be expected of science, the professions, the press, and other elements of civil society. Keeping corporate power in check depends on government policy, and keeping governmental power in check depends on constitutional design and the capacity of the courts to ensure that government operates democratically. And back of these, there must be a liberal democratic politics capable of producing majorities in elections.

An uneasy relationship between liberal politics and business is unavoidable. Liberalism seeks to maintain the creative dynamic of a capitalist economy that is essential for growth while insisting that firms abide by rationally crafted rules that reflect such wider social interests as the protection of the environment and the rights of labor, consumers, and investors. Experience has shown that business can adapt to these rules and thrive with them, but the struggle to enact them in the first place (and often to enforce them later) typically draws fire from both conservatives and business interests. Pluralism implies a diversity of influence but not necessarily an equality of political resources. As an interest group, business (or more abstractly, "capital") is qualitatively different from others. Governments depend on business to produce jobs and tax revenue, and if politicians destroy or weaken business confidence and drive investment abroad, they do so ultimately at their own peril. Marxists and radicals, as well as liberals in their moments of despair, say that this structural power of business and its resulting capacity to limit the political agenda contradict the pluralist picture of democratic politics as a fair contest. The alternative pluralist view claims that business consists not of one interest but of many, which are often in conflict with each other, and that even when business interests generally agree, they are not always able to get their way. Some historical situations fit the first picture of corporate dominance, others the second picture of a more level playing field. In the United States, business dominated in the Gilded Age but lost power in the Progressive era, dominated in the 1920s but lost power with the New Deal, and gained influence in the 1950s but lost it again in the 1960s and 1970s. In the last of these periods, just when many critics on the left were describing corporations as hegemonic, business suffered a sharp drop in public confidence and lost control over the agenda and outcome of national politics: Congress passed twenty-five major pieces of regulation in such areas as environmental and consumer protection, occupational health and safety, product liability, and employee rights. By

1980 business was on the road to recovering its influence, but most of the "new social regulation," albeit weakened, has remained ever since.[11]

This cyclical pattern has produced an evolving legal and administrative regime for preventing or limiting the damage that raw capitalism and unrestrained corporate power can do to society, the natural environment, democracy, and the integrity of the market itself. Markets cannot work well—indeed, they cannot work at all—without laws regarding property, contracts, and other aspects of economic relations and without courts to resolve the conflicts that inevitably arise. The issue is not whether to have government intervention, but what kind. As the Progressives and New Liberals argued a century ago, property carries obligations as well as rights, and liberty rightly conceived does not include a right to harm others. Regulation aims to control harms ("negative externalities") such as environmental pollution that go unpriced and therefore unchecked in the market and to prevent short-term interests in profit from outweighing such long-term interests as the sustainability of the environment and confidence in financial markets. The liberal discipline of corporate power rests on the idea that private corporations, like the state, need checks and balances, transparency, and contestability. Hence liberal support for the countervailing power of labor unions, consumer organizations, and environmental groups. Hence liberal support for laws that require certain forms of transparency, such as disclosure of product information to consumers and financial information to investors. Hence liberal support for enforcement of antitrust law to deter the creation of monopolies or, when monopolies arise for justifiable reasons, to bar predatory practices. Hence liberal support for limits on the ability of corporations to use the enormous resources under their control to buy political influence. "Democracy would not endure, "Arthur Schlesinger Jr. writes, "if private concentrations of wealth were permitted to become more powerful than the democratic state."[12]

But like science, the communications media, or any other institution, regulation too can go wrong. Liberals are concerned about due process in administrative law, not because of an obsessive proceduralism, but because such safeguards reduce opportunities for the misuse of power. The rationale for locating regulatory functions in independent agencies is to remove them from direct political control and to build in a role for scientific and professional judgment, which can then be subjected to independent criticism and evaluation. Like claims to scientific truth, the claims for every regulatory policy should be considered perpetually at risk of being disproved. As technologies and markets change, regulation that once made sense may become obsolete, or experience may show that some forms of regulation have costs that far exceed their benefits. During the 1970s, many of the same liberal reformers who supported environmental protection attacked the older systems of price regulation in such industries as transportation and telecommunications for inhibiting competition and innovation. Deregulation was originally a liberal cause.[13] As environmental regulation developed, liberals came to recognize that instead of setting uniform limits on polluters, they could achieve improvements in air quality more efficiently by creating a market in emissions rights. (Under such a system, owners of factories that reduce pollution below some standard can sell their right to greater emissions to another company for which meeting the standard would be more costly.) More generally, an effective liberal policy has to try to align private incentives and public purposes, rather than trying to suppress private incentives in the name of public purposes. The modern liberal discipline of power is not just about government regulation of corporations and markets; it also has to be a discipline of the regulatory state itself, using all the tools available—science, law, public discussion and accountability, and markets themselves.[14]

Liberalism, I suggested in part I, is based on a hypothesis—a gamble—that a state can be "strong yet constrained—indeed, strong *because* constrained." The constraints of constitutional liberalism generate that strength for both state and society through a variety of ways. For example, the division of powers requires consultation with other branches of government, which, when they perform their institutional role, criticize and double-check decisions and increase the chance of correcting mistakes. The rule of law limits arbitrary power and self-enrichment and thereby improves the reliability and creditworthiness of the state. Equal respect and equal rights for diverse religious groups facilitate stable social cooperation. I have tried to show in part II that modern democratic liberalism, as it expands the state, also expands the mechanisms for disciplining its power. By protecting the free development of science, the professions, the arts, and the media, modern liberalism has cultivated sources of innovation while simultaneously creating a more extensive system of social checks and balances. Rule-making for markets makes it possible to limit damage to the environment, the squandering of human resources, and the economic havoc of panics and depressions that were characteristic of unregulated capitalism. Equal respect and equal rights for racial, ethnic, and cultural groups not only serve their interests in liberty but also enable them to contribute more to society. A long line of conservative thinkers has seen the expansion of government as the death of liberty and the expansion of rights as the ruin of moral order. They were wrong. Modern liberalism has raised the equilibrium of power and liberty to a higher level, changed the moral order in ways that were necessary to build a more inclusive society, and thereby enlarged the social partnership on which modern democracy rests.

DID LIBERALISM GO WRONG IN THE SIXTIES?

Some readers may be prepared to accept much of what I have said thus far but still reject "liberalism" because they identify it with ideas that, in their view, the 1960s showed to be mistaken. The experience of that time did give rise to some legitimate concerns about what liberalism stands for and whether it works. The 1960s saw liberalism's peak influence, its strongest passions, and its deepest disappointments, and the legacy of that era continues to inspire, divide, and haunt liberals even now.

In mid-twentieth-century America, liberalism was both a philosophy of government and a philosophy of reform. Liberal ideas informed Democratic administrations—from Roosevelt's New Deal through the New Frontier of John F. Kennedy and the Great Society of Lyndon Johnson—as well as movements that sought to change government policy on behalf of such causes as equal rights for African Americans, women, and other groups, the protection of the environment, arms control negotiations with the Soviet Union, and an end to the Vietnam War.

During the 1960s, however, the strained but productive relationship between mainstream and opposition liberalism broke down as the war in Vietnam intensified and protest turned in a more radical (and in some respects illiberal) direction. Both sides of liberalism then suffered setbacks with the election of Richard Nixon in 1968 and Ronald Reagan in 1980. Ideologically, conservatism was ascendant during these years, though there continued to be liberal advances. Much of the growth in liberal programs identified with the 1960s actually occurred during the Nixon administration, and long after Earl Warren's tenure as chief justice (1953–1969) the Supreme Court continued to uphold and in some respects extend the precedents set in the Warren years. Nonetheless, after being elected president in 1976, Jimmy Carter was unable to carry out ambitious domestic initiatives, and after his election sixteen years later Bill Clinton had only limited success. On a variety of fronts, liberalism since the 1960s has found the road ahead blocked, though much of what earlier liberal reform accomplished is now hardly even controversial.

One simple explanation for the decline of liberal innovation is that liberalism failed, which in a political sense is surely true: liberal candidates lost national elections. But whether the 1960s showed that liberal principles were morally and politically wrong is another matter. The conservative story of the decade is simple: liberalism was tried, and it didn't work. With some historical perspective, however, this is a fairer assessment: the liberalism of the 1960s brought about an immense moral and political transformation that, for all its limitations, rectified long-standing injustices, expanded freedom and democracy, and helped to realize America's promise of opportunity and a decent life for millions of its people. In this fundamental sense, liberalism did work. Yet, because some of the policies failed or backfired, these changes came at a social and political cost, and part of the cost was to the Democratic Party and to liberalism itself.*

---

*I deal only with domestic policy here; for the discussion of foreign policy, see chapters 5 and 8.

Despite the economic progress since the Depression, America in the 1950s was still a deeply racist and unequal society. Black Americans were denied respect and opportunity and subject to segregation by law in the South and by social practice in the North. Discrimination against other racial and ethnic minorities was routine; quotas in the nation's immigration laws, for example, still institutionalized a bias in favor of northern and western Europeans. Except for a few token representatives, women were regarded as incompetent at anything outside the home and, with scarcely a thought, excluded from politics and public life, the professions, and other pursuits. State laws made homosexuality illegal, and public opinion considered it so shameful that the subject could not be openly discussed. The New Deal reforms and postwar economic growth had overcome mass poverty, but minority poverty remained a stubborn reality, with more than one-fifth of the population in 1960 below the poverty line. Despite America's general affluence, hunger and malnutrition still afflicted the poor, particularly in the rural South, and despite major advances in medical science, gains in health and life expectancy were limited. Millions lacked health insurance and access to health care; air and water pollution were uncontrolled; and the tobacco industry thwarted efforts to publicize the health effects of smoking.

Daunting political obstacles impeded reform in all of these areas. Black Americans were denied the right to vote in the South and had little representation elsewhere. Legislatures in many states had not been reapportioned for decades to reflect population change, and consequently cities were grossly underrepresented; in eleven states, less than 20 percent of the population could elect a legislative majority. Southerners in Congress used their control of key committees to block progress on civil rights and other issues at the national level. Powerful industries obstructed environmental and health legislation. And whenever reformers proposed action to deal with these problems, conservatives objected on grounds of states' rights, property rights, and the American way. They were content to do nothing. The liberals were open to change, and the troublemakers among them actively fought for it.

In an obstructed political system, where could the initiative come from? Partly from social criticism, the arts, and social movements that agitated for reform and brought about a shift in attitudes among the public at large. By the 1960s a more liberal climate of opinion prepared the way for national legislation, much of which finally moved through Congress after the Democratic landslide in 1964.[15] But until then, and for decades after, an institution that historically had hardly ever been a friend to social reform emerged as crucial in breaching the political barriers on the most difficult issues. This was the Supreme Court, and its role became an issue in itself. For how could liberals who believed in democracy also support the authority of unelected judges?

In fact, many liberals from the New Deal era believed that democracy was best served by courts that deferred to legislative policy judgments, in contrast to the long era when judges regularly struck down social legislation on the grounds of the sanctity of property rights and freedom of contract. In an otherwise minor Supreme Court decision in 1938, however, Justice Harlan Fiske Stone had appended a footnote that identified three exceptions requiring judicial scrutiny: legislation that appears to violate the Bill of Rights; legislation that restricts the democratic political process, impeding legislative change; and laws "directed at particular religions or national or racial minorities" because prejudice against them may "curtail the operation of those political processes ordinarily to be relied upon to protect minorities." According to this view, the courts have a legitimate role, not in limiting democracy, but in ensuring that the legislative and executive branches act democratically. Only if one thinks of democracy merely as simple majority rule are courts inherently undemocratic. But if democracy implies that all citizens, including minorities, must be able to make themselves heard, the Court's intervention in ensuring their rights under the Constitution fulfills and extends democracy, rather than limiting it.[16]

The judicial activism of the Warren Court needs to be understood in this context. Warren himself, the popular former governor of California, was a Republican, as was another key Eisenhower appointee, William J. Brennan. Beginning in 1954 with *Brown v. Board of Education*, in which it declared racially segregated schools unconstitutional, the Court handed down a series of decisions on behalf of the right of African Americans and other minorities to the equal protection of the laws. Beginning in 1962 with *Baker v. Carr*, in which it challenged Tennessee's failure to reapportion its state legislature for sixty years, the Court issued another series of decisions that established a rule of "one person, one vote" for state legislative districts. It also greatly expanded the guarantees of free speech and freedom of the press. In *New York Times v. Sullivan* (1964), for example, the Court said that the press could be held guilty of libel against a public official only when "actual malice" could be proven; in this particular case, the *Times* had published an advertisement by civil rights leaders that included criticism of the police in Birmingham, Alabama, though it never referred to the police chief, L. B. Sullivan, by name. If the Supreme Court had upheld the staggering libel judgment handed down by an Alabama court against the *Times*, national coverage of civil rights protests in the South—and thus the ability of African Americans to get themselves heard—would have been severely inhibited.

To be sure, not all the advances in civil rights and democracy during the 1960s came via the judiciary. The Warren Court was unable to agree that the Constitution prohibits discrimination in private employment, housing, and public accommodations. It took civil rights legislation adopted by Congress in 1964 as well as subsequent acts to bar such discrimination. In 1965 Congress also adopted the Voting Rights Act and passed new immigration legislation eliminating the old national-origins quotas. These actions would literally change the complexion of American society.

From 1954 to 1965, the struggle to overcome racism was the moral center of liberalism, but the rights revolution it set in motion went much further. The civil rights movement created a paradigm of moral authority and political action so compelling that it was adopted (and adapted) by movements on behalf of the rights of women, gays and lesbians, people with disabilities, and other groups. The Supreme Court also extended the conception of rights in new ways. In *Griswold v. Connecticut* (1965), in which it overturned a Connecticut law banning contraceptives, the Court declared that Americans have a right to marital privacy; two years later, in *Loving v. Virginia*, it overturned a Virginia law against interracial marriage; and in 1971, in *Roe v. Wade*, it struck down laws banning abortion on the ground that a woman's privacy rights include the control of her own body. In another line of decisions including *Miranda v. Arizona* (1966), the Court expanded the rights of police suspects and criminal defendants. And in yet other decisions regarding separation of church and state, it held, among other things, that organized prayer in public schools is unconstitutional. These decisions were all extensions of classical liberal strictures about the limitation of state power. But because an expanded right to privacy removed the government from the regulation of private relationships, the Court was advancing the modern movement toward a freer sexuality. Libertarians on the right had little objection to this aspect of the Court's work; they mainly wanted the Court to be more protective of property rights too. But to moral and religious conservatives, the Court's decisions on sexuality, abortion, and school prayer were outrages.

Another source of the emerging backlash against liberalism came from the means that reformers embraced to advance civil rights, such as the busing of children from one neighborhood to another to bring about school integration and the use of affirmative action to bring about greater equality in higher education and employment. Affirmative action originally developed as a way of carrying out antidiscrimination law and enforcing compliance by organizations such as crafts unions that excluded blacks through informal methods. It was not long, however, before racial and ethnic diversity in classrooms and workplaces became a value in its own right to be achieved through affirmative action. The original impetus of the civil rights movement was to remove race as a consideration in decisions; increasingly, the means adopted to achieve an equal and integrated society reemphasized race as a criterion. There was a logically defensible chain of reasoning that led from race-blind to race-conscious policies, but the result was at the very least a tension, if not an outright contradiction, between means and ends in the struggle to end discriminatory practices. Increasingly, the burdens of change seemed to fall on the innocent. Children forced to leave their neighborhood school and qualified white applicants passed over for jobs bore no personal responsibility for racist practices. The further liberalism moved from the original, compelling aim of eliminating discrimination against African Americans to other aims for other groups by means that harmed innocent bystanders, the more ambiguous the moral basis of the rights revolution became and the less political support it enjoyed.

Between 1965 and 1968, an increasingly intense backlash also developed against the "revolution in the streets": urban riots, campus revolts, the burning of draft cards in antiwar protests, and the rise of drug use and the counterculture. Some liberals condemned these developments, while others excused them or justified some aspects of the new radicalism but not others, and conservatives saw this sympathy, however qualified, as further evidence that liberalism was to blame for all the trouble. By this time, liberalism was being attacked from both directions—by radicals for being too conservative and by conservatives for being too radical. As young radicals saw it, liberally run institutions such as schools and universities were complicit in a stiflingly repressive culture, while conservatives said the same institutions were responsible for a culture that was wildly permissive. Radicals and conservatives, however, agreed on one point: liberal social programs were bound to be futile.

Like the rights revolution, the programs of the New Frontier and Great Society were a source of both the achievements of liberalism and the backlash against it. The prosperity and rising tax revenues of the 1960s allowed the Kennedy and Johnson administrations as well as governors such at Pat Brown in California to introduce new programs on a big scale. Although the War on Poverty looms over the historical memory of that era, most of the new social spending did not go for the poor. In budgetary terms, the biggest federal initiatives were for the elderly: the introduction of Medicare in 1965 and a major increase in Social Security benefits in the early 1970s. Health care generally absorbed a steadily increasing share of social spending. When Congress approved Medicare in 1965, it also created a second program, Medicaid, to finance medical care for the poor, albeit without covering all low-income Americans who lacked private insurance. But here too perceptions did not exactly reflect the fiscal realities: two-thirds of Medicaid expenditures went for nursing home patients, many of them middle-class seniors who had spent down their assets.

The antipoverty policies of the 1960s can be conveniently divided into two phases. Johnson's War on Poverty, the first of these, had "equality of opportunity" as its organizing principle and emphasized compensatory education and job training, along with community development. Among the leading programs were Head Start, a preschool program for disadvantaged children; the Elementary and Secondary Education Act of 1965 for the disadvantaged in school; and Job Corps, which provided training for the poor out of school. Whereas the social programs dating from the early twentieth century tried to prevent workers and their families from becoming destitute by buffering them against the economic risks of sickness, injury, old age, and unemployment, the War on Poverty aimed to improve the life chances of people who were already poor. This was inherently more difficult, as it involved changes in ways of thought and behavior that no one was certain how to bring about. As a result, some of the new initiatives were ineffective, and even those that yielded positive results did not do so quickly. Moreover, unlike Social Security and Medicare, which created a legal entitlement to benefits for all those who earned the right to qualify, the equal opportunity programs were funded by Congress on a limited and discretionary basis, and most of them reached only a fraction of the poor. Even a popular and successful program like Head Start received funds for only about 20 percent of eligible children. Funding these initiatives on a partial basis made sense at the beginning because they were experimental. But the equal opportunity programs should never have been expected to eliminate poverty; promising too much invited the verdict that the war was a failure.[17]

The trouble with the War on Poverty, according to many of its early liberal critics, was the government's reliance on services to the poor instead of the more direct method of income support. This was the rationale for a second wave of programs—many of them enacted or expanded at congressional initiative during the Nixon administration—creating a "safety net" to provide a basic level of material subsistence. In 1935, as part of the Social Security legislation, Congress had established a small benefit for children who had no working parent to support them, a situation at that time expected to arise primarily when a father died, leaving his widow to hold the family together. As late as 1961, this program—now called Aid to Families with Dependent Children (AFDC) and commonly referred to as "welfare"—was still relatively small, though it was growing as a result of rising rates of divorce and illegitimacy. The federal government paid for around two-thirds of the program's cost, but eligibility criteria and benefit levels were set by the states, some of which, particularly in the Deep South, were so restrictive as to leave the poor in conditions like those of the Third World. Many reformers wanted to change or replace AFDC entirely because the program was uneven in its coverage, aided only the nonworking poor (and hence discouraged recipients from taking a job), and was highly intrusive (caseworkers could inspect recipients' homes in the middle of the night to see if there was a "man in the house" capable of supporting the children). As an alternative to AFDC, some leading economists, including the conservative Milton Friedman as well as the liberal James Tobin, favored a "negative income tax" to provide the nonworking and working poor alike with a federally guaranteed minimum income (the tax subsidy being phased out gradually so as to preserve incentives to work). Both President Nixon and George McGovern, the Democratic presidential candidate in 1972, supported versions of this idea, but it never won popular support or congressional approval. In 1970, however, after widely publicized hearings about hunger and malnutrition in America, Congress built on a program adopted in 1964 and created a minimal version of a guaranteed income in the form of a national food stamp program for the poor. Two years later, also building on earlier measures, it adopted Supplemental Security Income, an initially small income-support program for the elderly, blind, and disabled poor. In addition, a program of rent subsidies enabled many of the poor to afford decent housing. Meanwhile, many of the states had increased welfare benefit levels, the courts had struck down the "man in the house" rule, and Congress had made it easier for the poor to receive welfare while earning a limited amount of money. From a fiscal standpoint, welfare (including both cash support and quasi-cash such as food stamps and housing subsidies) continued to be a small part of the welfare state—only 11 percent of social-welfare expenditures as of 1976. But from 1965 to 1976 the number of families on welfare had more than tripled—up from 1 million to 3.6 million—and this increase was widely viewed as evidence of the failure of the Great Society.[18] And, in fact, the growth of welfare did signal a failure: the equal opportunity programs of the War on Poverty were aimed at enabling the poor to earn a decent living, not to live idly off the taxpayers. Many reformers had hoped to change welfare to create incentives for employment (though they were unwilling to require work for fear that beneficiaries could not find jobs or stay employed), but no political consensus on an alternative developed.

From a material standpoint, the social programs of the 1960s and '70s did help to reduce poverty. After dropping from 30 percent to 22 percent during the 1950s, the poverty rate (as measured by standard federal criteria) fell to 13 percent in 1970. The official index, however, counts only cash income. Factoring in food stamps, housing subsidies, and medical coverage according to how much money the benefits saved recipients gives a more accurate picture. By this measure, according to estimates by Christopher Jencks, the poverty rate dropped from 29 percent in 1950 to 18 percent in 1965 to 10 percent in 1980.[19] Hunger and severe malnutrition in poor communities were virtually eliminated; overcrowded and dilapidated housing was drastically reduced; access to medical care for the poor sharply increased. Although there had been little gain in life expectancy in the decade before 1965, life expectancy rose by four years between 1965 and 1980, and age-adjusted mortality rates fell by 20 percent. Not surprisingly, the greatest decline in poverty occurred among the elderly, whose health and well-being also improved according to such criteria as longer life expectancy at age sixty-five and reduced days of bed-ridden disability. The elderly used to have higher poverty rates than other age groups, but by 1980 poverty was less common among the elderly than among those under sixty-five. Hardly anyone registered the significance of this change; together with Medicare and other reforms, Social Security had become the most successful antipoverty program of all. By a variety of measures—educational attainment, test scores in math and English, employment in higher-earning occupations, median earnings, home ownership—the historical disparities between black and white Americans were also significantly reduced.[20]

While law and social policy contributed to this progress, the decline in poverty during the 1960s reflected the strong economic growth of

those years. During the following decade, however, economic performance deteriorated sharply throughout the industrialized world. The
U.S. economy's total output continued to increase in the 1970s, but
only because the size of the labor force grew as the baby boom generation finished school and more women sought employment. For men,
real earnings per capita went down; for example, the median earnings
of men who were thirty-five to forty-four years old in 1973 dropped 15
percent (after inflation) in the next ten years. In many families, women
took paid jobs (sometimes because of their husband's employment
problems), but real median income per household hardly advanced at
all—and income inequality began to rise. Single-parent families did
much worse than families with two working adults. Under these conditions, the lack of further progress in reducing poverty was scarcely
surprising, nor was it proof (as conservatives contended) that social
programs were ineffective. Data on income before and after transfers
(income support programs) indicate that poverty rates would have
been substantially higher without government help. That, of course,
was the rationale for a safety net, and in that respect it worked.[21]

Increasingly, however, the debate about antipoverty policy was about
the moral condition of the poor rather than about their material condition. The main conservative objections to welfare were that it caused
idleness, discouraged marriage, subsidized illegitimacy, and thereby contributed to a cycle of moral irresponsibility and poverty from one generation to the next. This criticism was not new, but it gained plausibility
in an era when divorce, the share of births born to unmarried parents,
and single parenthood were rising in all classes and portrayals of poverty
focused on a ghetto underclass (about 10 percent of the poor) caught in
a self-perpetuating behavioral loop. During the 1980s, statistical analyses of welfare's effects on family structure did not bear out the claim that
welfare had increased the rate of illegitimate births.[22] But part of the
conservative critique was correct. By aiding the nonworking poor while
doing little for low-income workers, the safety net programs created incentives that discouraged work and personal responsibility. In some
states with generous welfare benefits, unskilled mothers could not expect to earn as much if they held a job as they could receive from the
state if they didn't work. The failure to pass universal health insurance

also produced an anomaly: the poor on welfare were eligible for Medicaid, while workers with low-wage jobs often had no health coverage. Other advanced countries avoided these incentive problems through universal health insurance and child allowances that parents did not lose by working or getting married. In this respect, the limitations of the American welfare state were partly responsible for welfare's perverse incentives. By providing greater benefits to poor people who didn't work than to poor people who did, welfare inverted the reasonable moral expectation that individual effort will receive its due reward.

The rise of the welfare population, moreover, seemed to fulfill the worst white stereotypes about black indolence. Race complicates virtually every aspect of American domestic policy, none more than welfare. Surveys have shown consistently strong public approval for some programs, such as Head Start, that the public associates with poor African Americans. White Americans associate welfare, however, not just with blacks but with blacks who don't work.[23] The political support for the program grew even more tenuous as it supported an increasing number of mothers with children born out of wedlock. To make matters worse, welfare was increasingly out of line with contemporary social norms about the role of women. The welfare system had developed at a time when few women with young children held paying jobs, but now that there were millions of working mothers, it no longer seemed reasonable to exempt women on welfare from paid employment so that they could stay home with their children.

By 1973 the expansion of cash welfare benefits was over, though Medicaid and housing subsidies continued to increase. During the rest of the 1970s, as inflation surged, the real value of welfare payments fell, and after Reagan's election in 1980, the new administration cut back antipoverty programs. By 1984 the average package of welfare and food stamps was worth 20 percent less than in 1972, and just 3 percent more than welfare alone had been worth in 1960. While many liberals simply denounced the cutbacks, a few began to call for reconstructing antipoverty policies on a more defensible foundation. Welfare, these reformers saw, was a dead end not just for its beneficiaries but also for any political effort to improve the lives of the poor. The American public could be generous toward the poor, but not if a program rewarded what most people thought was lazy and irresponsible behavior. The new approach accepted the legitimacy of reasonable work requirements for single mothers on welfare (as conservatives had demanded) but recognized that the jobs most beneficiaries could get would pay only poverty-level wages. A policy that genuinely sought to improve their lives, therefore, would not just require them to look for employment but aid them in the transition and boost the rewards of work. Although this new wave of thinking about antipoverty policy initially had no name or single champion, it eventually came to be associated with Bill Clinton. The key idea might be described as earnings support.

Unlike the equal opportunity and safety net approaches to reducing poverty, the earnings support approach was centrally concerned with the working poor, sought to get incentives right, and recognized that it was vital to align social policy with American values about work and responsibility. Economic as well as political realities dictated the focus on the working poor. Existing social policies, while relatively generous to the elderly and disabled, continued to do little for low-wage, able-bodied workers and their families at a time when the loss of industrial jobs had removed an important ladder of mobility into the middle class and the real wages of workers with less than a college education were falling. Policies that increased the rewards from low-wage work had the potential not just to help welfare beneficiaries get off the rolls but also to counteract the trend toward growing income inequality.

As a general goal, therefore, the new approach proposed that public policy should make it possible for every family with a full-time, year-round worker to escape poverty: "If you work, you shouldn't be poor." In view of global competition and the information revolution, improved education and training would be vitally important in achieving that goal over the long term. Here, once again, was the liberal emphasis on dual-purpose programs that served the aims of both economic growth and equality. But other antipoverty measures would be necessary for workers without a college education or special skills. Reformers particularly emphasized subsidized health insurance, a higher minimum wage, and an increase in what until that time was a relatively inconspicuous tax credit for earnings by low-income individuals with children, the Earned Income Tax Credit, originally established in 1975. Subsidized health coverage would relieve a major source of economic insecurity and personal bankruptcy for the working poor. A higher minimum wage combined with a larger Earned Income Tax Credit would also help "make work pay"—that is, guarantee that the rewards of work would be greater than those of welfare. As of the late 1980s, the tax credit augmented the earnings of a minimum-wage worker by only 14 percent, but its virtues were clear. Unlike welfare, it promoted work, carried no stigma, and required no large social-welfare bureaucracy to administer because it operated through the income tax system. The new approach also called for stricter enforcement of responsibilities for child support by absent fathers as well as measures to reduce teen pregnancy.[24]

As a candidate, when he called for "ending welfare as we know it," Clinton embraced this strategy, and as president, despite setbacks and compromises, he carried it out far more than is widely appreciated. His first budget in 1993 took a critical step, sharply increasing the Earned Income Tax Credit. Under the new provisions, a family of four with a minimum-wage worker received a tax credit boosting its income by 40 percent. A deal with Congress in 1996 raised the minimum wage by 21 percent (from $4.25 to $5.15 an hour). Although Clinton's Health Security Plan failed to pass Congress, changes in Medicaid eligibility and the adoption of a new children's health insurance plan later broadened public coverage of low-income working families. Other measures included an Access to Jobs initiative that subsidized transportation services to help those formerly on welfare get to work and a tax credit for businesses that hired former welfare beneficiaries. These were all crucial to the success of welfare reform.

Welfare reform itself turned out far differently from Clinton's original plan, which called for up to two years of education and training for recipients before requiring them to work, helped pay for child care, and subsidized community-service jobs for beneficiaries unable to find commercial employment. As a result of these provisions—and because budget forecasters assumed the program would not reduce the welfare rolls, only slow the rate of growth—the Clinton bill was projected to add significant costs to the federal budget. After the Republicans took control of Congress in 1994, however, they passed their own welfare reform legislation, which abolished AFDC and replaced it with a "block grant" to the states that froze spending at its existing level. The Republican approach pressed the states to make rapid cuts in the welfare rolls regardless of how many beneficiaries found work, omitted the two-year training period and last-resort jobs, and set a five-year lifetime limit on any family's receipt of all federal welfare aid. Most of Clinton's advisers wanted him to kill the legislation, but after vetoing the first two bills passed by Congress, the president signed a third one that limited the block grant to cash assistance and maintained food stamps and Medicaid as federal entitlements.

Many liberals predicted that the poor would fare badly under welfare reform, and perhaps the poor would have if it had not been for the increased Earned Income Tax Credit, higher minimum wage, expanded government health coverage, transportation subsidies, and preservation of food stamps and Medicaid. Above all, the strong economy of the late 1990s enabled the majority of women pushed off welfare to find jobs. Between 1996 and 2000, the number of families on welfare dropped from 4.5 million to a little more than 2 million, while the poverty rate among single mothers—counting food stamps and other aid—declined from 21 percent to 15 percent (before rising to 17 percent in 2003). The drop in state welfare costs was so sharp that it freed up state funds for child care and other services for the poor under the block grants fixed at 1996 levels. Overall, the number in poverty (as measured by the official index) dropped by 6.4 million during the Clinton years. Beginning around 1992, there were also declines in teen pregnancy and crime, and some of the worst-afflicted urban centers of the 1980s showed signs of recovery; welfare reform may have contributed to this turnaround. Since the mid-1990s, the poor have been expected to work, and when they do, they receive a supplement to their wages—the Earned Income Tax Credit—that is 100 percent federally funded and more substantial than the cash benefit that many state welfare programs had provided. The poor can now do what the old system prohibited: work full-time and receive additional public support to escape poverty. That is not to say the system is wholly satisfactory. As a result of a continuing shrinkage in employer-provided health coverage, the number of uninsured Americans has increased; child care for working mothers in low-wage jobs is still limited; and many of the poor who can no longer qualify for welfare are unable to find stable employment. In the ten years since 1996, Congress has failed to raise the minimum wage, allowing its real value to sink to the lowest level in half a century. But because the Clinton-era reforms showed it was possible to make progress on what had seemed an intractable problem, the way forward in dealing with poverty is clearer than it was during the decades of despair over welfare.[25]

Welfare was the most grievous domestic policy failure of 1960s liberalism. The correction of that failure did not require cutting off all government support of the poor, as some conservatives wanted. But it did require fundamentally redesigning that support to change the incentives and satisfy the public that work and responsibility would be expected and rewarded. There was less novelty in the reforms of the 1990s than it seemed. The president who first characterized cash assistance to the poor as a "narcotic" was not Reagan but Franklin D. Roosevelt, who did so in the context of a plea to Congress to create three million jobs. FDR structured his most successful program, Social Security, as an earned entitlement; to this day Americans qualify through work, and their benefits reflect what they have earned. Lyndon Johnson never intended the War on Poverty to expand welfare; the aim was "a hand up, not a handout." Replacing welfare with an employment-oriented, earnings-support system was therefore entirely in line with the liberal tradition. During the long battle over welfare, liberal advocates for the poor could have avoided a great deal of damage to their own cause by keeping in mind what the originators of the New Deal and the War on Poverty understood from the start.

Some critics of the liberalism of the 1960s see an exaggerated emphasis on rights as crucial to what went wrong afterward and accordingly describe the philosophy that emerged from that era as "rights-based liberalism." This is not a term I use. Rights are the legal means for claiming liberty in its various forms and are necessarily central to all versions of liberalism, not just to the liberalism of the Sixties. Disavowing or belittling the historic advances in rights brought about during the 1960s would also be a great mistake.

Nonetheless, the psychology of rights that developed in that era gave rise to a series of political problems. A liberalism that advances human rights, or even rights of citizenship, has an inclusive reach. But in the late twentieth century, as different groups claimed rights based on their particular identities, the rights revolution undercut social and political solidarity. Liberalism found itself increasingly divided from within. Soon there were many movements, yet no general liberal movement at all and a much diminished sense of an overall, greater good and public purpose.

Ordinary politics involves negotiation and compromise. Rights, however, are like trump cards that can be used to override the normal political give-and-take. Where constitutional rights are at issue, authority also passes into the courts. Inasmuch as the normal legislative means for protecting such rights have failed, there is a sound democratic logic to judicial intervention. But a hazy line distinguishes the judicial protection of democracy from the circumvention of the democratic process, and as the rights revolution went on, the courts intervened too often, and liberals became too dependent on them. For several decades it was easier to achieve goals by making constitutional arguments to judges than by building majority public support, winning elections, and passing legislation. Yet the imperatives of democratic politics cannot be avoided indefinitely; sooner or later, losing elections leads to losing control of the courts—and for liberals, that time has arrived. If liberalism is to move forward again, it will have to move on the basis of a majoritarian politics.

Some of the backlash against contemporary liberalism was unavoidable. The struggles on behalf of the rights of blacks and women upset a social hierarchy privileging white men: should it have been a surprise that many of them became more conservative? The acceptance of gays and lesbians and a freer sexuality contradicted the assumptions of many people who equated traditional moral rules about sex with morality itself: should it have been a surprise that they turned to conservative politics to restore what they felt was being lost? But as the case of welfare illustrates, liberals sometimes harmed their own cause by defending policies that were not working and that were politically unsustainable because they conflicted with widely shared moral values of personal responsibility. And these values were not like prejudice against gays—that is, values based on invidious social distinctions. On the contrary, they were values that a sensible liberalism upholds.

One of the glorious achievements of liberal societies is that they accommodate religious and cultural diversity and enable people with different moral ideals not just to live side by side but to flourish together. That is not to say, however, that a liberal state is morally neutral in a strong sense—neutral, that is, on all choices regarding human good—though some liberals and many critics of liberalism have interpreted it that way. In a familiar complaint, Francis Fukuyama writes that "liberal states do not refer their citizens to higher aims beyond the responsibilities of general civic-mindedness" but rather "leave them to do as they please. . . . This failure to address the question of the content of the good life is of course why liberalism works, but it also means that the vacuum that constitutes our freedom can be filled with anything: sloth and self-indulgence as well as moderation and courage, desire for wealth and preoccupation with commercial gain as well as love of reflection and pursuit of beauty, banality alongside spirituality."[26]

The reason why liberalism works, however, is not that it is silent on human good. A liberal government, like any other, must operate on the basis of substantive values, not just in the criminal law but in every phase of its activities. Its policies regarding public health and welfare are necessarily based on moral conceptions of human well-being. A liberal education is properly aimed at cultivating integrity and other aspects of character as well as intelligence. A liberal politics is premised on the belief that citizens and their representatives are capable of virtues such as reasonableness and a willingness to entertain new ideas. A liberal state cannot legitimately compel those under its authority to worship the same way, mouth an official ideology, or follow a preferred way of life. But neither can a liberal state legitimately be neutral between disease and health, sloth and effort, deceit and integrity, cowardice and courage. There are excellences and virtues that a liberal society must promote if it is to survive.[27] Far from being silent on the good, liberalism is intensely concerned with it, though that concern is not always fully expressed or best conveyed through the state.

Many people experienced the 1960s as an abandonment and collapse of moral values, and some liberals interpreted the breach of old moral rules as meaning that there were no limits and no restraints and that government had no business making any moral distinctions at all. But this was an error not only about the moral basis of liberalism but also about the significance of contemporary history. The enduring achievement of the 1960s was a moral transformation that led Americans to alter their conceptions of who is worthy of respect and what qualities and ideals they ought to try to realize in their society. For all the difficulties that have followed the 1960s, I cannot imagine that many people of even mildly liberal disposition would willingly return to the moral universe that preceded it. Yet the work begun at that time is unfinished, and the full promise of the new universe we inhabit remains unfulfilled. In realizing that promise, clarity about moral purposes and clarity about politics will go together.

III
THE LIBERAL PROJECT
OF OUR TIME

———

7

Up from Socialism

────────

IT USED TO BE AN ARTICLE OF FAITH AMONG BOTH SOCIALISTS AND communists that liberal democratic capitalism was merely a temporary phase in history's march toward a higher civilization and that one way or another, through revolution or reform, socialism would own the future. Then history made mischief with that vision, and instead of succeeding capitalism, socialism succumbed without a fight: Socialist parties in Western Europe abandoned even modest programs of state ownership and economic planning, China embraced capitalist enterprise, and in the revolutions that ended the global ideological warfare of the twentieth century, communist governments fell in Eastern Europe in 1989 and the Soviet Union itself crumbled two years later. Throughout the world, the socialist project of a planned economy and a classless society imploded as a credible ideal.

Ever since the early nineteenth century, socialism had been liberalism's chief rival as a framework for the creation of a more rational and egalitarian society. While modern liberals called for capitalism to be regulated, socialists called for it to be replaced by socializing the means of production through state or worker ownership of industry and state control over the allocation of investment. Besides viewing capitalism as chaotic and irrational because unplanned, socialists criticized liberal conceptions of equality as inadequate, holding up a more radical vision of equality of power and economic condition.

By the last quarter of the twentieth century, however, most parties calling themselves "socialist" in the capitalist democracies had largely given up on the idea of socializing the means of production as a way of advancing either economic rationality or equality and instead focused on providing broad social-welfare guarantees. Despite the Marxist grandparents on their family tree, they came to accept the basic economic institutions as well as political ideals associated with liberalism and offered an alternative only to policies adopted within the framework of a market economy. Meanwhile, the communist regimes that had socialized industrial production and investment failed to live up to their promise of creating a world of abundance and equality, not to mention that most ironic of Marx's utopian hopes, the "withering away of the state." By the time the Eastern European and Soviet regimes disintegrated, the dream that had originally inspired them was already dead.

The collapse of the socialist challenge put liberalism (in both the broad constitutional and contemporary American senses of the term) in a new position. Constitutional liberalism became the sole recognized basis of democracy: to establish a democratic state with international legitimacy meant adopting a constitution that guaranteed individual rights, including rights to private property, as well as free, competitive elections. Instead of referring to "liberal democracy," most writers and politicians just spoke of "democracy" as if no other kind was possible. Capitalism also no longer had any serious rival for global hegemony, and countries that had previously followed a policy of autarky or sharply restricted foreign investment now entered the world economy. Though important differences in policy and institutions remained, the global confrontation of hostile systems appeared to be over.

These developments gave rise not only to an understandable sense of relief in the West but also to a triumphalist certainty, especially on the right, about history's ultimate destination. Just after Marxist notions of historical inevitability had become ridiculous, some advocates of free markets and democracy proclaimed their own version of historical determinism according to which all the governments on earth were gravitating toward a single form. American free-market conservatives took the socialist collapse as proof of the endemic incompetence of the state, the errors of modern liberalism, and history's march upward toward their own laissez-faire ideals. Now they claimed to own the future, and in their vision—in this respect, the mirror image of Marxism—the single, overriding political imperative in the world, east and west, was to roll back the state, whether that involved privatizing the economy of Russia or Social Security in the United States. Any move toward less government was part of the same grand historical scheme, and a good thing.

Besides lumping together wholly dissimilar forms and roles of government, this view of political economy—called "neoliberal" outside of the United States, though Americans generally think of it as "conservative"—proved to be a poor guide to problems that soon seized the world's attention. In many of the postcommunist countries, the state was so weakened that it was unable to carry out such basic public functions as the control of crime, disease, and corruption. Failed states in the Third World were similarly unable to prevent networks of drug dealers, sex traffickers, and terrorists from operating in their territory. In these and other contexts, the view of the state as an evil to be minimized misstated the problem. Whether in its classical, eighteenth-century or modern democratic form, as I have emphasized throughout this book, liberalism has always been concerned with building effective and trustworthy public institutions; not even markets can function properly without them. If those who do business with one another cannot or will not trust the courts to resolve their disputes, they may call upon thugs to collect what they think they are due, and the rule of law gives way to the rule of force. And if citizens have no confidence in the effective ability of political leadership to address their problems, they will see no point to participating in politics even when they have the formal right to do so. Weak states are not a basis of liberty or democracy—they make it impossible to establish either. Part of the legacy of communism was a deep cynicism about the state that undercut the efforts to build well-functioning markets as well as new democratic institutions. Properly understood, the liberal project in the postcommunist (as in the postcolonial) world was not just to limit the state in its scope of action, but to transform it into an effective source of authority that could maintain the rule of law, earn the people's trust, and thereby create the conditions for a flourishing civil society, private economy, and democratic politics. And in some respects that meant creating state capacities such as an independent judiciary never developed by the previous communist regimes.

Moreover, while neoliberal economists claimed vindication from the fall of communism, the majority of the public in postcommunist societies did not necessarily favor an unfettered free-market system— indeed, the evidence from public opinion surveys is that most people did not. After all, the "normal" countries to their west that eastern Europeans yearned to emulate were modern welfare states, not throwbacks to nineteenth-century laissez-faire. In the immediate aftermath of communism's fall, neoliberal economists recommended not just a move to free markets but "shock therapy," an abrupt turn that included several distinct changes: immediate liberalization (decontrol) of both prices and trade, monetary stabilization, and rapid privatization of state enterprises. The adoption of these measures in whole or part by many of the postcommunist governments gave rise to the impression in the United States that the fall of communism was leading to a shift toward American-style capitalism. But other forces were at work leading in different directions. The central and eastern Europeans were not prepared to give up the state's role in protecting social welfare, and they were anxious to rejoin the community of western European nations, which itself was undergoing a change of historic proportions—the creation of a single European market and the pooling of sovereignty in a newly consolidated, transnational political entity, the European Union.

At its foundations, the European Union was a liberal project: it upheld and extended the principles of rule of law, human rights, and democracy, as well as free movement of goods, capital, and labor. Unlike free-market neoliberalism, however, a broad spectrum of European opinion represented in the Union also called for strong governmental protections of social rights within a market framework, and it was to this conception of a "social-market economy" (a term introduced by German Christian Democrats in the 1960s as an alternative to socialism) that eastern Europeans were most strongly attracted. In short, the postcommunist transition became another setting for the long conflict between two different visions of liberal democratic capitalism—the liberalism of laissez-faire and the liberalism of positive government. The term "transition" presumed a known destination. But not only were different kinds of liberal society possible; the legacies of the past and botched policies in the postcommunist era could produce regimes that were not liberal at all. And in much of the former Soviet Union that is precisely what happened.

The communist and socialist collapse also had political implications for liberalism in the United States. The conception of where liberalism stood on the mental map of politics changed. Liberalism had long been understood as a force of the center against conservatism on one side and socialism on the other, but with radicalism gone, many Americans now used the term "liberal" as a synonym for "left." The evolution of conflicts over foreign policy and cultural issues dating from the 1960s had contributed to this ambiguity, and the right-wing efforts to roll back regulatory and social-welfare programs beginning in the late 1970s had thrown liberals into a defensive alliance with what remained of left-wing progressives. After the fall of communism, "liberal" took the place of "communist" in the demonology of the American right. During the Cold War, despite McCarthyism, liberals and conservatives had been generally allied in their anticommunism, but conservatives now came to see liberals as their greatest adversaries and attacked them with greater venom than ever. "Now that the other 'Cold War' is over, the real cold war has begun," the neoconservative Irving Kristol wrote in 1993, referring to a "war" against liberalism.[1] After 1989 the liberal project had a new global urgency and relevance. But in a strange reversal of fortune from earlier in the twentieth century, liberals in the United States found themselves besieged from the right and beset with doubts even as the liberal ideals they espoused were experiencing a renaissance across the Atlantic.

AFTER 1989: THE POSTCOMMUNIST CHOICE

The fall of communism opened up new possibilities for a liberal democratic Europe on both sides of the line that had split the continent from

1945 to 1989. During the Cold War, as the strategists of Soviet containment had hoped, the West's prosperity and freedom had exerted a gravitational pull on Eastern Europeans. But from the rise of Solidarity in Poland in 1980, the influence also began to run in the reverse direction. With their emphasis on human rights, civil society, and democracy, the intellectuals and movements that resisted, satirized, denounced, and ultimately overthrew communist rule contributed to a renewal of liberalism all over Europe. France's "new philosophers" and other Western European intellectuals were already rediscovering the language of rights and liberty, and the movements in the East made it unmistakably clear how precious political freedom and other rights are. The popular revolutions of 1989 were not aimed at reforming communism; they repudiated it altogether. As some of the dissidents liked to point out, '89 was '68 turned upside down. Nothing so finished off Marxism as an ideological force as the realization that "state socialism" was beyond redemption. The communist system wasn't just unable to match Western living standards; it also created what Vaclav Havel, the new president of Czechoslovakia in 1990, called a "devastated moral environment" where saying one thing and thinking another, living without truth, had become habitual.[2]

The economic failures of the communist regimes were directly related to their organization of power. One of the ironies of Soviet-style revolutionary communism was that it gave rise to the least revolutionary of societies and that it ultimately stagnated and broke down because of the inability of the system it established to generate the kind of radical, productive innovation that keeps capitalism in perpetual motion. In principle, the communist leadership was free to do whatever it wanted because the powers of the state had no limits—not the rule of law, internal checks and balances, or individual rights. ("Communism means not the victory of socialist laws, but a victory of socialism over any law," the first president of the USSR Supreme Court wrote in 1927.)[3] By centralizing economic decisions and suppressing an independent civil society, however, the communist regimes for decades choked off the sources of initiative, enterprise, dynamism, criticism, and self-correction that might have helped to renew their own economic and political life.

The consequences of tightly coupling economics and politics were not immediately apparent. In its early decades, the Soviet Union was able to use mass-production technology from the West and forced industrialization to achieve impressive rates of economic growth. By the 1970s, however, the geriatric leadership in Moscow and its satellites epitomized a pervasive torpor affecting the economy and entire society. As the historian Stephen Kotkin has emphasized in his account of the Soviet collapse, while technological change and the oil shocks of the 1970s forced a wrenching readjustment in the advanced capitalist societies, Soviet communism did not undertake any comparable economic restructuring. Wedded to an increasingly obsolete and inefficient industrial gigantism, it failed to shift production toward services and information, adopt flexible manufacturing, reengineer firms, or play any significant role in the electronics and computer revolutions. Even with its economy in decline, the Soviet Union might have continued plodding along if it had not been involved in global geopolitical competition. But as it fell further behind the West, much of the elite panicked, and when the generational change in leadership finally came, it brought a leader to the top, Mikhail Gorbachev, who attempted to retrench on military spending and to reform communism from within, only to unleash forces that brought down the Soviet empire and the Soviet state itself. Gorbachev's signal that he would not use force to prop up the communist regimes in Eastern Europe sealed their doom.[4]

Unlike the countries in southern Europe, Latin America, and east Asia that since the 1970s had moved from authoritarianism to democracy, the states that emerged from the Soviet collapse faced the dual challenge of establishing both democratic institutions and a market economy. Adding further complications, three of the original communist states—the Soviet Union, Yugoslavia, and Czechoslovakia—broke up into twenty-two independent states, making a total of twenty-seven new governments. The legacies of communism posed daunting obstacles to reform. The shift to the market implied a massive reallocation of capital and labor because of industrial obsolescence and the underdevelopment of services and a radical change in prices because the communist regimes had kept ordinary necessities artificially cheap. State revenue previously drawn from the state-owned economy would now have to come from taxes. The transition to capitalism also required the establishment of laws and norms regulating private property, contracts, corporate governance, financial markets, and other aspects of economic society that had been present only in a distorted form or missing entirely under communism. To transform both property and politics, moreover, there was a need not just for specific kinds of legislation but for courts and administrative agencies capable of enforcing the rule of law.[5]

Reformers agreed that all of these problems needed to be addressed, but they differed as to how fast to proceed, in what sequence, and how much priority to give the various elements of the transformation. The pacing and methods for privatizing state enterprises provoked especially sharp disagreements. Privatization of large-scale industry was not the only means of creating a private sector. By establishing clear property rights, liberalizing entry into markets, allowing for small-scale privatization of trade and services, and ensuring a positive climate for investment, the state could also promote the formation of new businesses and entry by foreign firms. Fearful, however, that any delay in privatizing the industrial behemoths might allow the communists to regain control, the advocates of shock therapy called for selling off state industry on a rapid schedule, over the objection of critics who argued that enterprises should first be restructured and that more time was needed to establish corporate governance laws, banking regulation, and other legal underpinnings of a market economy. These disagreements reflected deeper differences in views of the state. The advocates of shock therapy argued that if only the state would disgorge its assets and get out of the way, markets would spring up, while the gradualists were wary of seeming shortcuts to capitalism that might undermine long-term development.[6]

The first postcommunist decade saw successes and failures. In general, the countries traditionally thought of as belonging to central Europe, such as Poland, Hungary, and Slovenia, fared the best in achieving economic growth and stable democratic institutions, while the countries to the east, including Russia and other former Soviet republics, experienced the greatest economic difficulties and were most likely to remain authoritarian. Historical differences help to explain the gap.

Communist rule in central and Eastern Europe had lasted only about four decades, compared to three-quarters of a century in Russia. Perhaps partly for that reason, during communism's final decades an independent civil society reemerged as a stronger force in some of the central European countries than in the Soviet Union and helped to facilitate the transition. But history was not necessarily fate. As the Polish and Czech experiences illustrate, postcommunist political and policy choices also critically affected economic performance. The new Polish state, like others in central and eastern Europe, became a multiparty parliamentary government rather than a presidential system. After early steps in shock therapy led to a drop in GDP of 35 percent, parliamentary elections in 1993 brought to power a social-democratic coalition led by former communists, who slowed down the privatization of state industry but in other respects continued the reform program. Within a few years the Polish economy had recovered and then surpassed its earlier level. In contrast, partly because of a precipitous mass-privatization program, the Czech Republic fared much worse during the 1990s.[7]

Reform's greatest failure came in Russia. After early steps in shock therapy, President Boris Yeltsin used tanks in 1993 to shut down a recalcitrant Parliament, obtained ratification of a new constitution giving him powers to rule by decree, and then used those powers to pursue a program that included large-scale, rapid privatization. At the time, American economic advisers and the International Monetary Fund (IMF) supported Yeltsin's moves; eager to see privatization proceed on the fast track, they weren't about to shy away from a little market Bolshevism. But the concentration of powers in the presidency undercut liberal democracy in Russia, and the economic program proved to be a disaster. Russia's GDP shrank by 54 percent from 1990 to 1999, and industrial production fell by almost 60 percent (compared to a drop of 24 percent during World War II). The toll in human life was catastrophic: life expectancy fell by six years during the first half-decade of transition, with the higher mortality concentrated among working-age men. After first insisting that things were on the right track, neoliberal reformers blamed the disaster on the legacies of Russia's communist past, but these difficulties were known at the time. As a variety of studies have shown, shock privatization bore a heavy onus of responsibility for the economic implosion. Because Russians could not afford to buy the state economy—for one thing, after prices were decontrolled, hyperinflation hit 2,250 percent in 1992, wiping out the value of personal savings—the government offered vouchers to individual citizens at nominal cost to buy shares in privatized companies. To win over managers and workers, however, the program awarded them 51 percent of the shares (under a system that provided little protection to minority-shareholder interests). As a result, privatization brought no new capital or managerial talent to restructure firms just when trade liberalization put them in competition with more efficient producers abroad. From 1995 to 1998, an even worse method of privatization, known as "loans for shares," gave control of twenty-nine of Russia's most valuable companies to insiders with close ties to the government. As various commentators pointed out, it was as if Russia's new government sought to validate the old communist line that private property was theft.

The pervasive looting of the Russian state led many commentators to attribute the problems to the culture of corruption that had been endemic to communism. But the incentives created by the privatization program itself made it rational to acquire state property at cheap prices, strip the assets, and transfer the proceeds to safe havens abroad. What Russia needed was massive investment; what it got was massive capital flight. The rate of investment plummeted to a fraction of what it had been under communism. After hitting bottom in 1999—the year after the government defaulted on its debts—the Russian economy began to recover, and by 2005 GDP was back up to its level fifteen years earlier. But the recovery came mainly from rising prices for raw materials exports, not from industrial restructuring. Instead of decoupling politics and the economy, the new regime has brought them back together under an interlocking directorate, Kremlin, Inc., which now controls both the government and powerful corporations such as the oil-and-gas giant Gazprom and the mass media that Gazprom owns. This system of undemocratic state capitalism bears little resemblance to the liberal capitalist democracy that reformers thought they were creating.[8]

The early programs of rapid, mass privatization proved to be a disaster throughout the postcommunist world.[9] Instead of paving a shortcut to capitalism, free-market zealotry contributed to one of the great economic and political catastrophes of modern history. In 2001 the free-market economist Milton Friedman said that a decade earlier he would have just had three words of advice to countries making the transition from socialism: "Privatize, privatize, privatize. . . . But I was wrong. It turns out that the rule of law is probably more basic than privatization." The rule of law, however, is not the only imperative; as the political scientists Juan Linz and Alfred Stepan put it in a review of the postcommunist experience, "Effective privatization entails less state *scope* but greater state *capacity*." The neoliberal reformers failed to appreciate the need for that greater capacity, and their own strategy undermined it.[10]

One of the principal reasons that things worked out better in central and eastern Europe was that the prospect of membership in the European Union provided a constrained framework for liberal state-building that was missing in the former Soviet Union. To qualify for the EU, the new central and eastern European governments had to adopt thousands of pages of laws and regulations—the EU's *acquis communautaire*—and demonstrate a commitment to rule of law, democracy, and human rights, including respect for the rights of minorities. The economic advantages of joining the EU helped to keep illiberal forces in check. By providing a ready-made package of rules, the EU also removed a variety of potentially divisive issues from political debate. Remarkably, despite their long resentment of Soviet control, the central and eastern Europeans accepted tutelage from western Europe, particularly from Germany, admired as the prototype of a social-market economy. It was here that the two contemporary transformations of Europe came together.

SOCIAL-MARKET
LIBERALISM IN THE NEW EUROPE

The creation of a European liberal order on a continental scale has been the quiet, underappreciated revolution of our time. Differences in terminology ought not to diminish or confuse the significance of this achievement. Many Europeans use the term "liberal" interchangeably with "neoliberal" to refer to a political economy that relies on the logic of the market. The contrast is usually with a social-democratic or social-market economy in which the state plays a stronger role in social welfare, and bargains struck between representatives of organized business and labor provide a high level of economic coordination. This distinction highlights important differences in the workings of capitalism between the Anglo-American economies, on the one hand, and those in Nordic and continental Europe, on the other. Whether closer to the free-market or social-market models, however, all of these societies are liberal, constitutional democracies, and in recent decades even the social-market countries have adjusted their economic policies in a market-oriented direction. The resulting hybrid is perhaps best thought of as social-market liberalism.[11] Recent attempts to update social democracy as the "third way" or "neoprogressivism" also typically emphasize such characteristically liberal ideas as competition, choice, and pluralism. In its intellectual and political life, Europe has become distinctly more liberal than at any time at least since 1914. Throughout the continent, except for the Balkans, aggressive nationalism has given way to a politics of conciliation, and the major political parties operate within the bounds of a constitutionalist consensus. Nowhere is this general turn toward a continental liberal order more apparent than in the pooling of sovereignty in the European Union, with its commitment to the free movement of capital, goods, and labor as well as the rule of law, democracy, and human rights.

After the disillusionment with socialism, the conventional wisdom was that all grand schemes and utopian visions were dead. But in any other historical period, the idea of a borderless and democratic Europe, willing to put aside old rivalries for the sake of peace and prosperity, would have seemed utopian indeed. Today the Union has gone far beyond the aim of advancing free trade among the six original members of the Common Market. Not only has it eliminated most customs barriers among its twenty-five member states and created a single currency; it has also taken over such critical matters as environmental, agricultural, and competition policy and begun to coordinate foreign relations and defense. The European Court of Justice has become the final authority on European law, accepted by the domestic courts in each member country. Under the

Maastricht Treaty of 1993, the citizens of those countries are also European citizens and enjoy the protection of their rights under European law. If the full depth and breadth of the Union's reach had been voted on at one time, its radical significance might have been more widely appreciated—but it probably would never have been approved. Step by step, integration has spilled from one area over into another, and in the face of competitive pressures from the United States and east Asia, the leaders of the major European states have repeatedly decided that their national interest lies, not in pulling back, but in pushing economic and political integration forward. Although the defeat of the proposed European Constitution in 2005 reflected public uneasiness about globalization and immigration, there does not appear to be any threat to the basic European constitutional settlement, which has vested certain critical functions in the EU while retaining others for the individual member states. All along, integration has been chiefly an elite project, conducted with popular consent rather than enthusiasm. The project could never have advanced as far it has, however, if there had not been a widely shared tendency toward ideological convergence. The decline of right-wing authoritarianism, most notably in southern Europe in the mid-1970s, removed one kind of barrier. The decline of the socialist left in Western Europe during the 1970s and '80s removed another.[12]

The economic crisis of the mid-1970s triggered a far-reaching shift in European politics that facilitated continental integration on liberal principles. For roughly three decades after 1945, the interventionist state in Western Europe turned in an exceptionally strong economic record; indeed, the social-market economies grew faster, on average, than the free-market economies in that period. The forms of state intervention varied. For example, Sweden had generous welfare-state benefits but little state-owned enterprise, whereas Italy had a large state-owned sector but more limited social spending. During these years, neither higher public expenditures nor more extensive public enterprise appeared to be a drag on growth. Then, in the 1970s, inflation, unemployment, and government deficits all soared. The performance of state-owned enterprises also sharply deteriorated, partly because of politically driven decisions in the face of rising macroeconomic troubles. Afraid of exacerbating unemployment or precipitating strikes, governments declined to close unprofitable factories, mines, and other operations. Worried about inflation, they held down the prices charged by state enterprises. And because of limits on public-sector borrowing, they stinted on capital investment. Although not as grave as the failures of the centrally planned economies, the declining performance of state-owned enterprise in the West reflected the same underlying problem. Economic restructuring required disinvesting in unprofitable industries and obsolete technologies, but governments often found it politically difficult to impose immediate and highly visible costs, such as factory shutdowns, lost jobs, and higher prices, for the sake of distant and uncertain gains from long-run growth. The "soft budget constraint" of state ownership—the ability to run persistent losses—invites delay in making hard decisions.

But in Western Europe, unlike the East, change came through the normal political process. In Britain the failure of Labour governments during the mid-1970s to deal with rising unemployment and persistent strikes led to a Conservative victory in 1979 under Margaret Thatcher, who rejected her own party's earlier accommodation with the interventionist state and proceeded to retrench on public spending and initiate a broad sell-off of the nationalized industries. When Labour returned to power under Tony Blair in 1997, the party had finally eliminated the clause in its 1918 constitution promising to nationalize the means of production, and it no longer threatened to reverse Thatcher's privatization program. To emphasize the change, Labour rebranded itself "New Labour." ("New Liberal" would have been just as accurate.) In France the Socialist Party under François Mitterrand swept the presidential and parliamentary elections in 1981 and at first proceeded along traditional socialist lines, nationalizing banks and industrial enterprises and raising wages and reducing working hours. But the program was a fiasco, in 1983 Mitterrand reversed course, and even the Socialists later sold off companies they had nationalized only a few years earlier. These reversals completed a long evolution. Originally concerned with changing how wealth is produced, European socialists came to settle for changes in its distribution—and in doing so gave up on the idea of socialism as an alternative to capitalism.

All across Europe (and in much of the rest of the world) there was a wave of privatization through the 1980s and '90s that reflected both long- and short-term developments. Technological change had undermined the case for state ownership in some sectors, such as telecommunications, that had long been regarded as "natural monopolies," while rising deficits pressured governments to sell state-owned assets as a means of fiscal relief. By and large, these one-by-one sales of state-owned firms were more successful than the mass privatizations in former communist countries, as they did not require the sudden, wholesale creation of an institutional framework for a market economy (though in some cases, particularly where competition was limited or nonexistent, governments needed new regulatory capacities). In earlier decades, individual European states had attempted to generate economic growth by building up key companies as "national champions." A growing consensus, however, regarded this strategy as a failure and concluded that European firms could become more globally competitive only if they achieved the economies of scale that an open, continental market would allow them to reach. Rising concern about competitiveness was a key factor in the agreement by members of the European Community during the mid-1980s to create a single European market by 1992 (the year the Community was renamed the European Union), and rules adopted as part of that process barred governments from subsidizing their own firms to the disadvantage of competitors based in other countries. But if governments had to treat all enterprises the same, there was little reason for state ownership. In a sense, political leaders during the 1980s and '90s faced a choice between the residual vision of socialism and an emerging vision of Europe, and they chose Europe.

The significance of the privatization movement should not be overstated. While selling off public enterprises, European governments did not abandon the welfare state. After 1980 governments reined in the generosity of social programs, but expenditures still continued to rise as a share of GDP, albeit more slowly. Despite greater receptiveness to neoliberal policies on the center-right, Europe was not about to convert to what was widely seen as American-style capitalism. Even while rejecting socialism in favor of economic integration on liberal principles, European leaders reaffirmed their commitment to social-market policies at home.

That course, according to the conventional American criticism, condemns the European to a chronic debility, "Eurosclerosis," the regrettable result of a misguided tendency to value equality over economic growth. In this familiar view, high taxes and social benefits reduce incentives to work and invest, leading to slower growth and lower living standards, to the disadvantage even of the poor. The data, however, do not bear out that simple story. From 1960 to 1980, as already mentioned, there was no trade-off, at least in macroeconomic outcomes, between equality and growth: the countries with larger, more egalitarian social expenditures grew faster. Contrary to the conservative argument, the pro-growth effects of social spending (for example, through education and training) outweighed whatever negative effects higher taxes and expenditures may have had on incentives. From 1980 to 2000, however, when rates of economic growth fell in both Europe and North America, the decline was greater in the social-market economies than in the United States. American critics have seized especially on the low rate of job creation in some European countries, notably Germany and France, as evidence for the error of Europe's ways.[13]

Yet the picture even for the recent period is complicated by other considerations. The slightly larger gains in GDP in the United States in recent decades have not been broadly shared; real earnings for Americans below the median have been virtually stagnant since the mid-1970s. Meanwhile, other aspects of the standard of living have diverged. On average, Europeans have shorter workweeks and take longer vacations than do Americans, who put in many more working hours per year, in some cases taking second jobs. Americans now have the longest work year of all the economically advanced societies, including Japan. If compared according to output per hour, the western European social-market economies are nearly as productive as the United States, and workers in three European countries generate more value.[14] European workers also have retained more secure health and pension benefits. Whether the U.S. pattern of stagnant wages, longer hours, declining fringe benefits for health care and pensions, and higher per capita GDP counts as a point in America's favor is a matter of judgment (and perhaps class perspective). On the whole, Europeans seem to be expressing different values, choosing to take the rewards of an affluent society in the form of more free time and greater security rather than more money. Stronger labor unions have also given voice to those preferences. Many Americans who face high levels of stress from trying to raise children while they and their spouses both work full-time, and often overtime, would appreciate a shorter workweek, but career demands and labor-market realities in America don't make that option readily available.

The slow rate of job creation is a genuine problem in much of Europe, though seven of the social-market economies during the early 2000s actually outperformed the United States in that respect. Where employment growth has lagged, the cause seems to be rigid labor-market regulation and heavy reliance on payroll taxes, which especially depress the expansion of low-paid, private-sector service jobs. Rather than overturning the entire social-market model, these countries could adjust their regulations and alter the mix of taxes in line with the policies of neighbors that have generated stronger employment growth.[15]

The primary purposes of social policy are to narrow the inequalities generated in the marketplace and to reduce the impact on personal security and life chances of adverse events such as sickness, disability, and unemployment. In pursuing those objectives, the European social-market countries have clearly had more success than the United States. Recent decades have seen a rise in market-generated income inequality virtually everywhere, but the social-market economies have done more to counteract that trend. America has the highest poverty rate among the economically advanced societies—two to three times the level of the social-market economies according to a standard that puts poverty at or below 40 percent of median disposable income (which corresponds roughly to the official poverty line in the United States).[16] And the gap between European and American policy could not be more stark in reducing the economic insecurity resulting from illness. The European social-market countries provide universal health insurance, while about one in six Americans has no health coverage and many more are underinsured, even though the United States spends about 16 percent of GDP on health care, compared to a range of 8 to 11 percent of GDP in social-market Europe. The gap arises, not because Americans receive more medical care, but rather primarily because they pay higher prices for drugs, physicians' services, hospital care, and insurance.[17] Compared with the United States, Europe saves about 5 to 8 percent of GDP from its lower health care costs, plus an additional 5 percent of GDP from lower defense spending. These reduced burdens contribute to its ability to shoulder more egalitarian policies in other areas. Fiscal and political pressures for retrenchment are unlikely to abate in Europe, particularly because of the aging of Europe's population. The growing numbers of immigrants may also undermine the sense of social solidarity that underlies the welfare state. But the protection of social rights is now a strongly embedded element of the ideals that Europeans identify with their way of life, as distinct from America's.

In maintaining a social-market economy while creating a continental liberal order, Europe has devised a new way of balancing the interests in fairness and growth. The individual member states of the European Union have retained control over taxation, social policy, education, and culture, while accepting a free-trade regime for the continent and ceding to the Union the central role in constituting markets (that is, setting the economic rules of the game). This compromise is an effort to adapt to the global economy without sacrificing individual nations' democratic institutions, cultural traditions, or hard-won socioeconomic compromises.

The European Union, however, has made only halting progress in defense and foreign policy, and its members have enjoyed the luxury of low military expenditures not only because they have put aside old enmities but also because NATO (and behind it the United States) has provided guarantees of security. The Europeans have become devoted to international law, some American conservative critics say, because they have retreated from the Hobbesian realities of power into an illusory paradise.[18] But as the Iraq War has shown, American conservatives have been prone to their own illusions about the promotion of democracy through military force. By comparison, the Europeans seem positively hard-nosed.

Part of the reason for harsh American conservative criticism of Europe is that the debate in the United States about Europe is a displaced domestic argument. The achievement of European social-market liberalism violates the premises that conservatives want Americans to accept in approaching social and economic choices at home. But even American conservatives, if they have any historical perspective, ought to recognize that Europe's establishment of a socially stable, democratic peace on the continent is an enormous benefit to the entire world, including America. In the promotion of liberal democracy, no country or international organization comes close to the achievement of the European Union. If it fails in eastern Europe or breaks down entirely, Americans will come to appreciate just how valuable it has been.

AMERICAN LIBERALISM WITHOUT A LEFT

The international socialist collapse had domestic reverberations in America, but the situation in the United States was different from Europe's. American socialism was incapable even of collapsing for the simple reason that as a political movement it was already dead. Communists and socialists had made up the old left of the 1930s, and socialists had been one of several influences along with other radicals of varying hues, from libertarian to Maoist, in the new left of the 1960s. By the 1980s and '90s, however, there was no radical left to speak of in America, except in the academy and cultural life. And this displacement of the left, from politics to culture, did not work in liberalism's favor.

In the wider political arena, liberalism appeared as if it were the left, the earlier identification of liberalism with the mainstream of the democratic tradition was lost, and many public figures with liberal views no longer felt comfortable with the label. Conservatives made every effort to identify liberalism with cultural radicalism, and as defenders of civil liberties and equal rights for women, blacks, and gays, liberals seemed to many Americans, particular white men, to advocate every one else's rights and interests but their own. Meanwhile, in the precincts of the academy where an adversarial left continued to thrive, intellectuals of varying tendencies sought to fashion a critique of liberal philosophy and politics that was no less radical than socialism but avoided the embarrassment of being associated with socialist economics. Communitarians picked up the old Marxist criticism of liberal rights and individualism, and postmodernists denied the validity of the basic categories of liberal thought. While the liberal achievements of the Progressive era, the New Deal, and the Great Society were under attack in the main theater of politics from free-market conservatives, liberalism also faced challenge in the sphere of ideas from a left that was trying to reinvent itself in a postsocialist world.

The relationship of American liberalism to the left has always been ambivalent. While sharing some common ground with socialists and populists, liberals have favored a more circumscribed role for the state and often deplored the unwillingness to compromise, sentimental delusions, tendency to romanticize "the people," susceptibility to authoritarianism, and occasional violence on the left. Unlike the socialist ideal, the liberal conception of equality does not call for a classless society. Economic inequalities are acceptable in a liberal framework if over time they redound to the advantage of all, including the poor, and are not so great as to undermine democracy. At times liberals have worried that the radical left would alienate potential supporters of liberal causes or, if left-wing third parties ran their own political candidates, that they would splinter progressive votes (as in the 2000 presidential election). Nonetheless, there has also been a productive tension between liberals and the left. Radical movements have often been quicker to take up the cause of the socially marginalized and sometimes broken through barriers to reform that liberals mistakenly accepted as unchangeable. As liberalism is a practical philosophy of government and politics, liberals are perennially vulnerable to charges from the left that they have violated sacred ideals for the sake of profane compromises—and sometimes the accusations are justified. Even when they are not, the mere existence of an uncompromising left has indirectly afforded liberals the rhetorical advantage of representing themselves as the reasonable center. Liberals sometimes lose their patience with the impatience of the left. But in attempting to defeat entrenched interests, liberalism without a left is missing a punch.

The liberal attitude toward socialism from the nineteenth to the mid-twentieth centuries reflected this ambivalence. While hostile to the Marxist vision of proletarian revolution, some of the major figures in liberal thought searched for a synthesis of liberalism and socialism that could preserve individual liberty while extending democracy into the economy. For example, John Stuart Mill, who defended laissez-faire as a first principle, took a deep interest in socialist experiments during the mid-1800s and thought it might be possible to reconstruct industry with the ownership of firms shared by labor rather than solely belonging to capital. But he believed that competition among firms was essential whatever their ownership and that the most desirable system would be the one "consistent with the greatest amount of human liberty and spontaneity." John Dewey, less tentative than Mill, argued in 1935 that it was necessary to use socialist means to advance liberal ends, which "can now be achieved *only* by reversal of the means to which early liberalism was committed"—that is, by the introduction of "organized social planning." Dewey also advocated democracy in the workplace. Cooperatives for farmers, consumers, and workers have been an important part of the populist and socialist traditions, and some advocates of "economic democracy" continue to call for an alternative to capitalism based on various forms of cooperative and self-managed organizations. Hoping to make both politics and the economy more participatory, they adhere to the old radical maxim that "the cure for the ailments of democracy is more democracy."[19]

As attractive as the ideas of economic and participatory democracy may be, they have suffered from some of the same difficulties in coping with economic change that have beset centrally planned economies and state-owned enterprises. Employee cooperatives do not respond flexibly to pressures for disinvestment and restructuring because the workers want to protect their jobs, nor do cooperatives of any kind respond quickly to opportunities for expansion, which typically require new investment and threaten to dilute current members' control. The happy vision of worker ownership is that participation will be emotionally fulfilling; the dreary reality, however, is that employee control often generates frustration and conflict because employees are far more likely than investors to have sharply conflicting interests.[20] As a result, even though there have been many viable cooperative organizations, they have been outstripped in most economic sectors by investor-owned enterprise. If an economy were entirely based upon cooperatives, it would likely become a stagnant backwater; consequently, a government that attempted to create such an economy would likely be voted out of office. Economic democracy may therefore be inconsistent with political democracy.

More generally, the theory of participatory democracy is unrealistic about human energies and interests. Oscar Wilde's famous remark that the problem with socialism is that it takes too many evenings is not just the view of an ironic aesthete. Few people can sustain the enthusiasm for meetings that participatory democracy requires. Democracy generates rules, which are the only way for majorities to communicate their will without devoting all their waking hours to common decisions. Yet rules imply bureaucracy, and who would say that "the cure for the ailments of democracy is more bureaucracy"? This was a central problem for socialism, and it does not disappear when socialism goes by other names.

Democracy at the level of the enterprise, however, is certainly more benign than central planning. Cooperatives often mobilize altruism for productive purposes, compensate for the limitations of the market, and expand pluralism in the economy. In some kinds of conventional enterprises, less hierarchical structures with more employee participation have advantages in performance. In recent years, the Internet has led to networked forms of collaboration in the development of open-source software, public-domain knowledge bases such as Wikipedia, and a variety of online communities. The Internet reduces the Oscar Wilde problem: contributors to a virtual cooperative can participate at their convenience and do not have to suffer through long meetings (though if Wilde himself were alive today, he might find other entertainment online). Networked collaboration represents an increasingly important form of economic organization, particularly because knowledge is so central to economic growth. But noncommercial organization still seems more likely to supplement conventional patterns of enterprise and association than to become the basis of an alternative political and economic system.[21]

Much the same may be said of efforts to make "community" into the central principle of progressive politics. Though often presented as a comprehensive alternative to liberal thought, communitarianism has at best been a supplement or a corrective to tendencies within liberalism since the 1960s. The standard communitarian case against liberalism identifies it with hyperindividualism. According to one form of the argument, liberal thought erroneously imagines society to be composed of isolated individuals; according to a second form, individuals in liberal society really are miserably isolated from one another, and that is the source of the crisis of modern life. As an antidote to this toxic individualism, the communitarians call for a reaffirmation of social ties and obligations, which they see as an inherently positive value. Some reject the concept of individual rights altogether, while others hold that rights are just one of several values and should not be regarded as superior to the common good.[22]

The point of departure for this analysis is a misreading of liberal philosophy. Liberalism is well acquainted with the existence of society, and far from being oblivious to the value of community and social ties, liberal principles aim to protect civil society from being dominated by the state and to allow the many communities in a modern society to develop freely. Liberals are keenly aware of two phenomena that the communitarians ignore: disagreement and power. Although some values are widely shared, people frequently have different ideas about what would be good for the community. Liberalism does not reject the concept of the common good; one merely has to consult the major works in the liberal tradition, as well as laws and judicial opinions, to see frequent references to the "common" or "public good," "general welfare," or "public interest." But it is not self-evident where that good, welfare, or interest lies, and liberalism seeks to protect rights against the state partly to ensure a free and open process for discovery of the interests that citizens have in common. In a world with deep moral disagreements, the wisest course is not to stipulate shared values as a premise but to facilitate means of social cooperation whether or not the divide can be bridged. Moreover, experience has taught that if rights are protected only when they serve the common good (as those in power understand it), rights may have no protection at all. Rights certainly do not always trump other interests. In the liberal constitutional tradition, however, when the government seeks to override a fundamental right, it must demonstrate a compelling reason and narrowly tailor the exception. Whether most of those attracted to communitarianism genuinely want to repudiate that framework altogether seems doubtful. Despite their often apocalyptic language and broad indictment of liberal rights, the communitarians have typically proposed only modest amendments to current law and policy. Communitarianism has also had little to say about most constitutional, economic, and foreign policy questions, so it has not offered a comprehensive alternative to liberalism.[23]

Nonetheless, the emergence of communitarianism in the 1980s and '90s responded to a real political problem in the United States. During the previous decades, liberals had been so emphatic about civil liberties and the rights of minorities that many people were persuaded that liberalism had lost sight of the demands of personal responsibility and the interests of society as a whole. The same was true, to some extent, of social democracy in Europe, especially Britain. The remedy, however, was not to repudiate the tradition of equal liberty, but to restore ideas of responsibility, reciprocity, and the common good to a central place in liberal and social-democratic argument. The liberal project was never about a mere aggregation of special interests, but liberal politics had often been conducted as if that were true. In the struggle against free-market conservatism, this was a crucial point. Liberals had to reassert an ethic of responsibility—not least of all among those with the greatest power and wealth in the world.

8

Statecraft and
Danger in a New World

────────

THE COLLAPSE OF THE SOVIET UNION IN 1991 GAVE RISE TO A NEW reality, A new illusion, and a new temptation in geopolitics. The reality was that no nation could seriously challenge the dominance of the United States; the illusion was, at first, that because America as well as other liberal democracies no longer faced a traditional strategic threat, they faced no threat at all. September 11, 2001, shattered that daydream, exposing the vulnerability of advanced societies to networks of terrorists who can put modern technology at the service of old hatreds.

Then came the temptation. As the world's unchallenged superpower, the United States was now able to act unilaterally not just in its immediate defense but to change the international status quo by overturning regimes it deemed to be potential threats and exempting itself from treaty obligations and international norms it no longer viewed as expedient in the pursuit of its own interests. In a unipolar world, America seemingly had no need of the blessing of international institutions, the cooperation of allies, or the approval of international public opinion. The temptation was to act like an imperial power; Prometheus could stop playing pygmy, as the conservative columnist Charles Krauthammer put it. Free at last, the unshackled colossus could dispense with niceties, stride across the globe, and, in the name of democracy, try to impose a "benevolent" hegemony in remote countries with rogue or failed states.[1] This is the course that the United States under George W. Bush has pursued, only to discover that the rest of the world does not trust America's power and good intentions or bend so easily to its will.

Accompanying the unilateral assertion of American power abroad has been a unilateral assertion of executive power at home. Externally, the unilateralist impulse has swept aside international alliances, law, and institutions; internally, it has swept aside constitutional checks and balances in foreign affairs, defense, and security, however much developments in those areas might impinge on domestic society. Multilateralism and separation of powers are mechanisms of obligatory consultation. The common element in the unilateralism of the Bush presidency has been an attenuation of both—consultation with allies and consultation with other branches of government.

In defense and foreign affairs, neither kind of consultation is imperative under all circumstances. If the United States comes under attack, the president as commander in chief has the obligation as well as indisputable authority to defend the country, and no alliance or treaty overrides the nation's sovereign right of self-defense. Like the Constitution, a treaty is not a suicide pact. And while separation of powers is an aspect of a constitutional government with well-established practices for resolving conflicts, multilateral institutions operate only by mutual agreement among states and do not have the same depth of commitment or means of enforcement. The same logic, however, underlies separation of powers and multilateralism. The rationale is that institutionalized consultation, whether domestic or international, contributes to a democratic state's power as well as its responsible use—first, by enlisting cooperation, coordinating action, and sustaining mutually beneficial partnerships; and second, by reducing the likelihood of arbitrary, impulsive, narrowly self-interested, and imprudent decisions. These ideas, particularly about separation of powers, are not alien to conservatism. To the conservative American unilateralist, however, the system of international institutions merely provides the weak with ways to limit the strong and thereby undercuts America's great and wholesome power. To the liberal internationalist, in contrast, these mechanisms function like internal checks and balances as enabling constraints—they create legitimate and effective power even as they limit it. They foster shared expectations that enable independent states to cooperate with each other. And the United States as the dominant force in multilateral institutions has more to gain than to lose from the order they can help establish.

At an earlier unipolar moment—the end of World War II, when the United States had sole possession of atomic weapons and the other major economies of the world lay in devastation—America chose to pursue security through cooperation, and Franklin Delano Roosevelt, Harry Truman, and the "wise men" of the early Cold War led the way in founding new international institutions and multilateral alliances. September 11 could have opened another era of creative liberal-internationalist statecraft. The United States has not been alone in facing threats from radical Islamist terrorism, nor is that the only form that new threats to international security are likely to take. The same advances that strengthen the connections of the world economy—the Internet, global trade, air travel—can also serve as vectors of destruction from distant and obscure sources, whether criminal networks, cyberterrorists, or pandemic viruses. Every nation's security depends therefore on how well other governments work internally and cooperate with each other. But instead of seizing the opportunity for a new international statecraft, the Bush administration responded unilaterally in ways that have generated more hostility toward the United States than support for its global leadership.

In framing the rationale for his policies, Bush has drawn on elements of the liberal internationalist tradition, particularly the idea that the foreign policy of the United States should reflect its values as well as its interests and that it is in America's interest to promote democracy. The distinctive character of Bush's policy comes from adopting this Wilsonian vision, while downgrading the international cooperation that Wilsonians have advocated to achieve it and emphasizing instead an assertive nationalism and reliance on force drawn from the "Jacksonian" tradition in American foreign policy, as the historian Walter Russell Mead calls it.[2] Liberal internationalists disagree not about the general goals of defending American security and promoting democratic values and institutions, but about whether Bush's approach is the most effective way to realize those aims. Contrary to its critics, the liberal internationalist tradition—that is, the kind of internationalism that liberal administrations and public figures have practiced and advocated since the 1940s—is not a preachy moralism based on a naive devotion to international law and vagrant hopes of international cooperation. Rather, it offers an alternative theory of how a liberal democracy such as the United States can most effectively create and sustain its power, and responsibly exercise it, to the mutual benefit of its own people and those of other countries.

Every external threat to a liberal democracy poses a challenge not just to its security but to the values and institutions that are freedom's true foundation. Changed conditions in the world also require a sober assessment of the balance between national resources and foreign commitments; as Walter Lippmann wrote years ago, the United States, like any other nation, "must maintain its objectives and its power in equilibrium, its purposes within its means and its means equal to its purposes."[3] An effective response to new threats may well require altering longstanding security policies. But danger arouses fear, fear distorts good judgment, and political leaders are often eager to capitalize on public anxiety by shedding the restraints, and self-restraint, that a liberal state and multilateral institutions require. An overreacting government can threaten a liberal society's freedoms at home, while an overreaching government can exhaust its power abroad and, instead of making good on its commitments, elicit a self-defeating backlash against them. On September 11, Americans discovered that they faced new dangers from outside. But it was not long before they discovered that they also faced dangerous tendencies from within.

THE TWO FACES OF UNILATERALISM

New international and domestic political conditions allowed Bush to adopt a foreign policy that broke sharply with his predecessors. The unilateral use of American military power to bring about regime change and remake the world was exactly what the hard-line conservatives of the late

1940s and '50s had in mind when, instead of accepting containment and deterrence, they called for "rolling back" communism in Eastern Europe and Asia. Throughout the Cold War, however, this impulse was held in check by the risks of provoking World War III and by the patent need of the United States to maintain strong alliances against the Soviet Union. Domestic political alignments also helped to maintain a foreign policy that had a liberal internationalist foundation. Even during Republican administrations, Democrats usually controlled Congress, and there was a strong tradition of bipartisanship in foreign policy. The end of the Cold War, the virtual disappearance of liberals from the Republican Party, and the advent of an all-Republican government with the 2000 election created the conditions that allowed the Bush administration to repudiate multilateralism in international relations and bipartisanship at home. These tendencies were evident from the administration's early months, when it withdrew from negotiations begun under Clinton over North Korea and the Middle East, rejected treaties such as the agreement on antipersonnel land mines, and disparaged the value of international institutions. Rather than changing their attitude toward international cooperation, 9/11 provided Bush and his principal advisers on foreign affairs (the "vulcans," as Condoleezza Rice named them) with the rationale and public support the president needed to act on his views about America's role and to lay claim to expansive executive powers.[4]

The neoconservatives, despite their later identification with Bush's foreign policy, formed only a small faction within the administration, though they represented a critical intellectual influence from the outside. While the neoconservatives favored making democracy promotion and regime change a priority, the vulcans were generally exponents of a hard-line, nationalist foreign policy who had expressed skepticism during the Clinton years about using America's power to advance human rights, viewed the world in traditional power-politics terms, and saw states such as China as the principal emerging challenges. Terrorism was not a prominent concern of theirs; neither were they concerned with creating beachheads for democracy in the Middle East. But 9/11 aligned the priorities of the vulcans with those of the neoconservatives, and both groups shared the premise that the United States had to adopt a more muscular posture and assert its global primacy.

The key elements of this assertive unilateralist worldview are that international alliances and institutions hamstring the United States because other countries do not share America's interests or are too timid
to resort to force, and that the United States ought to take full advantage of its military superiority and use it, not just to respond to attacks
but proactively to take the fight to the enemy. Unilateralists differ from
isolationists in that they favor engagement with other countries, but
like isolationists, they want to minimize entanglements with international institutions. Rather than negotiate with regimes they abhor, they
seek to replace them, and rather than rely on permanent alliances and
be bound by joint decisionmaking, they prefer that the United States set
its own course, organize temporary "coalitions of the willing," and
thereby retain complete freedom of action. These were the premises on
which Bush took the nation to war in Afghanistan and, by a much less
defensible chain of reasoning, led the United States into Iraq.

Although Bush presented the Afghan and Iraq wars as seamlessly
linked, the differences between them were fundamental. Like the Gulf
War in 1991, the Afghan War was a just and appropriate response to
aggression.* After being attacked by Al Qaeda, the United States had

---

*Lest the reader think these are only retrospective judgments, I should emphasize
that these were the views I took at the time. In "No Vietnam" (*The New Republic*,
February 19, 1991), written before U.S. ground troops moved into southern Iraq, I
argued that liberals ought to support the Gulf War. And in "The War We Should
Fight" (*The American Prospect*, October 21, 2001), written shortly after 9/11, I argued in favor of overturning the government in Afghanistan as well as striking Al
Qaeda's camps there: "To leave the Taliban in control might well be to repeat the
mistake we made of leaving Saddam Hussein in power at the end of the Gulf War."
In regard to both of those conflicts as well as intervention in the Balkans during
the 1990s, I could have been fairly characterized as a "liberal hawk." But as the
Bush administration prepared to go to war with Iraq in 2002, it seemed to me that
the government had failed to pursue alternatives sufficiently, lacked the necessary
legitimacy for an invasion, and could become mired in a colonial occupation, on
which grounds I was extremely skeptical ("No Choice But War?" *The American
Prospect*, October 7, 2002) and soon outright opposed ("A Reckless Rush to War,"
The American Prospect, October 21, 2002, written with my fellow editors, Robert
Kuttner and Harold Meyerson).

ample grounds for invading Afghanistan in pursuit of Al Qaeda's leaders and training camps, for overturning the regime that harbored them, and for supporting a new government that did not abet terrorism and was broadly representative of Afghan society. The Afghan War was a legitimate war on terrorism; indeed, it was because of Afghanistan that the phrase "war on terrorism" did not at first seem merely metaphorical. The case for the war was especially compelling because the Taliban regime had lost its popular support as well as international legitimacy and was already facing an armed insurgency that could supply much of the force on the ground. Under the circumstances, Bush's decision to go to war enjoyed strong backing at home and from the world community, including a resolution of support by NATO. In a sign of things to come, however, the president spurned offers of international military cooperation, except from Britain and Australia. But at least in the short run, victory in Afghanistan was so swift, and the costs in American casualties were so low, that the administration's strategy raised few questions.

It was in Iraq that the limitations of Bush's strategic vision became painfully apparent. Although the president and members of his administration repeatedly cast Iraq as part of the war on terrorism, the connection was based either on a false premise (that Saddam Hussein had some responsibility for 9/11) or on a speculative hypothesis (that his regime might someday give terrorists weapons of mass destruction, assuming that he could acquire them). The confusion of 9/11 and Iraq was hardly accidental: the administration cultivated it to legitimate the war. It also generally conflated terrorism and rogue states in support of its claim that American defense strategy had to move to a first-strike policy. The National Security Strategy adopted by the administration in 2002 stated: "Given the goals of rogue states and terrorists, the United States can no longer solely rely on a reactive posture as we have in the past. The inability to deter a potential attacker, the immediacy of today's threats, and the magnitude of potential harm that could be caused by our adversaries' choice of weapons do not permit that option."[5] The plain implication was that the United States had no choice but to strike first against Iraq—and for that matter, against Iran and North Korea, the two other members of the "axis of evil" that Bush identified after 9/11.

But while containment and deterrence cannot stop terrorists, they may prevent states, even rogue regimes, from threatening other nations' security. There is a crucial distinction, moreover, between preemptive action (that is, against an imminent threat) and preventive war (against a mere potential threat). When facing a threat that is substantial and immediate, the United States has a right well recognized in international law to strike preemptively and, if need be, unilaterally against terrorists or states that support them. But whether a potential threat will materialize in the future is inherently difficult to predict, and the high probability of error creates a correspondingly high risk of starting wars with regimes that are not true threats or that, if contained and deterred, might eventually collapse, like the Soviet Union, or become more cooperative, like Libya. An announced policy of preventive war also gives other states a rationale for initiating wars on mere suspicion; the United States can scarcely arrogate to itself the right to wage preventive war without expecting that other nations will invoke that right as well. Preemptive action must always be an option when threats develop, and preventive action may in certain circumstances also be justified. But elevating preemption, much less prevention, into a doctrine risks increasing the "nervousness" of weapons and the likelihood of international crises escalating into wars before alternatives have been fully explored.[6]

There is no need, however, to imagine the dangers of preventive war and of the doctrine that Bush proclaimed as the new basis of American strategy; the Iraq War showed what can go wrong. In the run-up to the invasion, the president justified it mainly on preventive grounds—specifically, to prevent Saddam Hussein's government from developing weapons of mass destruction. It was only shortly before the war that Bush began portraying it as a crusade for democracy. Like Afghanistan, Iraq was also supposed to be an easy war: the fighting would be over quickly, American soldiers would be hailed as liberators, Iraqi oil would largely pay for the country's reconstruction, and there would be no new taxes, a draft, or other burdens for Americans to bear—indeed, as in no previous war, the public could continue to enjoy tax cuts. "Nothing is more important in the face of a war than cutting taxes," the House majority leader Tom DeLay declared in March 2003 as the war approached.[7]

All the crucial premises of the Iraq War, however, turned out to be mistaken: Iraq had neither weapons of mass destruction nor an active program to develop them, and the war was easy only in the early going. The administration's errors were more profound than underestimating the necessary troop deployments. It failed to think through the political consequences of giving power in Iraq to a Shia majority that had ties with Iran; it failed to anticipate the ethnic and regional fracturing of Iraq; and it failed to see the contradiction between calling for democracy throughout the Middle East and inflaming popular majorities there against the United States. If the general purpose was to prevent rogue states from developing nuclear weapons, the war was plainly a failure. By implicitly threatening Iran and North Korea while tying down the U.S. military, the war gave both of those countries the motivation as well as the opportunity to accelerate their nuclear programs, which they did. And when North Korea exploded a bomb in 2006, there developed the very situation that the United States had been trying to avert—a rogue state that might sell nuclear weapons to terrorists. As America became mired in Iraq, Bush belatedly turned to multilateral negotiations in the hope of getting Iran and North Korea to give up their nuclear weapons programs, but there was a contradiction between the previously declared policy of regime change and the interest in disarmament negotiations. No state facing an existential threat is likely to agree to disarm.

The point here is a more general one than the Bush administration's strategic incompetence. In the debate over Iraq and foreign policy generally, conservatives have portrayed themselves as strong and liberals as weak. But the policies of a conservative administration, enthusiastically supported by nearly all conservatives, have been a failure *in their own terms*: those policies have not added to America's power—they have consumed it. They have not built on the goodwill toward America after 9/11—they have squandered it. The conservative project has undermined American power and influence in other ways as well. The tax cuts that conservatives sought and Bush delivered have created a dependence on foreign borrowing—from China, among other countries—while the administration's energy policies have increased American dependence on foreign oil. The Bush administration originally rejected multilateral cooperation and a series of international treaties on the grounds that they would limit America's freedom of action. But the Iraq War, mounting deficits, and deepening energy dependency have limited America's freedom of action in far more damaging ways.

In its 2002 National Security Strategy, the administration declared it was American policy to prevent the emergence of any rival power. Such a stance guarantees rising anxiety abroad about American primacy; the idea that the United States can impose a "benevolent global hegemony" without inspiring resentment and countermeasures is an illusion. Acting alone, the United States is sure to spur other countries, even traditional allies, to do what they have already begun doing: to strengthen their own partnerships, such as the European Union, separate from and perhaps increasingly in opposition to the United States. The kind of aggressive unilateralism pursued by Bush during his first term also ensures that American taxpayers will bear most of the military burden of maintaining world order. Ultimately, unilateralism in foreign policy is unsustainable: unipolar moments do not last indefinitely, and this one will be all the shorter under the policies Bush has followed. Unilateralism is not a formula for the perpetuation of American power any more than it is a formula for global peace and security.

The counterpart to Bush's unilateralist foreign policy has been the unilateral exercise of executive power at home at the expense of the other branches and of constitutional rights. The expansion of presidential powers in wartime is scarcely unusual, and several wars have seen grave infringements of liberty, such as the repression of dissent and violence against German Americans during World War I and the internment of Japanese Americans in concentration camps during World War II. Nothing has helped end earlier bouts of repression so much as the fact that the wars themselves came to a close, and nothing has now so exposed American liberties to indefinite jeopardy as the conception of a "war on terrorism" with no end.[8] Moreover, Bush has made claims of unlimited power that are unprecedented even in wartime, attempting to remove both the courts and Congress from their constitutional roles. He has claimed an inherent power, for example, to imprison citizens whom he determines to be the nation's enemies without obtaining a warrant, letting them hear the charges against them, or following other safeguards against wrongful punishment guaranteed by the Bill of Rights. He has similarly claimed an inherent power to conduct surveillance of citizens deemed by officials to be suspicious, again without a warrant. Under his administration, the government has engaged in inhumane treatment of prisoners that amounts to torture, and when Congress banned such treatment, Bush signed the law but said he would interpret it in a way that was consistent with executive prerogatives and "the constitutional limitations on the judicial power." Such signing statements have become routine for Bush, enabling him to avoid a formal veto while saying, in effect, that he is not bound to enforce the law. He regards international treaty obligations as matters entirely in his discretion. Although the Constitution says treaties are the "supreme law of the land," the president has abrogated treaties in whole or in part on his own, without any action by Congress.

More dangerous than any of the specific abuses is the theory of inherent powers that Bush and conservative lawyers have invoked to justify his actions. In this view, the president has sole authority over all matters related to foreign affairs, defense, and national security, except for the congressional power of the purse. The president can do whatever is required for the nation's security—take the nation to war, imprison enemies, use torture in interrogations—and if Congress disapproves, it can cut off funding. Once war is under way, however, Congress cannot realistically cut off funds for troops in the field. And without the independent eye of the courts, the prospects for abuse of power are enormous. The difficulty with this theory of the unitary executive is analogous to the one that Justice Robert H. Jackson articulated when he dissented from the majority in *Korematsu*, the infamous Supreme Court decision in the midst of war (1944) upholding the constitutionality of the military order to intern Japanese Americans. Once racial discrimination is accepted, Justice Jackson wrote, "the principle then lies about like a loaded weapon ready for the hand of any authority that can bring forward a plausible claim of an urgent need."[9] The principle of unlimited executive power now lies about like a loaded weapon for a future president with even less respect for individual rights.

Americans have been slow to react to Bush's actions because the great majority of them no more identify with the Arabs who have been the chief targets of antiterrorism measures than the majority in the 1940s identified with their fellow citizens of Japanese descent. But the liberties under attack and the constitutional role of Congress and the courts protect all citizens. Those constraints do not make the abuse of power impossible, but they make it less likely. Liberals ought not to be the only ones concerned about preserving such checks on the president. Just as Americans ought to look to the day when the United States is not hegemonic, so Republicans who have supported Bush's usurpations ought to be careful about the precedents they set for the day when they no longer control the executive branch. Unipolar moments aren't perpetual in domestic politics any more than they are internationally.

POWER THROUGH PARTNERSHIP

Three days after September 11, a former president of the United States declared, "Just as Pearl Harbor awakened this country from the notion that we could somehow avoid the call to duty and defend freedom in Europe and Asia in World War II, so, too, should this most recent surprise attack erase the concept in some quarters that America can somehow go it alone in the fight against terrorism or in anything else for that matter." That was the view of George Bush Sr.[10] His son saw things differently.

Political conditions in 2001 allowed the turn toward unilateralism in U.S. foreign policy, but they did not necessitate it. Another president could have used the historical moment to solidify America's alliances and to organize more effective international cooperation against terrorism and other threats to security. The United States could have fought the war in Afghanistan successfully—indeed, possibly brought it to a more successful conclusion by capturing Osama bin Laden at Tora Bora in November 2001—without becoming mired in the Iraq War. America not only lost a historic opportunity after 9/11 for a new liberal internationalist statecraft but now faces problems that have become far more difficult as a result of the spiral of antagonism with the Islamic world and the rise in anti-American sentiment elsewhere that Bush's policies have engendered.[11]

The repair of America's partnerships and the restoration of its good name require different policies and a different spirit. The United States cannot approach other countries insisting, as Bush did after 9/11, that they have to decide for themselves whether they are "with us or with the terrorists"; after all, other nations may reasonably want to know whether America is with them. Surely there are joint interests in stopping terrorism. And there are also joint interests in the global environment, alternative sources of energy, the control of pandemics, and global economic security. The United States has done itself no good by spurning any agreement on global warming. An America that wants other countries to stand "with us" in fighting terrorism will have to stand with them on matters such as global climate that they legitimately regard as vital to their welfare and even their survival.

Every great disaster in foreign policy has a bitter afterlife, not just abroad but at home as well. One of the indirect costs of the Iraq War is that it has made Americans skeptical about the aim of promoting democracy and human rights. And just as the Vietnam War led many Americans—particularly liberals—to an overly broad rejection of force, so the Iraq War has lent credence to a reflexive hostility to the use of American power. Some on the left today seem to think it would be better if the United States were divided into happy little welfare states with no military power—a North American Scandinavia. But that is not the right inference to draw. American power has been, and can again be, a positive influence in the world. The preemptive and preventive use of force may also be necessary to thwart genuine threats, and the entire international community stands to benefit from the spread of liberal democratic values. Promoting democracy is certainly not an all-purpose remedy to the world's problems, especially if democracy is interpreted as consisting merely of elections. Democracies are not immune to aggressive nationalism; indeed, new democracies have been especially prone to it. But if democracy is understood as including constitutionalism, the rule of law, and respect for individual rights, including the rights of minorities—if democracy is understood, that is, as liberal democracy—the long-term advantages for peace and global security, as well as economic development, are reasonably clear.[12] A liberal foreign policy ought to support liberal democracy, however, without slipping into the democratic imperialism advocated by neoconservatives and liberal backers of the Iraq War. Democracy imposed deliberately through war was never a reasonable proposition.

Success in the Cold War came as a result of containment, deterrence, multilateralism, and patience—liberal policies tempered by realism. To be sure, the Cold War offers only an inexact parallel for the challenge of terrorism. Even in this new struggle, however, the legacy of international institutions from the Cold War provides a foundation and a model for further efforts. But that is all that they are: to support international cooperation is not necessarily to be satisfied with the institutions that attempt to achieve that cooperation today. Although many of its technical divisions such as the World Health Organization are effective, the United Nations itself has resisted reform, and the International Monetary Fund has often aggravated economic problems through its adjustment policies. The time may have come for a new "concert of democracies" and for new international financial institutions to remedy the failures of the existing system.[13]

As the world's greatest power, the United States has exceptional leverage in shaping the rules and institutions of the international order. The liberal alternative to assertive nationalism and neoconservatism is not to abandon power for cooperation, but to seek additional power and security through a system of partnerships with other countries. That system, moreover, is best founded on the basis of social partnership at home. It is far easier to sustain public support for trade and cooperation with other countries if a nation's own citizens feel that they share in its prosperity and that the good being pursued by the government includes what is good for them. At home and abroad, a liberal government ought to convey the same idea: we're in this together.

9

In This Together:
The Democratic Partnership Now

───────

B$_{\text{EFORE THE}}$ 2006 $_{\text{ELECTION}}$, A$_{\text{MERICAN LIBERALISM SEEMED TO BE}}$ teetering on the edge of political irrelevance. The election brought it back from the brink, but the results were less a victory for liberals than a defeat for conservatives. Just as a liberal Democratic administration wounded itself in the 1960s through a failed war, so a conservative Republican administration after 2001 damaged its own cause by the same means. Republicans also overreached by identifying themselves fully with the religious right. Conservatism itself now seems spent, riddled with internal divisions and recriminations, just as liberalism did for a long time.

Yet America has not returned to the political environment that existed before the conservative ascendancy. The air remains bitter with ideological acrimony, and political conflict now reaches into aspects of American society that used to be off limits to partisan hostilities.

During the mid-twentieth century, the absence of deep ideological divisions was widely thought to be one of the distinguishing features of American politics, and even when the 1960s brought an outburst of ideological politics, there remained a broad consensus about institutions, public and private, built largely on liberal foundations. By the beginning of the twenty-first century, however, not just politics but law, religion, journalism, education, and other arenas of American life were rife with ideological tension and rancor. The driving force in that heightened conflict came from the right, and the stakes increased. The issue was no longer only a reversal of Great Society programs and the decisions of the Warren Court as it had been in the earlier stages of conservatism's revival. Emboldened by their political triumphs between 2000 and 2004, conservatives at the highest levels of government sought to undo limits on executive powers and other basic constitutional restraints, attacked key elements of modern liberal policy such as progressive taxation and Social Security, and undermined liberal principles regarding such institutions as science, religion, and education.

While the immediate source of jeopardy to liberal policies was the Democrats' loss of predominance, the revolution of contemporary Republicanism was the reason that the change in the partisan balance had so great an impact. Energized by a conservative movement at its base, the GOP became a far more ideologically driven party, and in an age of rising inequality and declining unions, the Republicans enjoy significant financial and organizational advantages. Together, the right, the rich, and the Republican leadership have combined to create a formidable political machine. On the Democratic side, despite the many causes and constituencies, there has been no liberal or progressive movement comparable in political resolve or material support. The question for the Democrats is not whether they can win elections—2006 showed they can—but whether they can achieve the organizational strength and intellectual coherence to create a durable majority and lead the country in a progressive direction. For liberals especially, the two sides of the problems are intertwined: if liberalism is to regain the influence it once enjoyed, it can do so only through a renewal of both its principles and the practical basis of its politics.

At its best, modern liberalism has stood for inclusive, democratic partnerships at home and abroad. Those partnerships are both means and ends. They supply the political power for realizing the ends of a free and just society and a secure world. And the partnerships themselves express the core liberal values of mutual respect and equality.

This inclusive vision was missing from the classical liberal tradition. In the eighteenth century, constitutional liberalism provided the foundations of a powerful yet constrained state, but it excluded the majority from participation and full citizenship. In the nineteenth and early twentieth centuries, laissez-faire economics provided a framework of law and policy for industrial capitalism's dynamic growth, but it left most working people in insecurity and poverty. In the same era, while often favoring reform at home, liberal imperialists supported Western colonialism. But in the first decades of the twentieth century, when the old liberal order of constitutional government, classical economics, and colonialism went up in flames amid total war and the Great Depression, fascism or communism could easily have emerged from the wreckage to dominate the world.

Modern liberalism, however, transformed its classical inheritance into a genuinely democratic politics that proved stronger and more effective in both war and peace than its critics expected. Liberals now called for true political equality for all, aimed to bring raw capitalism under control in the interests of an expanded circle of opportunity, and supported national self-determination for all peoples and new forms of cooperation among states to promote democracy, human rights, and international peace and security. Every step of the way, right-wing critics objected to these movements toward a wider democratic partnership, but as of the mid-twentieth century liberals had won the argument decisively and built an electoral majority in support of it. The prevailing view in the liberal democracies held that the extension of political and social rights and economic regulation was not only just, but also the basis of a more productive and powerful society. And cooperative international organization, far from being a naive delusion, was plainly necessary to meet the twin threats posed by communism, on the one hand, and nuclear extinction, on the other.

In the United States, however, what seemed to be a solid liberal consensus disintegrated during the 1960s and subsequent decades as liberals supported efforts to expand democracy's inclusive reach beyond its old limits. Equal rights for African Americans, women, gays and lesbians, and other groups long subject to discrimination; public spending to reduce poverty; the regulation of business to protect health and the environment; the deregulation of private sexual life, literature and the arts, and other forms of cultural expression—each of these followed directly from the liberal commitment to an equal right to freedom. And each aroused a hostile reaction—from whites, particularly in the South, who felt liberalism and the Democratic Party were no longer on their side; from business, which had always regarded government spending and regulation suspiciously; and from moral and religious conservatives, who mobilized new political energy in their long struggle against liberal modernity. While a growing conservative movement close to the Republican Party assembled these groups into a broadened coalition, liberals fragmented into myriad issue- and identity-based causes.

The social movements and reforms that liberalism advocated and advanced in the second half of the twentieth century have rectified historic injustices, enlarged the scope of freedom, and, despite their limitations, changed America for the better. But the model of liberal politics forged in the 1960s has been played out: the old political majority is gone. Single-issue causes can no longer direct their protests and proposals to a sympathetic Congress with large and secure Democratic majorities, and they can no longer turn to the federal courts with much hope of advancing constitutional claims. The impulses in foreign policy produced by the Vietnam War have long ceased to be relevant to the world. The liberalism of the mid-twentieth century could back stronger rights of free expression and personal autonomy without losing much support among the more traditionally minded because of the unambiguous achievements of Roosevelt, Truman, and Kennedy in leading the country during World War II and the early Cold War and delivering prosperity and economic security. That reservoir of goodwill, however, vanished after Vietnam and the stagflation of the 1970s. Yet liberal groups pushed ahead, calling upon the courts to impose policies on unwilling majorities at the cost of an increasingly intense backlash. For some time the imperative has been clear: liberalism has no way to advance without a majoritarian politics capable of restoring the kind of inclusive democratic partnership that was the basis of modern liberalism's achievements.

Competing visions of a new American political majority emerged from the 1960s on both the right and the left. In 1969 Kevin Phillips argued that the Republican Party would dominate electoral politics as a result of a pair of overlapping developments. The Democratic Party's embrace of black interests had opened the South to the Republicans, while rapid economic and population growth in the Sunbelt presaged a continuing shift of power toward the most reliably conservative region of the country.[1]

A second theory, the progressive vision of a New Politics, also proposed a strategy for a new majority based on a long-run trend: the spread of more liberal social and cultural attitudes. Instead of emphasizing traditional lunch-bucket concerns, the New Politics foresaw a potential for Democrats to add a new generation of supporters by championing such causes as civil rights, feminism, the quality of the environment, consumer protection, broader political participation, and openness in government.

Which theory was right? In a sense, both were. After Nixon's election, the Republicans capitalized on their opportunities in the Sunbelt, drew more of their leadership from the region, and remade themselves into a more conservative party. The South's partisan switch affected voting for president more quickly than voting for Congress because of the inertial force of congressional incumbency. And while Democrats hung on to congressional seats in the South, the New Politics—sometimes described as a postindustrial progressivism—brought the Democrats new vitality as well as new voters elsewhere in the country. They were consequently able to keep control of Congress for another quarter-century after Phillips's forecast, for a total run of sixty-two years (1932 to 1994), about twice the duration of typical party regimes in American history.

As a result of these conflicting developments, neither party was able to monopolize national power from 1968 to 2000. For twenty-six out of those thirty-two years, the United States had a divided government, with one party in possession of the presidency and the other party controlling at least one house of Congress. Roughly matched in strength, Democrats and Republicans each had the capacity to win a national electoral majority. The parties exchanged regional bases: New England and California trended toward the Democrats, as the South moved toward the Republicans. A gender gap opened up as Democrats drew more support from women, Republicans from men. And while Democrats could sometimes assemble majorities from whites and minorities combined, Republicans typically had an edge among native-born whites.

Rising to parity, however, is different from falling to the same point. The Republicans sensed that they were riding a wave, and it gave them confidence. When they won control of Congress in 1994, they were mainly completing the takeover of southern seats they had begun decades earlier, but the impact was much greater than that of earlier Republican gains. Democrats had long used the advantages of an incumbent congressional majority to offset Republican business support, but after 1994 the GOP had both, and a party system that had been roughly balanced passed a tipping point. Moreover, changes in congressional rules, particularly in the House, allowed the leadership to control proceedings much more tightly than had been the case during most of the earlier Democratic era. In the past, conservative Democrats from the South often joined with Republicans to thwart liberal legislation, but under the new system the GOP congressional leadership generally kept moderate Republicans in line. The 2000 presidential election proved to be a tipping point of another kind. The Republicans took full control of the entire federal government for the first time since 1932 (other than a brief period at the beginning of Eisenhower's presidency). And rather than moderating their positions, as might have been expected given George W. Bush's failure to win the popular vote and their narrow margins in Congress, the Republicans carried out a far more radical program in both domestic and foreign affairs than observers expected or thought possible. In cutting taxes while going to war in Iraq, the Republicans defied the entire history of wartime finance.

Despite close margins in voting and party identification, the balance of political power after 2000 swung sharply toward the right. The Bush administration was able to use the patriotic awakening and sense of national emergency following September 11 not only to solidify its support but also to gain acceptance of policies, such as the Iraq War and expanded presidential powers and government surveillance, which would otherwise likely have been politically inconceivable. At least during Bush's first term, Republicans in Congress showed more internal discipline than Democrats had under Clinton. Similarly, the wider network of conservative interest groups, think tanks, and media coordinated their efforts more effectively than had been characteristic of their progressive counterparts under Democratic presidents. But there were also deeper forces at work in the consolidation of conservative Republican power.

As the distribution of income and wealth have become increasingly unequal, the political power of groups at the top of American society has grown. They have the discretionary funds to spend on political contributions, and Republican candidates and conservative causes generally get more of that money in a period when the cost of campaigns has soared and politics has become more money-centered than ever. Moreover, because all those who run for office, Democratic as well as Republican, have to devote increased time to soliciting donations from affluent contributors, the "ears" of the political system as a whole are cocked in the direction of wealth.[2]

The long-term atrophy of political activism and civic participation in America has also affected Democrats far more than Republicans. The most productive eras of liberal reform in the twentieth century—the Progressive era, the New Deal, and the 1960s—were all periods of public ferment when new types of civic action emerged. Whenever the public is disengaged, however, there is little to counter the pressure exerted by business and the wealthy, and liberal politics and more egalitarian policies suffer as a result. The decline of labor unions has particularly weakened the Democrats because the money and ground troops provided by unions are vital to the party, and the unions have a substantial effect on their own members' voting. But while the proportion of Americans belonging to unions has dropped, the Republicans have benefited from the heightened political arousal of Christian conservatives. Public opinion has not shown any overall shift in a conservative direction.[3] But conservatism has benefited from an edge in organized advocacy.

The Iraq War has also highlighted another change: the disappearance of the old dynamic between war and equal rights. Modern warfare has in the past had two seemingly contradictory effects on liberal democracy at home: while repeatedly putting civil liberties in jeopardy, war has promoted democratization. As I have emphasized in earlier chapters, the modern liberal state emerged from a long history of meeting the challenges of war. In seventeenth- and eighteenth-century England, the need to raise armies and obtain new revenue led kings to concede authority to Parliament; in nineteenth- and twentieth-century America and Europe, the demands of large-scale warfare similarly led governments to concede new rights of citizenship as a way of generating popular loyalty and re-warding sacrifice. In the United States the expansion of voting rights to African Americans after the Civil War, to women after World War I, and to eighteen-year-olds during the Vietnam War exemplified the pattern. Wars also led to expanded economic regulation and social welfare provision, much of which remained once the wars ended, while the wartime infringements of individual rights were typically reversed afterward. Liberal democracies have generally not gone to war against each other. But more often than not, they have prevailed in wars against undemocratic states. And during the mid-twentieth century their struggles with totalitarian regimes led them to become both more democratic and more liberal.[4]

The kind of highly technological war recently waged by the United States, however, no longer requires mass enlistment or popular mobilization and consequently has not generated pressure on the government to expand rights or social benefits. The war in Iraq and the "war on terror" have all the illiberal effects of wars in the past but none of their egalitarian and democratizing consequences. The Bush administration was able to avoid asking for any kind of domestic sacrifice, not a draft or even a delay in tax cuts, and thereby avoided large-scale protest against the war's costs, even when it proved to be based on false premises. In the past, wars have led to long-term increases in civic engagement. But although the Americans who came of age during World War II have since voted and participated in civic activities at a higher rate than both earlier and later generations, the Iraq War is unlikely to produce this kind of aftereffect. Civic activism was low going into the war, and the war seems unlikely to change the pattern.

There are, however, long-run trends in American society that may work in the Democrats' favor and create new possibilities for progressive politics. In the next quarter-century, according to Census Bureau projections, Hispanics will represent 45 percent of U.S. population growth, raising their share of the total population from 13 percent in 2000 to 20 percent by 2030.[5] Tighter immigration policy could slow down this process, but the projected increase partly reflects the relatively low median age and high birth rate among Hispanics compared to other Americans.

Although no one can be certain of future voting patterns, ethnic groups' early partisan attachments generally tend to stick, and except for the Republican-leaning Cuban Americans, Hispanics tend to be strongly Democratic and seem likely to remain so. Thus far they have represented a much smaller percentage of the electorate than of total population because of low turnout and the relatively large number who are too young to vote or lack citizenship. But as their median age increases and more become citizens because they have naturalized or were born in the United States, the Hispanics' share of the electorate should grow faster than their share of the population. (The creation of a permanent guest-worker population would counter that development.) Even with policies curbing immigration and restricting access to citizenship, some of the states in the Sunbelt where Hispanic population growth is especially high seem likely to flip back from the Republicans to the Democrats.

Demography is not destiny; trends in population, the economy, and public opinion only open up political possibilities. The growth of the elderly population could provide an advantage to the party most strongly identified with protection of Social Security and Medicare. The greater social tolerance among the young, particularly toward gays, could mean that over time the conservative cultural backlash will lose its force. And perhaps most important, the stagnation in real incomes among all but those at the upper end of the scale could enable the Democrats to recover some of the support they have lost among white working- and middle-class families.

The disparity in who benefits from economic growth has become one of the most striking social facts of our time. A rising tide is supposed to lift all boats—economic growth and rising productivity should bring greater prosperity for all—but it hasn't been working that way. During George W. Bush's first term, while incomes at the top boomed, median family income actually declined. The top 1 percent alone in 2004 received 36 percent of all the growth in national income that year. The concentration of income and wealth at the top has returned to patterns not seen in America since before the 1930s.[6]

But would a Democratic administration make any difference? The previous half-century of experience suggests that it would. Although there has been a long-term trend toward rising income inequality, the two parties have affected that trend in opposite ways. From 1948 to 2001, there were five Democratic and five Republican presidents. During that time, according to research on pretax income by the political scientist Larry Bartels, there was no difference between Democratic and Republican administrations in the rate of income growth for families near the top at the ninety-fifth percentile, but incomes down at the twentieth percentile rose four times more rapidly under Democratic than under Republican presidents. Every Republican administration saw an increase in income inequality: incomes rose more for families at the eightieth percentile than for those at the twentieth percentile. In contrast, income inequality declined during four out of five Democratic administrations (all but Jimmy Carter's): incomes at the twentieth percentile increased more than those at the eightieth did. The primary explanation for these differences in pretax income, according to Bartels, is macroeconomic policy. On average, economic growth was 30 percent higher and unemployment 30 percent lower under the Democrats than under the Republicans. Tight labor markets benefited lower- and middle-income families more than those at the top.[7]

These patterns understate the differences between Republicans and Democrats because living standards also depend on policies toward taxes and noncash benefits that aren't reflected in pretax money income. Republican policies have chiefly boosted the after-tax income of people in the upper brackets. The fully phased-in Bush tax cuts, for example, provided an average annual cut of $19 (in 2004 dollars) for families in the bottom 20 percent; a cut of $652 for those in the middle 20 percent; and a cut of $136,398 for people with incomes over $1 million.[8] The benefits of reduced estate taxes flow entirely to the most affluent and perpetuate concentrations of great fortunes from one generation to the next in what the billionaire Warren Buffet calls the "lucky sperm club." The "flat tax" favored by many conservatives would eliminate progressive taxation of income altogether by imposing the same rate on all wage-earners as on the rich, freeing dividends, interest, and capital gains from all taxation, and thereby shifting the tax burden from capital to labor. While Democratic tax policies have narrowed the gap in market-generated incomes, Republican tax policies have increased that disparity and, if conservatives were to achieve their full aims, they would increase inequality further.

The same is true of Republican policies toward noncash benefits, which include government-sponsored health programs such as Medicare and Medicaid as well as health coverage paid for by employers. Since the battle over national health insurance under Truman, Democrats have been the primary force calling for publicly financed health insurance for all or for requirements that firms cover their employees, whereas Republicans have generally opposed such measures. Many Americans who have supported the conservative position have not seen any need for government intervention because their jobs carried good health benefits. In recent decades, however, the "private welfare state" has been shrinking: fewer firms offer health and pension benefits, and those that do have shifted costs to their employees and required them to assume more of the risk. From 2001 to 2004, the number of jobs providing health coverage declined by 5 million.[9] While Democratic policies would block or counteract the shifting of risk to individuals, Republican policies would extend that process further through individual health savings accounts and the privatization of Social Security.

The erosion of health benefits particularly affects young workers, many of whom are finding it difficult to achieve the economic security and middle-class standard of living that their parents enjoyed at the same stage of life. The long-term decline in real wages for young men with less than a college education has diminished their ability to support a family and sustain a stable marriage. Although young parents typically need two incomes today, little has been done nationally to require changes in the workplace that would help them fulfill their family responsibilities. The one notable reform was the unpaid family-leave legislation passed over Republican opposition during the first year of the Clinton administration. But the United States, nearly alone among advanced countries, has no provisions guaranteeing paid sick leave or paid leave after childbirth.

Growing inequality, economic insecurity, and stress on working families scarcely register as issues for Republicans, who have trouble even acknowledging the evidence that inequality is on the rise, much less that their own policies contribute to the trend. The problem is not just that there is a growing gap between rich and poor. There is also a widening gap between those at the very top and everyone else, as the median-income family—the average family—has failed to receive close to a proportionate share of economic growth. In 1965 the average chief executive officer of an American corporation made 24 times as much as the average worker; now the average CEO makes 262 times as much— and keeps more of it, thanks to Republican tax cuts in the intervening years. A century ago, prominent men of wealth, many of them Republicans, recognized that the progressive income tax and estate tax were in the wider interests of society. Though there still are such people, the Republican Party now speaks on behalf of the interests of a part of the upper class that has no sense of those wider social responsibilities, nor any hesitation or the least shame about concentrating wealth in their own hands. While preaching moral responsibility, discipline, and abstinence to the poor, they want a government that gratifies their own appetites, and conservatives have been eager to provide it to them on the false premise that a winner-take-all-and-keep-all economy is the only way for the nation to prosper.

The inattention to rising inequality and insecurity is part of a more general pattern of conservative moral and political default. On a wide range of issues, Republicans have abdicated the responsibilities of national leadership for the sake of political advantage in an ideologically driven attack on the capacities of government. Stewardship of public finance is one of the responsibilities long associated with the very meaning of the word "conservative." In slashing taxes and precipitating deficits, however, the administrations of both Reagan and the younger Bush hoped to force changes in policy that they would otherwise be unable to enact. Public opinion surveys regularly show that, by wide margins, Americans favor more resources for such purposes as health care and education, and Republicans have been unwilling to challenge that preference directly. But deficits have the happy effect, from the standpoint of conservatives who want to "starve the beast," of making it appear regrettably necessary to cut social programs and completely unthinkable to undertake new initiatives to deal with such problems as the millions of Americans without health insurance. Conservatives once opposed deficits in the name of "sound finance," and some still do: during the late 1980s and early 1990s, pressure from balanced-budget conservatives helped bring about the budget agreements and corrective tax increases that stanched the fiscal hemorrhages produced by Reagan's early tax cuts. But the more radical conservatives lately in power under Bush have concluded, in Dick Cheney's phrase, that "deficits don't matter," except for the convenient purpose of constricting the public agenda.

It is true that government deficits of moderate size are not the unpardonable sin that conservatives said they were when Democrats were in office. Whether deficits are defensible depends on how public money is spent and the prospects for future budgetary balance. Because of the return that public investment yields to society, expenditures for new physical infrastructure, scientific research, and a better educated, healthier, and more productive workforce may justify government borrowing. Deficits to counter a recession or to finance a war may also be necessary for short-term reasons. But neither of these justifications apply to the Bush administration, which took the government from record surpluses to record deficits in record time. The Republicans cut taxes precisely to inhibit social spending regardless of whether it is economically productive, and the deficits they have generated are not short-term or self-correcting. Rather, they have created a deep, structural gap between revenues and expenditures that is projected to grow to unsustainable levels as the population ages and the costs of Social Security and Medicare increase. And because the public strongly supports both of those programs, the Republican strategy has prepared the ground for a fiscal crisis of epic proportions that will deplete the capacity of government to meet any contingency.

The failure of conservative leadership to confront long-term problems forthrightly applies equally to energy and the environment. America's need to wean itself away from oil—and from fossil fuels generally—has been apparent for decades. Dependence on imported oil exposes the United States to obvious economic risks and political threats and distorts calculations of the national interest in the making of foreign policy. And America's use of fossil fuels is a central factor in the production of greenhouse gases. Scientific reports about the dangers of global warming first reached the White House when Carter was president, and since that time the scientific consensus in favor of that view has become overwhelming. Although Carter proposed the first steps to deal with global warming just before he left office, the Reagan administration ignored the problem, and ever since conservatives have preferred denial and inaction to a realistic assessment of the scientific evidence and a commitment to the technological investments, economic adjustments, and international agreements that are going to be needed to sustain a livable world.

The influence of global-warming deniers in the Republican Party of the Bush era reflects two corrosive forces eating away at the intellectual force of contemporary conservatism: corporate special interests (in this case, chiefly the oil industry, which has financed critics of the scientific consensus on climate change), and a contempt for science long harbored by the far right and especially by religious conservatives. During the 1970s it seemed that the Republicans had embraced both science and environmentalism. But as the GOP has moved right, it has reverted to an older right-wing suspicion that the scientific community is a gigantic intellectual conspiracy—a view that panders to populist suspicions and conveniently serves business interests close to the party that want to avoid regulation.[10]

Nowhere have the claims of contemporary conservatism proven more hollow and misleading than on the very foreign policy and defense issues its own leaders see as vital to U.S. national security. Conservatives have cultivated an image of being tough and realistic, ready and willing to use military force to advance America's interests. But rather than augmenting American power, they have dissipated it. During the lead-up to the Iraq War, the Bush administration overstated the dangers of Saddam Hussein's regime, understated the ease of changing Iraq, and consequently set in motion a train of perverse consequences whose end is not yet in sight. The war was supposed to display the overwhelming might of the United States, to keep weapons of mass destruction out of the hands of America's enemies, and to turn the Middle East in a more democratic direction that would be more friendly to the West. Instead, the war has shown the limits of American military capabilities, plunged Iraq into civil war, enlarged Iran's influence, encouraged Iran to pursue its nuclear ambitions and North Korea to fulfill them, and brought the Middle East no closer to peace or democracy. As the disaster has unfolded, Bush and his principal advisers have denied facts that were plain to all observers, as if the power of positive thinking could rule events. It cannot be said that the perverse effects of the war were unforeseen; experts in the government, as well as the war's public critics, warned of them beforehand. But the administration's disregard of critical experts and conflicting intelligence was typical of a strain of conservatism that distrusts professionals and scientists and regards intellectual complexity as a barrier to black-and-white moral judgments and the simple logic of force in matters of national security.

Brilliant as they have been in achieving political power, the Republicans of the Bush era have shown little of that genius in using it. A conservatism that does not want to hear about inequality or the sinking fortunes of the middle class, or about dangers to the global environment, or about fiscal recklessness, or about gaping flaws in plans for war may prevail in the short run, but the realities will sooner or later make themselves felt as they did in 2006. A great nation cannot long be governed by wishful and simplistic thinking, denial, obfuscation, and deceit. Costs mount, grievances accumulate, and there comes a reckoning.

To be sure, not all of what has gone grievously wrong under Bush has been inherent in conservative philosophy. For example, Bush's claims of unilateral presidential powers to conduct surveillance without a court warrant and to imprison without trial anyone, including U.S. citizens, whom the executive alone identifies as "enemy combatants" have blatantly violated constitutional principles held dear by thoughtful conservatives and liberals alike. But recent Republican policies have not been an idiosyncratic expression of conservative politics. The conservative movement has long agitated for just what Bush has given them: a comprehensive attack on the social and economic capacities of government at home while asserting the nation's military power abroad. Republicans in Congress have stood behind the president on the central points of his agenda. The upward tilt of the tax cuts, the favors for business interests, the expansion of executive powers—none of these has produced a serious split in Republican ranks. The conservative movement and the Republican Party have not just been indifferent to growing economic inequality, environmental deterioration, and long-term fiscal problems—they have obstructed progress on each of these fronts. If Americans are going to get a national leadership that takes on those challenges, they are going to get it, as a practical matter, only from a new Democratic political majority.

The conservative default is liberalism's opportunity—an opportunity to rebuild a political majority by showing how liberal ideas make sense for America and by reopening a conversation with people who believe that liberals have not shown any concern or respect for them. At the heart of any such effort must be a program for shared prosperity to counter the trends toward rising inequality, insecurity, and stress on working families that the Republican policies have accentuated. But no politics can live on bread alone. The public's concerns are inextricably moral and material; our standard of living depends on the safety of our neighborhoods as well as our wages. Whether economics or values matter more is a false choice and a futile debate, like arguing whether white or black matters more in picking out a zebra. Anyone who worries about the institution of marriage, for example, ought to be receptive to changes in employer policies, the availability of preschool education, and other reforms that would help parents meet their obligations at work and at home. And anyone who favors those reforms ought to make the argument that they are good for stable marriages. Liberals ought to contest conservatives for the very ground the right claims as its own—morality and patriotism. What is the protection of the global environment if not a moral concern? What are efforts to preserve constitutional liberties if not a patriotic devotion to the true basis of America's greatness? Liberalism should appeal for support on the straightforward basis that conservative economic policies do not serve the interests of the great majority of people. But liberalism ought to do more than that—it ought to remind us of our responsibilities and the power of our traditions and call us to greater interests and purposes than our own.

Nothing has to be reinvented, yet everything has to be reimagined. Constructive ideas for new policies are not wanting, but liberals have to think differently about what those policies are about and how they can be achieved. The era of single-issue progressive causes, each agitating—and litigating—separately, is finished. Liberals have to make the case for progressive policies on the basis of the nation's shared interests and common future. National crisis has in the past often supplied the sense of a common citizenship and the imperative demand to put the greater good ahead of one's own. The task of political leadership now is to evoke that same sentiment: "We are all in this together."[11] This is the work of rebuilding democratic partnerships: a social partnership at home that includes working- and middle-class families, and a partnership with other liberal democracies in defense of our common values and security.

The practical politics that goes with these objectives, however, is not simply a redoubled commitment to public purposes. Today there is a Democratic project and a liberal project, and it is a mistake to confuse them. The Democrats' once-sturdy congressional majority disappeared in 1994 with the loss of southern seats not held by liberals in the first place. To reestablish that majority, as the 2006 election showed, requires the acceptance of ideological diversity within the party, particularly in the South, the Midwest, and the Rocky Mountain states. As the Republicans have moved right, they have created opportunities for the Democrats to absorb alienated moderates and independents. Liberals should neither expect nor try to make the Democratic Party as ideologically exclusive as the Republican Party has become. During the 1930s and '60s, liberals were able to realize many of their aims through a Democratic Party that had plenty of moderates and conservatives. Liberals can again serve their ideals best by providing energy and vision to the Democrats without demanding adherence to a checklist of liberal positions.

Here liberals have much to learn from Bill Clinton's presidency. The central challenge in the 1990s was formulating a program that could realize progressive aspirations under severe fiscal pressures and radically changed economic and social conditions, including a globalized economy, a wave of technological innovation, and rising income inequality. Many liberals chafed at Clinton's caution, but his program responded effectively to the difficult conditions of the time, setting the stage for an era of sustained prosperity, fiscal recovery, and significant reductions in poverty and social pathology. Clinton also artfully defused tensions associated with racially charged issues such as affirmative action. He was stymied, however, on such critical goals as health reform, lost the political initiative in his second term as a result of scandal, and failed to turn the success of his policies to the long-term institutional advantage of the Democratic Party.

The economic and fiscal conditions today bear a resemblance to those of the early 1990s. Republican rule has again aggravated economic inequalities and created a deep structural deficit that will sooner or later require the Democrats to act as the responsible parent in the American political family. But this is a dreary role to play—making gloomy forecasts, protecting established progressive programs and policies, and totaling up the public's bill—unless Democrats have the imagination and courage to turn trouble into opportunity. For example, they ought to frame the challenges of energy and the environment as a chance for America to take a leading role in the technological innovations and new industries that all nations will need for a sustainable world economy. Rather than merely reforming Medicare to keep it afloat, the Democrats ought to reopen the battle for universal health insurance. And rather than just defending Social Security, they ought to be calling for a New Deal for the Young. Many of the forces now affecting the economy come to bear hardest on young people starting out in life: the soaring cost of a college education; the difficulty in finding jobs that provide a middle-class income and benefits; the escalation in housing prices; and the conflicts between the demands of work and family life. After World War II, the GI Bill provided a great boost to young veterans and their families by helping them with higher education, job training, health care, and home mortgages. This was in keeping with the established pattern of war and social policy: a society that asked a great deal of its youth did more in return afterward. But America today asks little and does little, when it ought to be asking more of its young and doing more for them. It ought to make national service a routine experience—for some in their late teens, for others after college—and in return it should help young people invest in their educations, careers, businesses, and homes. A New Deal for the Young—a Young America program—would not provide something for nothing. Like Social Security, its benefits would be earned. And because of its focus on youth, it would be a way of helping Americans, individually and collectively, become more productive as well as more secure.

The premise of a Young America program is the inclusive conception of freedom and power that is at the core of modern liberalism. An increasingly unequal America that exposes so many of its young to poverty and insecurity cannot be the strong and prosperous nation all Americans want it to be. Government, however, can be the means for expanding the horizon of freedom, creating opportunity, and making a society both more powerful and more just.

In much of the postcommunist and postcolonial world, the liberal project is still the creation of constitutional democracy, and liberalism remains an intellectual tradition without deep social and historical roots. But in the United States the idea that everyone enjoys an equal right to life, liberty, and the pursuit of happiness is part of the national tradition. The story of America is of a nation that has grown greater and stronger by becoming more diverse and inclusive and extending the fruits of liberty more widely among its people. American liberals do not have to invent something new or import a philosophical tradition from abroad. They have only to reclaim the idea of America's greatness as their own.

Notes

INTRODUCTION

1. In saying that liberals share political principles while disagreeing about their foundations, I mean only to bracket the foundational questions for purposes of defining liberalism. The idea that a liberal polity does not require comprehensive moral agreement is itself a particular position within liberalism, associated with John Rawls. See his *Political Liberalism*, expanded ed. (New York: Columbia University Press, 2005); and for discussion, see the essays in Shaun P. Young, ed., *Political Liberalism: Variations on a Theme* (Albany: State University of New York Press, 2004). For efforts to define liberalism or simply to describe it in its historical variety, see John Gray, *Liberalism* (Minneapolis: University of Minnesota Press, 1986); J. G. Merquior, *Liberalism, Old and New* (Boston: Twayne Publishers, 1991); Stephen Holmes, *Passions and Constraint: On the Theory of Liberal Democracy* (Chicago: University of Chicago Press, 1995); Jeremy Waldron, "Theoretical Foundations of Liberalism," *Philosophical Quarterly* 37 (1987): 127–50; and, still useful, L. T. Hobhouse, *Liberalism* (New York: Oxford University Press, 1911). Listing the elements of a conception of "man and society" shared by "all variants of the liberal tradition," Gray writes that liberalism is "*individualist*, in that it asserts the moral primacy of the person against the claims of any social collectivity; *egalitarian*, inasmuch as it confers on all men the same moral status and denies the relevance to legal or political order of differences in moral worth among human beings; *universalist*, affirming the moral unity of the human species and according a

secondary importance to specific historical associations and cultural forms; and *meliorist* in its affirmation of the corrigibility and improvability of all social institutions and political arrangements" (*Liberalism*, x). A merit of this list is that it allows for divergent tendencies within liberalism that have put one aspect ahead of others or tempered one with another (say, individualism with egalitarianism). Some in the academy tend to equate liberalism with individualism alone—or with adherence to the idea of "negative liberty"—also often attributing to liberalism an insistence on analyzing society (or the public) entirely in terms of individuals, as if liberalism were logically incompatible with any kind of sociological understanding. Needless to say, I reject these interpretations.

2. My formulation of the first and third of these responsibilities reflects the influence of Ronald Dworkin's conception of two principles of human dignity—the principles of "personal responsibility" and of "intrinsic value." See Ronald Dworkin, *Is Democracy Possible Here? Principles for a New Political Debate* (Princeton, N.J.: Princeton University Press, 2006), ch. 1.

3. I owe this phrasing to the nineteenth-century French writer Jules Simon, *La politique radicale* (Paris: Librairie Internationale, 1868): "Un pouvoir fort, mais restreint,—fort, parce qu'il est restreint" (35).

CHAPTER 1

1. This approach to conceptualizing power attempts to reconcile the competing perspectives derived from Max Weber, Talcott Parsons, and some of their critics. For an analysis (curiously reversing his own earlier views in critical respects), see Steven Lukes, *Power: A Radical View*, 2nd ed. (New York: Palgrave Macmillan, 2005).

2. Stephen Holmes, "The Liberal Idea," *The American Prospect*, no. 7 (Fall 1991): 86 (summarizing an insight of Jean Bodin); see also Stephen Holmes, *Passions and Constraint: On the Theory of Liberal Democracy* (Chicago: University of Chicago Press, 1995).

3. Unpacking this definition could take a book in itself. It is intentionally worded so as to apply to both an individual and a nation or some other community. Freedom includes liberty as I have defined it here. In its modern liberal usage, however, freedom also includes the idea of self-realization—that is, not being thwarted in developing one's true capabilities. The two terms "liberty" and "freedom" are often interchangeable, but their use has

varied through history. For a fascinating history of the American conceptions of the two terms, see David Hackett Fischer, *Liberty and Freedom* (New York: Oxford University Press, 2004).

4. See Jose Mariá Maravall and Adam Przeworski, eds., "Introduction," *Democracy and the Rule of Law* (New York: Cambridge University Press, 2003). The following discussion draws on other essays in the volume, particularly Stephen Holmes, "Lineages of the Rule of Law," 19–61.

5. For recent contrasting views on the relationship of republicanism and liberalism, see Quentin Skinner, *Liberty Before Liberalism* (New York: Cambridge University Press, 1998), and Vickie B. Sullivan, *Machiavelli, Hobbes, and the Formation of a Liberal Republicanism in England* (New York: Cambridge University Press, 2004). Skinner's argument reflects his premise, derived from Isaiah Berlin, that liberalism conceives of liberty exclusively in negative terms; see Holmes, *Passion and Constraint*, for an alternative view. In the American context, the work of Bernard Bailyn, J. G. A. Pocock, and Gordon Wood in the 1960s and '70s led to a rediscovery of republicanism—and a corresponding devaluation of liberalism—that spread from the Revolutionary era into succeeding periods and led to the idea that these were two incompatible traditions. But as Bailyn himself later wrote, the ideas of the American Revolution did not reflect "something scholars would later call 'civic humanism' or 'classical republicanism,' nor were these ideas felt to be incompatible with what would later be described as 'liberalism.'" See "The Central Themes of the American Revolution," in Bailyn, *Faces of Revolution: Personalities and Themes in the Struggle for American Independence* (New York: Knopf, 1990). For a brilliant account of the recent historiography of republicanism, see Daniel Rodgers, "Republicanism: The Career of a Concept," *Journal of American History* 79 (1992): 11–38.

6. This section draws on the classic discussions in Charles Howard McIlwain, *Constitutionalism, Ancient and Modern* (Ithaca, N.Y.: Great Seal Books, 1947), and Guido de Ruggiero, *The History of European Liberalism* (New York: Oxford University Press, 1927).

CHAPTER 2

1. John Lord Sheffield, *Observations on the Commerce of the American States* (London, 1784), 238.

2. Michael Mann, "The Autonomous Power of the State: Its Origins, Mechanisms, and Results," in John A. Hall, ed., *States in History* (Oxford: Blackwell, 1986), 109–36 [quotation: 114].

3. For this chapter's discussion of 1688, I have relied primarily on Mark Kishlansky, *A Monarchy Transformed: Britain, 1603–1714* (New York: Penguin Books, 1996); R. A. Beddard, *The Revolutions of 1688* (New York: Oxford University Press, 1991); John Miller, *The Glorious Revolution*, 2nd ed. (New York: Addison Wesley Longman, 1997); J. G. A. Pocock, ed., *Three British Revolutions: 1641, 1688, 1776* (Princeton, N.J.: Princeton University Press, 1980), especially the essays by Lawrence Stone and Lois Schwoerer; and W. A. Speck, *The Reluctant Revolutionaries: Englishmen and the Revolution of 1688* (New York: Oxford University Press, 1988). The view that the Glorious Revolution was merely a coup comes most famously from Christopher Hill; see, for example, his essay in Pocock, *Three British Revolutions*.

4. William H. McNeill, *The Pursuit of Power: Technology, Armed Force, and Society Since A.D. 1000* (Chicago: University of Chicago Press, 1982), ch. 3. [quotation: 89]. For general background, see Geoffrey Parker, *The Military Revolution: Military Innovation and the Rise of the West, 1500–1800*, 2nd ed. (Cambridge: Cambridge University Press, 1996), and Bruce D. Porter, *War and the Rise of the State: The Military Foundations of Modern Politics* (New York: Free Press, 1994), ch. 3.

5. Otto Hintze, *The Historical Essays of Otto Hintze*, ed. Felix Gilbert (New York: Oxford University Press, 1975); John Brewer, *The Sinews of Power: War, Money, and the English State, 1688–1783* (New York: Knopf, 1989); Charles Tilly, ed., *The Formation of National States in Western Europe* (Princeton, N.J.: Princeton University Press, 1975); Thomas Ertman, *Birth of the Leviathan: Building States and Regimes in Medieval and Early Modern Europe* (Cambridge: Cambridge University Press, 1997). The following account is particularly indebted to Brewer's *The Sinews of Power*.

6. For an anatomy of these political divisions, see Lawrence Stone, "The Results of the English Revolutions of the Seventeenth Century," in Pocock, ed., *Three British Revolutions*, 23–108.

7. Brewer, *The Sinews of Power*, ch. 4; Henry Roseveare, *The Financial Revolution, 1660–1760* (New York: Longman, 1991), pt. II. Brewer and Roseveare build on P. G. M. Dickson, *The Financial Revolution in England: A Study in the Development of Public Credit, 1688–1756* (New York: St. Martin's Press, 1967).

8. Kishlansky, *A Monarchy Transformed*, 304; Brewer, *The Sinews of Power*, 130–31.

9. Brewer, *The Sinews of Power*, xix.

10. After a period when historians disparaged Locke's impact in America and insisted on the priority of "republican" rather than "liberal" influences, the pendulum has swung back toward a more balanced view. On the question of the legitimacy of revolution, however, the Americans invoked Locke far more than any other figure. For the empirical evidence, see Steven M. Dworetz, *The Unvarnished Doctrine: Locke, Liberalism, and the American Revolution* (Durham, N.C.: Duke University Press, 1990).

11. For this view of the Revolution, see Gordon S. Wood, *The Radicalism of the American Revolution* (New York: Knopf, 1992). The American Revolution also brought about another kind of revolution—in communications; see my *The Creation of the Media: Political Origins of Modern Communications* (New York: Basic Books, 2004), chs. 2 and 3.

12. Bernard Bailyn, *The Ideological Origins of the American Revolution* (Cambridge, Mass.: Belknap Press of Harvard University Press, 1967), esp. ch. 3; James H. Read, *Power Versus Liberty: Madison, Hamilton, Wilson, and Jefferson* (Charlottesville: University Press of Virginia, 2000).

13. Gordon S. Wood, *The Creation of the American Republic* (1969; Chapel Hill: University of North Carolina Press, 1998), 132–49; see also Gordon S. Wood, *The American Revolution: A History* (New York: Modern Library, 2002). I draw on Wood's accounts in the succeeding paragraphs as well, while favoring an interpretation of the Constitution's origins that places more emphasis on the fiscal and military incapacity of the Confederation and on the challenges posed to the early republic by the international state system.

14. Max M. Edling, *A Revolution in Favor of Government: Origins of the U.S. Constitution and the Making of the American State* (New York: Oxford University Press, 2003), 82. On the inability of the Confederation even to pay for shipping the Treaty of 1783, see John M. Murrin, "Gordon S. Wood and the Search for Liberal America," *William and Mary Quarterly*, 3rd ser., 44 (July 1987): 598.

15. John J. McCusker and Russell R. Menard, *The Economy of British America, 1607–1789* (Chapel Hill: University of North Carolina Press, 1991), 367–73, 376.

16. Edling, *A Revolution in Favor of Government*, 8–10.

17. Robert McGuire, *To Form a More Perfect Union: A New Economic Interpretation of the United States Constitution* (New York: Oxford University Press, 2003), 53.

18. Roger H. Brown, *Redeeming the Republic: Federalists, Taxation, and the Origins of the Constitution* (Baltimore: Johns Hopkins University Press, 1993), 236; Edling, *A Revolution in Favor of Government*, chs. 13 and 14.

19. McGuire, *To Form a More Perfect Union*, 6; Charles A. Beard, *An Economic Interpretation of the Constitution of the United States* (New Brunswick, N.J.: Transaction Publishers, 1998).

20. See Ira Katznelson, "Flexible Capacity: The Military and Early American State-building," in Ira Katznelson and Martin Shefter, eds., *Shaped by War and Trade: International Influences on American Political Development* (Princeton, N.J.: Princeton University Press, 2002), 82–110. My interpretation of the formation of the liberal state—in this and later chapters—owes a great deal to the entire line of work in American political development that emphasizes international influences. On the general explanation for democracies' success in war, see Dan Reiter and Allan C. Stam, *Democracies at War* (Princeton, N.J.: Princeton University Press, 2002).

CHAPTER 3

1. The analysis here of classical liberalism, with its emphasis on the crucial importance of separations and boundaries and the rules governing when they can be crossed, draws on ideas from structural anthropology. I made an earlier effort along these lines in "Social Categories and Claims in the Liberal State," in Mary Douglas and David Hull, eds., *How Classification Works* (Edinburgh: Edinburgh University Press, 1992), 154–79.

2. The quoted phrase comes from an 1832 definition of "public" by George Cornewall Lewis: "Public, as opposed to private, is that which has no immediate relation to any specified person or persons, but may directly concern any member or members of the community, without distinction"; George Cornewall Lewis, *Remarks on the Use and Abuse of Some Political Terms* (1832; Oxford: Clarendon Press, 1898), 175. For discussions citing this definition, see Brian Barry, *Political Argument* (London: Routledge and Kegan Paul, 1965), 190–91, and Stanley I. Benn and Gerald F. Gaus, "The Liberal Conception of the Public and the Private," in Stanley I. Benn and Gerald F. Gaus, *Public and Private in Social Life* (New York: St. Martin's

Press, 1983), 31–66. Benn and Gaus provide a subtle schema for understanding the manifold different "levels" and "modes" of the public-private distinction in what they refer to as the "individualist" and "organic" models of liberal political thought. An earlier discussion of mine about these issues appears in "The Meaning of Privatization," *Yale Law and Policy Review* 6 (1988): 6–41.

3. Gerald Frug, "The City as a Legal Concept," *Harvard Law Review* 93 (1980): 1059–1154.

4. Albert O. Hirschman, *The Passions and the Interests: Political Arguments for Capitalism Before Its Triumph* (Princeton, N.J.: Princeton University Press, 1977). On the questions of self-interest and moral character, see Stephen Holmes, *Passions and Constraint: On the Theory of Liberal Democracy* (Chicago: University of Chicago Press, 1995), ch. 2 ("The Secret History of Self-Interest"), and Stefan Collini, "The Idea of 'Character' in Victorian Political Thought," *Transactions of the Royal Historical Society*, 5th ser., 35 (1985): 29–50.

5. John Stuart Mill, "Considerations on Representative Government," in *On Liberty and Other Essays* (New York: Oxford University Press, 1998), 255 (ch. 3).

6. John Locke, *Second Treatise*, XII, para 143; on the elements of the rule of law, see Lon Fuller, *The Morality of Law* (New Haven, Conn.: Yale University Press, 1964). The following discussion draws on M. J. C. Vile, *Constitutionalism and the Separation of Powers*, 2nd ed. (Indianapolis: Liberty Fund, 1998).

7. Gordon J. Schochet, "From Persecution to 'Toleration,'" in J. R. Jones, *Liberty Secured? Britain Before and After 1688* (Stanford, Calif.: Stanford University Press, 1992), 122–57.

8. Leonard W. Levy, *The Establishment Clause: Religion and the First Amendment*, 2nd ed. (Chapel Hill: University of North Carolina Press, 1994), 52–60.

9. For this analysis of religious economies, see Roger Finke and Rodney Stark, *The Churching of America, 1776–1990* (New Brunswick, N.J.: Rutgers University Press, 1992), and Rodney Stark and Laurence R. Iannoccone, "A Supply-Side Reinterpretation of the 'Secularization' of Europe," *Journal for the Social Scientific Study of Religion* 33 (1994): 230–52. For comparative background, see Stephen V. Monsma and J. Christopher Soper, *The Challenge of Pluralism: Church and State in Five Democracies* (Lanham, Md.: Rowman and Littlefield, 1997).

10. Locke, *Second Treatise*, ch. 5.

11. Adam Smith, *An Inquiry into the Nature and Causes of the Wealth of Nations* (New York: Modern Library, 1937), 423, 14, 423. For background, see also Elie Halévy, *The Growth of Philosophic Radicalism*, tr. Mary Morris (Clifton, N.J.: A. M. Kelley, 1972); Lionel Robbins, *The Theory of Economic Policy in English Classical Political Economy*, 2nd ed. (London: Macmillan, 1978); Emma Rothschild, *Economic Sentiments: Adam Smith, Condorcet, and the Enlightenment* (Cambridge, Mass.: Harvard University Press, 2001); and D. P. O'Brien, *The Classical Economists Revisited* (Princeton, N.J.: Princeton University Press, 2004).

12. Adam Smith, *The Theory of Moral Sentiments* (Indianapolis: Liberty Fund, 1982), 81; Smith, *Wealth of Nations*, 628.

13. Smith, *Wealth of Nations*, 98, 78–79.

14. Ibid., 142, 674, 250; Rothschild, *Economic Sentiments*, 52–71.

15. *Wealth of Nations*, 651, 737; Robbins, *Theory of Economic Policy in English Classical Political Economy*, 34–67.

16. For a review of the British historical debate, see Arthur J. Taylor, *Laissez-faire and State Intervention in Nineteenth-Century Britain* (London: Macmillan, 1972); on the American story, see Arthur M. Schlesinger Jr., *The Cycles of American History* (Boston: Houghton Mifflin, 1986), ch. 9.

17. Morton J. Horwitz, *The Transformation of American Law, 1780–1860* (Cambridge, Mass.: Harvard University Press, 1977), ch. 2; see also James Willard Hurst, *Law and the Conditions of Freedom: In the Nineteenth-Century United States* (Madison: University of Wisconsin Press, 1956).

18. Immanuel Kant, "The Metaphysics of Morals" (1797), in Immanuel Kant, *Political Writings*, 2nd ed., ed. Hans Reiss, tr. H. B. Nisbet (New York: Cambridge University Press, 1970), 133; Kant, "Idea for a Universal History with a Cosmopolitan Purpose" (1784), ibid., 45.

19. Joseph Priestley, *Essay on the First Principles of Government* (London, 1768), 13.

20. Adam Ferguson, *An Essay on the History of Civil Society*, ed. Fania Oz-Salzberger (New Brunswick, N.J.: Transaction Publishers, 1980), 207. On the concept of civil society, see John Ehrenberg, *Civil Society: The Critical History of an Idea* (New York: New York University Press, 1999).

21. Benjamin Constant, "The Liberty of the Ancients Compared with That of the Moderns," in Benjamin Constant, *Political Writings*, tr. and ed. Biancamaria Fontana (New York: Cambridge University Press, 1988),

309–28 [quotations: 316, 311, 318, 327]. For background and analysis, see Stephen Holmes, *Benjamin Constant and the Making of Modern Liberalism* (New Haven, Conn.: Yale University Press, 1984), 28–52.

22. Alexis de Tocqueville, *Democracy in America*, tr. Henry Reeve (New York: J. & H. G. Langley, 1840), vol. 2, bk. 2 [quotations: 104, 106, 111, 114, 119, 120].

23. Paul Starr, *The Creation of the Media: Political Origins of Modern Communications* (New York: Basic Books, 2004).

24. Karl Marx, "On the Jewish Question," in Karl Marx and Frederick Engels, *Collected Works* (New York: International Publishers, 1975–), 3:164.

25. De Tocqueville, *Democracy in America*, 117.

26. Constant, "The Liberty of the Ancients Compared with That of the Moderns," 326.

27. John Stuart Mill, "On Liberty," in *On Liberty and Other Essays* (New York: Oxford University Press, 1998), 15; idem, "Considerations on Representative Government," 447, 453, 455 (ch. 18). See Uday Singh Mehta, *Liberalism and Empire: A Study in Nineteenth-Century British Liberal Thought* (Chicago: University of Chicago Press, 1999).

28. Carol Pateman, *The Sexual Contract* (Stanford, Calif.: Stanford University Press, 1988); Mary Wollstonecraft, *A Vindication of the Rights of Men with A Vindication of the Rights of Woman and Hints*, ed. Sylvana Tomaselli (New York: Cambridge University Press, 1995); Christine Fauré, *Democracy Without Women: Feminism and the Rise of Liberal Individualism in France*, tr. Claudia Gorbman and John Berks (Bloomington: Indiana University Press, 1991).

CHAPTER 4

1. On voting rights in the United States, see Alex Keyssar, *The Right to Vote: The Contested History of Democracy in the United States* (New York: Basic Books, 2000), 83. Regarding citizenship more broadly, see T. H. Marshall, *Citizenship and Social Class, and Other Essays* (Cambridge: University Press, 1950); Dennis F. Thompson, *The Democratic Citizen: Social Science and Democratic Theory in the Twentieth Century* (London: Cambridge University Press, 1970); and Reinhard Bendix, *Nation-Building and Citizenship*, 2nd ed. (New Brunswick, N.J.: Transaction Publishers, 1996).

2. The key general works on the sources of democracy from the eighteenth to the mid-twentieth centuries include Seymour Martin Lipset, *Political Man: The Social Bases of Politics* (Garden City, N.Y.: Doubleday, 1960); Barrington Moore, *Social Origins of Dictatorship and Democracy: Lord and Peasant in the Making of the Modern World* (Boston: Beacon Press, 1966); and Dietrich Ruesdchemeyer, Evelyne Huber Stephens, and John D. Stephens, *Capitalist Development and Democracy* (Chicago: University of Chicago Press, 1992). For a recent effort to provide a unified theoretical account of democratization, emphasizing the critical importance of income equality and the mobility of capital, see Carles Boix, *Democracy and Redistribution* (New York: Cambridge University Press, 2003).

3. *The Times* (London), April 18, 1833; cited as the epigraph to Robert McKenzie and Allan Silver, *Angels in Marble: Working Class Conservatives in Urban England* (Chicago: University of Chicago Press, 1968).

4. Stanislav Andreski, *Military Organization and Society* (1954; Berkeley: University of California Press, 1968); Sherman quoted in Keyssar, *The Right to Vote*, 88.

5. Bernard Mandeville, "An Essay on Charity, and Charity-Schools," in *The Fable of the Bees, or Private Vices, Publick Benefits* (Indianapolis: Liberty Fund, 1988), 1:331.

6. Arthur M. Schlesinger Jr., *The Cycles of American History* (Boston: Houghton Mifflin, 1986), ch. 9; Carter Goodrich, *Government Promotion of American Canals and Railroads, 1800–1890* (New York: Columbia University Press, 1960); Charles S. Morgan, "Problems in the Appraisal of the Railroad Land Grants," *Mississippi Valley Historical Review* 33 (1946): 443–54.

7. S. G. Checkland, *British Public Policy, 1776–1939: An Economic, Social, and Political Perspective* (New York: Cambridge University Press, 1983), 27, 75–77, 127–34, 211–12.

8. Melvin Dubofsky, *Labor in America: A History*, 6th ed. (Wheeling, Ill.: Harlan Davidson, 1999).

9. On the historical background of the Liberal Party, see Kenneth O. Morgan, *The Age of Lloyd George* (New York: Barnes and Noble, 1971); David Powell, "The New Liberalism and the Rise of Labor, 1886–1906," *Historical Journal* 29 (1986): 369–93; Alan Sykes, *The Rise and Fall of British Liberalism, 1776–1988* (New York: Longman, 1998).

10. L. T. Hobhouse, *Liberalism* (New York: H. Holt, 1911) [quotations: 129, 31, 29, 132, 122–23, 90]; Michael Freeden, *The New Liberalism: An*

Ideology of Social Reform (Oxford: Clarendon Press, 1978); Stefan Collini, *Liberalism and Sociology: L. T. Hobhouse and Political Argument in England, 1880–1914* (New York: Cambridge University Press, 1979).

11. On the comparative point, see Morton Keller, "Regulation of Large Enterprise: The United States Experience in Comparative Perspective," in Alfred D. Chandler Jr. and Herman Daems, eds., *Managerial Hierarchies: Comparative Perspectives on the Rise of the Modern Industrial Enterprise* (Cambridge, Mass.: Harvard University Press, 1980), 161–79.

12. Herbert Croly, *The Promise of American Life* (Cambridge, Mass.: Harvard University Press, 1965); Wilson and Roosevelt quoted in Schlesinger, *The Cycles of American History*, 237.

13. This section draws on an earlier work of mine: "The Rediscovery of the First Amendment," ch. 8 of *The Creation of the Media: Political Origins of Modern Communications* (New York: Basic Books, 2004). Additional supporting evidence, including citations, may be found there.

14. John Stuart Mill, "On Liberty," especially ch. 3, in *On Liberty and Other Essays* (New York: Oxford University Press, 1998).

CHAPTER 5

1. David Lloyd George, *War Memoirs of David Lloyd George, 1915–1916* (Boston: Little, Brown, 1933), 189.

2. For the idea of treating the years 1914 to 1990 as a single era involving simultaneous ideological and strategic challenges (though not for the analysis that appears here), see Phillip Bobbitt, *The Shield of Achilles: War, Peace, and the Course of History* (New York: Knopf, 2002). Bobbitt calls it the "long war." I prefer the "long crisis" because the term encompasses the Depression. But then Eric Hobsbawm calls it the "short twentieth century"; Hobsbawm, *Age of Extremes: The Short Twentieth Century, 1914–1991* (London: Michael Joseph, 1994).

3. For the various writers referred to, see James Burnham, *The Managerial Revolution* (New York: John Day, 1941); Joseph A. Schumpeter, *Capitalism, Socialism, and Democracy* (New York: Harper, 1942); Friedrich A. Hayek, *The Road to Serfdom* (Chicago: University of Chicago Press, 1944); George Orwell, *Nineteen Eighty-Four* (London: Secker & Warburg, 1949); Reinhold Niebuhr, *Moral Man and Immoral Society* (New York: Charles

Scribner's Sons, 1932); and Arthur Schlesinger Jr., *The Vital Center: The Politics of Freedom* (1949; New York: Da Capo, 1988). For Niebuhr's measured response to Hayek, see Alan Brinkley, *The End of Reform: New Deal Liberalism in Recession and War* (New York: Knopf, 1995), 159–60. The liberal anxieties about state power after World War II, far from being a new phenomenon, paralleled the anxieties after World War I that had given rise to the ACLU. Nonetheless, Schlesinger and others portrayed the emerging generation of liberals as more sober and cautious about the state than their elders had been.

4. Brinkley, *The End of Reform*, 7. The following discussion of the New Deal also draws on Richard Hofstadter, *The Age of Reform: From Bryan to FDR* (New York: Vintage Books, 1955); Steve Fraser and Gary Gerstle, eds., *The Rise and Fall of the New Deal Order, 1930–1980* (Princeton, N.J.: Princeton University Press, 1989); Gary Gerstle, "The Protean Character of American Liberalism," *American Historical Review* 99 (1994): 1043–73; and Daniel T. Rodgers, *Atlantic Crossing: Social Politics in a Progressive Age* (Cambridge, Mass.: Belknap Press of Harvard University Press, 1998), 409–84.

5. Roosevelt quoted in Rodgers, *Atlantic Crossings*, 423.

6. U.S. Department of Commerce, *Historical Statistics of the United States: Colonial Times to 1970* (Washington, D.C.: U.S. Bureau of the Census, 1975), 1:224, 2:1105.

7. Aaron L. Friedberg, *In the Shadow of the Garrison State: America's Anti-Statism and Its Cold War Grand Strategy* (Princeton, N.J.: Princeton University Press, 2000).

8. Paul Starr and Gösta Esping-Andersen, "Passive Intervention," *Working Papers for a New Society* (July–August 1979).

9. Bruce D. Porter, *War and the Rise of the State: The Military Foundations of Modern Politics* (New York: Free Press, 1994); Alan T. Peacock and Jack Wiseman, *The Growth of Public Expenditure in the United Kingdom*, 2nd ed. (London: Allen & Unwin, 1967); Andrew Shonfield, *Modern Capitalism: The Changing Balance of Public and Private Power* (New York: Oxford University Press, 1965).

10. Mary L. Dudziak, *Cold War Civil Rights: Race and the Image of American Democracy* (Princeton, N.J.: Princeton University Press, 2000); Willkie quoted, 7; Myrdal quoted, 8.

11. Robert Putnam, *Bowling Alone* (New York: Simon & Schuster, 2000), ch. 14.

12. Tony Smith, *America's Mission: The United States and the Worldwide Struggle for Democracy in the Twentieth Century* (Princeton, N.J.: Princeton University Press, 1994), ch. 5, Roosevelt quoting Balkan proverb, 120; John Lewis Gaddis, *The Long Peace: Inquiries into the History of the Cold War* (New York: Oxford University Press, 1987), chs. 3–6 [quotation: 158–59].

13. Robert Divine, *Second Chance: The Triumph of Internationalism in America During World War II* (New York: Atheneum, 1967), 48–49; Smith, *America's Mission*, 118–19. The text of the Atlantic Charter appears at http://usinfo.state.gov/usa/infousa/facts/democrac/53.htm.

14. On the developments in this period, see Divine, *Second Chance.*

15. On the significance of the transformation of Germany and Japan, see Smith, *America's Mission*, ch. 6.

16. Rudolf von Albertini, "The Impact of the Two World Wars on the Decline of Colonialism," in Tony Smith, ed., *The End of the European Empire: Decolonization After World War II* (Lexington, Mass.: D. C. Heath & Co., 1975), 3–19.

17. Wm. Roger Louis, *Imperialism at Bay: The United States and the Decolonization of the British Empire, 1941–1945* (New York: Oxford University Press, 1978); Smith, *America's Mission*, 124–28.

18. Schlesinger, Introduction, *The Vital Center*, xix.

19. See Gaddis, *The Long Peace*, chs. 2 and 6, esp. 60, 150–51.

20. Samuel P. Huntington, *The Third Wave: Democratization in the Late Twentieth Century* (Norman: University of Oklahoma Press, 1991), 19–21. In Huntington's conception, each "wave" of democratization has been followed by a "reverse wave" in a two-steps-forward-one-step-back pattern; the shift toward authoritarianism beginning in the late 1950s was the second reverse wave, paralleling the first reverse movement during the 1920s and '30s.

21. Ibid. On democratic transitions, see Guillermo O'Donnell, Phillipe C. Schmitter, and Laurence Whitehead, *Transitions from Authoritarian Rule*, 4 vols. (Baltimore: Johns Hopkins University Press, 1986); Juan J. Linz and Alfred Stepan, *Problems of Democratic Transition and Consolidation: Southern Europe, South America, and Postcommunist Europe* (Baltimore: Johns Hopkins University Press, 1996).

22. Adam Przeworski, *Democracy and Development: Political Institutions and Material Well-being in the World, 1950–1990* (Cambridge: Cambridge University Press, 2000).

23. Walter Russell Mead, *Special Providence: American Foreign Policy and How It Changed the World* (New York: Knopf, 2001), 9.

CHAPTER 6

1. Adam Przeworski et al., *Democracy and Development: Political Institutions and Material Well-being in the World, 1950–1990* (Cambridge: Cambridge University Press, 2000).

2. Among the early exponents of the authoritarian-advantage thesis were Walter Galenson, *Labor and Economic Development* (New York: Wiley, 1959); Karl de Schweinitz, "Industrialization, Labor Controls, and Democracy," *Economic Development and Cultural Change* 4 (1959): 385–404; and Samuel P. Huntington, *Political Order in Changing Societies* (New Haven, Conn.: Yale University Press, 1968). For a full critique, see Morton H. Halperin, Joseph T. Siegle, and Michael M. Weinstein, *The Democracy Advantage: How Democracies Promote Prosperity and Peace* (New York: Routledge, 2005), and Przeworski et al., *Democracy and Development*.

3. Peter H. Lindert, *Growing Public: Social Spending and Economic Growth Since the Eighteenth Century*, vol. 1, *The Story* (New York: Cambridge University Press, 2004).

4. Jonas Pontusson, *Inequality and Prosperity: Social Europe Versus Liberal America* (Ithaca, N.Y.: Cornell University Press, 2005), chs. 1 and 7.

5. Adam Smith, *An Inquiry into the Nature and Causes of the Wealth of Nations* (New York: Modern Library, 1937), 651.

6. Judith Shklar, "The Liberalism of Fear," in Nancy Rosenblum, ed., *Liberalism and the Moral Life* (Cambridge, Mass.: Harvard University Press, 1989), 21–38; T. M. Scanlon, "When Does Equality Matter?" paper presented at the Princeton University Center for Human Values, Princeton, N.J., December 1, 2005.

7. Of course, much depends on the extent to which differences in rewards are ultimately to "everyone's advantage" and on how much protection against bad luck can be provided without creating additional social costs (the problem of "moral hazard"). The central text in contemporary liberal thought about these questions is John Rawls, *A Theory of Justice* (Cambridge, Mass.: Harvard University Press, 1971). See also Amy Gutmann, *Liberal Equality* (Cambridge: Cambridge University Press, 1980),

and Ronald Dworkin, *Sovereign Virtue: The Theory and Practice of Equality* (Cambridge, Mass.: Harvard University Press, 2000).

8. Benjamin M. Friedman, *The Moral Consequences of Economic Growth* (New York: Knopf, 2005), esp. ch. 4 [Smith quoted, 49].

9. I borrow the argument here from my earlier book, *The Creation of the Media: Political Origins of Modern Communications* (New York: Basic Books, 2004), esp. 7–12.

10. Walter Lippmann, *Liberty and the News* (New York: Harcourt, Brace and Howe, 1920), 64.

11. For the debate over the power of business in liberal democracies, see Charles Lindblom, *Politics and Markets: The World's Political Economic Systems* (New York: Basic Books, 1977), and David Vogel, *Fluctuating Fortunes: The Political Power of Business in America* (New York: Basic Books, 1989).

12. Arthur M. Schlesinger Jr., *The Cycles of American History* (Boston: Houghton Mifflin, 1986), 243.

13. See, for example, Martha Derthick and Paul J. Quirk, *The Politics of Deregulation* (Washington, D.C.: Brookings Institution Press, 1985).

14. For discussion of these issues, see Cass R. Sunstein, *Free Markets and Social Justice* (New York: Oxford University Press, 1997).

15. Tom W. Smith, "Liberal and Conservative Trends in the United States Since World War II," *Public Opinion Quarterly* 54 (1990): 479–507; Benjamin I. Page and Robert Y. Shapiro, "Effects of Public Opinion on Policy," *American Political Science Review* 77 (March 1983): 175–90; Gerald C. Wright Jr., Robert S. Erikson, and John P. McIver, "Public Opinion and Policy Liberalism in the American States," *American Journal of Political Science* 31 (1987): 980–1001.

16. Morton J. Horwitz, *The Warren Court and the Pursuit of Justice* (New York: Hill and Wang, 1998), ch. 5; the case is *Carolene Products Co. v. United States* (1937). The following discussion of the Warren Court draws on Horwitz's account and on Bernard Schwartz, ed., *The Warren Court: A Retrospective* (New York: Oxford University Press, 1996).

17. For discussions and evaluations of the War on Poverty and subsequent programs, see James T. Patterson, *America's Struggle Against Poverty in the Twentieth Century* (Cambridge, Mass.: Harvard University Press, 2000); Christopher Jencks, *Rethinking Social Policy: Race, Poverty, and the Underclass* (Cambridge, Mass.: Harvard University Press, 1992); Sheldon H. Danziger and Daniel H. Weinberg, eds., *Fighting Poverty: What Works*

and What Doesn't (Cambridge, Mass.: Harvard University Press, 1986); John E. Schwartz, *America's Hidden Success: A Reassessment of Twenty Years of Public Policy* (New York: Norton, 1983); and Edward Zigler and Susan Muenchow, *Head Start: The Inside Story of America's Most Successful Educational Experiment* (New York: Basic Books, 1992).

18. Social Security Administration, "Annual Statistical Supplement, 2005" (February 2006), table 9G, available at: www.ssa.gov/policy/docs/statcomps/supplement/2005; David T. Ellwood, *Poor Support: Poverty in the American Family* (New York: Basic Books, 1988), 39.

19. Jencks, *Rethinking Social Policy*, 74.

20. See my "Health Care for the Poor: The Past Twenty Years," in Danziger and Weinberg, *Fighting Poverty*, 106–32. On the reduction in black-white disparities, see "Summary and Conclusions" in Gerald David Jaynes and Robin M. Williams Jr., eds., *A Common Destiny: Blacks and American Society*, for the Committee on the Status of Black Americans, Commission on Behavioral and Social Sciences and Education, National Research Council (Washington, D.C.: National Academy Press, 1989), 3–32.

21. On the economic record of the 1970s and its relationship to poverty and other trends, see Jencks, *Rethinking Social Policy*, 75–79, and Ellwood, *Poor Support*, 52–57.

22. Ellwood, *Poor Support*, 57–62, summarizes the evidence of the time: single parenthood rose while welfare benefits were declining after 1973; state-to-state variations in welfare benefits did not explain variations in out-of-wedlock births; and births out of wedlock grew as a share of total births among African Americans primarily because of a precipitous drop in the rate of births to married couples. More recent data suggest that welfare may have had some impact on single parenthood, but the effect was relatively small compared to other factors.

23. Martin Gilens, *Why Americans Hate Welfare: Race, Media, and the Politics of Antipoverty Policy* (Chicago: University of Chicago Press, 1999).

24. David Ellwood did more than anyone else to formulate this new strategy; see his *Poor Support*. For his later views on what happened to that strategy, see David T. Ellwood, "Welfare Reform as I Knew It: When Bad Things Happen to Good Policies," *The American Prospect* (May–June 1996): 22–29. Ellwood incorporated ideas originally advanced by conservatives; see particularly Lawrence Mead, *Beyond Entitlement: The Social Obligations of Citizenship* (New York: Free Press, 1986). The Clinton policies

also built on legislation adopted in 1988, the Family Support Act. Regarding the crucial importance of education and training, Robert B. Reich was particularly influential; see his *The Work of Nations* (New York: Knopf, 1991). On the history of welfare reform in the Clinton years, see Jason DeParle, *American Dream: Three Women, Ten Kids, and a Nation's Drive to End Welfare* (New York: Viking, 2004), esp. chs. 6 and 7.

25. Christopher Jencks, "Liberal Lessons from Welfare Reform," *The American Prospect* (Summer 2002, special supplement): A9–13; Christopher Jencks, Scott Winship, and Joseph Swingle, "Welfare Redux," *The American Prospect* (March 2006): 36–40.

26. Francis Fukuyama, "A Reply to My Critics," *The National Interest* (Winter 1989): 21–28 [quotation: 28].

27. On this view of liberalism, see William Galston, *Liberal Purposes: Goods, Virtues, and Diversity in the Liberal State* (New York: Cambridge University Press, 1991), and Stephen Macedo, *Liberal Virtues: Citizenship, Virtue, and Community in Liberal Constitutionalism* (New York: Oxford University Press, 1990).

CHAPTER 7

1. Irving Kristol, *Neoconservatism: The Autobiography of an Idea* (New York: Free Press, 1995), 486; Kristol's essay "Memoirs of a 'Cold Warrior,'" which contains this passage, originally appeared as "My Cold War," *The National Interest* (Spring 1993): 141–44.

2. Timothy Garton Ash, *The Magic Lantern: The Revolution of '89 Witnessed in Warsaw, Budapest, Berlin, and Prague* (New York: Vintage Books, 1993), 151, 137. See also Gerald Marzorati, "Europe Reclaims Its Liberal Language," *New York Times*, July 7, 1990.

3. Quoted in Harold J. Berman, *Justice in the USSR* (New York: Vintage, 1963), 26.

4. Stephen Kotkin, *Armageddon Averted: The Soviet Collapse, 1970–2000* (New York: Oxford University Press, 2001).

5. For general analyses of these questions, see Juan J. Linz and Alfred Stepan, *Problems of Democratic Transition and Consolidation: Southern Europe, South America, and Post-Communist Europe* (Baltimore: Johns Hopkins University Press, 1996); Jon Elster et al., *Institutional Design in Post-Communist Societies: Rebuilding the Ship at Sea* (New York: Cambridge University Press,

1998); David Stark and Laszlo Bruszt, *Postsocialist Pathways: Transforming Politics and Property in East Central Europe* (New York: Cambridge University Press, 1998); and Michael Mandelbaum, ed., *Postcommunism: Four Perspectives* (New York: Council on Foreign Relations, 1996).

6. On the internal divisions among policymakers in the West, see Joseph E. Stiglitz, *Globalization and Its Discontents* (New York: Norton, 2002), 133–65. Stiglitz writes: "The gradualist critics of shock therapy not only accurately predicted its failures but also outlined the reasons why it would not work. Their only failure was to underestimate the magnitude of the disaster" (141).

7. On the eastern European economic and political experiences, see Jeffrey Sachs, *Poland's Jump to the Market Economy* (Cambridge, Mass.: MIT Press, 1999); Elizabeth Pond, *The Rebirth of Europe*, 2nd ed. (Washington, D.C.: Brookings Institution Press, 2002), 105–34; Linz and Stepan, *Problems of Democratic Transition and Consolidation*; Elster et al., *Institutional Design in Post-Communist Societies*; and Ivan Szelenyi and Lawrence King, "Postcommunist Economic Systems," in Neil Smelser and Richard Swedberg, eds., *Handbook of Economic Sociology*, 2nd ed. (Princeton, N.J.: Princeton University Press, 2005), 205–29.

8. On the political economy of postcommunist Russia, see Stiglitz, *Globalization and Its Discontents*, 133–65; Peter Reddaway and Dmitri Glinski, *The Tragedy of Russia's Reforms: Market Bolshevism Against Democracy* (Washington, D.C.: U.S. Institute of Peace Press, 2001); Lawrence R. Klein and Marshall Pomer, eds., *The New Russia: Transition Gone Awry* (Stanford, Calif.: Stanford University Press, 2001); and Jerry F. Hough, *The Logic of Economic Reform in Russia* (Washington, D.C.: Brookings Institution Press, 2001). For a narrative, see Chrystia Freeland, *Sale of the Century: Russia's Wild Ride from Communism to Capitalism* (New York: Crown Business, 2000). The role of Gazprom is described in Andrew E. Kramer and Steven Lee Myers, "Workers' Paradise Is Rebranded as Kremlin Inc.," *New York Times*, April 24, 2006.

9. See a series of studies by Lawrence King, including "Shock Privatization: The Effects of Rapid Large-Scale Privatization on Enterprise Restructuring," *Politics and Society* 31 (March 2003): 3–30, and Lawrence King, David Stuckler, and Patrick Hamm, "Rapid Large-Scale Privatization and the Postcommunist Mortality Crisis," unpublished paper.

10. Friedman quoted in Francis Fukuyama, *State-Building: Governance and World Order in the Twenty-first Century* (Ithaca, N.Y.: Cornell University

Press, 2004), 19; Linz and Stepan, *Problems of Democratic Transition and Consolidation*, 436. For a general analysis of the relationship between state capacity and liberty, see Stephen Holmes, "What Russia Teaches Us Now: How Weak States Threaten Freedom," *The American Prospect* 33 (July–August 1997): 30–39.

11. As an expression of this hybrid, consider article I-3 of the proposed European constitution: "The Union shall work for the sustainable development of Europe based on balanced economic growth and price stability, *a highly competitive social market economy*, aiming at full employment and social progress, and a high level of protection and improvement of the quality of the environment" (emphasis added).

12. On the explanation for growing integration, see Robert O. Keohane and Stanley Hoffman, "Institutional Change in Europe in the 1980s," in Robert O. Keohane and Stanley Hoffman, eds., *The New European Community: Decisionmaking and Institutional Change* (Boulder, Colo.: Westview Press, 1991), 1–39. On the European "constitutional settlement," see Andrew Moravcsik, "The European Constitutional Compromise and the Neofunctionalist Legacy," *Journal of European Public Policy* 12 (April 2005): 349–86; and Andrew Moravcsik, "Europe Without Illusions," *Prospect* (July 2005). On Europe's recent development, I am generally indebted here to Pond, *The Rebirth of Europe*, and to Tony Judt, *Postwar: A History of Europe Since 1945* (New York: Penguin, 2005). For background to the following discussion of public enterprises and privatization, see Richard Pryke, *The Nationalised Industries: Policies and Performance Since 1968* (Oxford: Martin Robertson, 1981); Bernardo Bortolotti and Domenico Siniscalco, *The Challenges of Privatization* (New York: Oxford University Press, 2004); and John Waterbury and Ezra Suleiman, eds., *Public Enterprise and Privatization* (Boulder, Colo.: Westview Press, 1990), which includes my own "The New Life of the Liberal State: Privatization and the Restructuring of State-Society Relations," 22–54.

13. On the comparative performance of social-market and what he calls "liberal market economies," see Jonas Pontusson, *Inequality and Prosperity: Social Europe Versus Liberal America* (Ithaca, N.Y.: Cornell University Press, 2005), esp. chs. 1 and 7.

14. Ibid., 11–12.

15. Ibid., 9, 171–81.

16. Lane Kenworthy, "Do Social-Welfare Policies Reduce Poverty?" *Social Forces* 77 (1999): 1119–39. Even using the same fixed standard for

measuring poverty, Kenworthy shows that the tax and spending policies of the social-market countries achieve a substantially greater reduction in poverty than do such policies in the United States.

17. Gerard F. Anderson et al., "Health Spending in the United States and the Rest of the Industrialized World," *Health Affairs* 24 (July–August 2005): 903–14; Uwe E. Reinhardt, Peter S. Hussey, and Gerard F. Anderson, "U.S. Health Care Spending in an International Context," *Health Affairs* (May–June 2004): 10–25.

18. Robert Kagan, *Of Paradise and Power: America and Europe in the New World Order* (New York: Knopf, 2003).

19. John Stuart Mill, *Principles of Political Economy*, 8th ed. (London: Longmans, Green, Reader, and Dyer, 1878), bk. 2, ch. 1; John Dewey, *Liberalism and Social Action* (New York: G. P. Putnam, 1935), 40; John Dewey, *The Public and Its Problems* (1927; Athens, Ohio: Swallow Press, 1991), 144, 146. For a contemporary example of the case for economic democracy, see Gar Alperovitz, *America Beyond Capitalism: Reclaiming Our Wealth, Our Liberty, and Our Democracy* (Hoboken, N.J.: John Wiley, 2005).

20. See Henry Hansmann, *The Ownership of Enterprise* (Cambridge, Mass.: Harvard University Press, 1996).

21. For an analysis, see Yochai Benkler, *The Wealth of Networks: How Social Production Transforms Markets and Freedom* (New Haven, Conn.: Yale University Press, 2006).

22. The major communitarian works include Michael Sandel, *Liberalism and the Limits of Justice* (New York: Cambridge University Press, 1982); Alasdair MacIntyre, *After Virtue* (Notre Dame, Ind.: Notre Dame University Press, 1981); and Roberto Mangabeira Unger, *Knowledge and Politics* (New York: Free Press, 1975). For two trenchant critiques, see Stephen Holmes, *The Anatomy of Antiliberalism* (Cambridge, Mass.: Harvard University Press, 1993), esp. 176–84; and Amy Gutmann, "Communitarian Critics of Liberalism," *Philosophy and Public Affairs* 14 (1985): 308–22.

23. Holmes notes the "schizophrenic tone" of many communitarian works: "A high-pitched jeremiad fizzles into tiptoed retreat. After total criticism of the ontological foundations of liberalism and dire warnings about the collapse of Western civilization, we are treated, say, to limp advice about tightening up pornography laws"; Holmes, *The Anatomy of Antiliberalism*, 181. For a good example of the discrepancy between premises and program, see Michael Sandel, *Democracy's Discontent: America in Search of a Public Philosophy* (Cambridge, Mass.: Harvard University Press, 1996).

CHAPTER 8

1. Charles Krauthammer, "A New Policy," *Washington Post*, June 8, 2001; Robert Kagan and William Kristol explicitly call for a "benevolent global hegemony" in the introduction to their edited volume *Present Dangers: Crisis and Opportunity in American Foreign and Defense Policy* (San Francisco: Encounter, 2000), 6.

2. Walter Russell Mead, *Special Providence: American Foreign Policy and How It Changed the World* (New York: Knopf, 2001).

3. Walter Lippmann, *U.S. Foreign Policy: Shield of the Republic* (Boston: Little, Brown, 1943), 7.

4. On the historical origins of Bush's foreign policy, see Ivo H. Daalder and James M. Lindsay, *America Unbound: The Bush Revolution in Foreign Policy* (Washington, D.C.: Brookings Institution Press, 2003); James Mann, *The Rise of the Vulcans: The History of Bush's War Cabinet* (New York: Viking, 2004); and Francis Fukuyama, *America at the Crossroads: Democracy, Power, and the Neoconservative Legacy* (New Haven, Conn.: Yale University Press, 2006).

5. "The National Security Strategy of the United States" (Washington, D.C.: White House, September 2002), 19.

6. See G. John Ikenberry and Anne Marie Slaughter, "Forging a World of Liberty Under Law: U.S. National Security in the 21st Century" (Princeton, N.J.: Woodrow Wilson School of Public and International Affairs, Princeton University, 2006), 31–32; Fukuyama, *America at the Crossroads*, ch. 3. For some of the language in this paragraph and elsewhere in this chapter, I draw on passages that I originally wrote for the article "The Liberal Uses of Power" (co-authored by Robert Kuttner and Michael Tomasky), *The American Prospect* (March 2005): 20–22.

7. "Congress Daily PM," *National Journal*, March 12, 2003.

8. I draw some of this discussion from my column "Bush v. Constitution," *The American Prospect* (March 2006): 3. See also an article in the same issue by Gordon Silverstein, "All Power to the President," 49–53, reviewing John Yoo, *The Powers of War and Peace: The Constitution and Foreign Affairs After 9/11* (Chicago: University of Chicago Press, 2006).

9. *Korematsu v. United States* 321 U.S. 760 (1944).

10. Daalder and Lindsay, *America Unbound*, 79.

11. For the data on public opinion abroad, see Andrew Kohut and Bruce Stokes, *America Against the World: How We Are Different and Why We Are Disliked* (New York: Times Books, 2006).

12. For the general case, see Morton H. Halperin, Joseph T. Siegle, and Michael M. Weinstein, *The Democracy Advantage: How Democracies Promote Prosperity and Peace* (New York: Routledge, 2005); but for the argument that new democracies are prone to aggressive nationalism and war, see Edward D. Mansfield and Jack Snyder, *Electing to Fight: Why Emerging Democracies Go to War* (Cambridge, Mass.: MIT Press, 2004), and Amy Chua, *World on Fire: How Exporting Free Market Democracy Breeds Ethnic Hatred and Global Instability* (New York: Doubleday, 2003). Fareed Zakaria holds that the priority should be constitutional liberalism, not democracy. Although the two are historically separable (as I have argued throughout this book), I do not believe they can be separated any longer. A government that had a classically liberal constitution, but no popular participation, would likely be unstable—and not liberal in any sense that would be accepted today. See Zakaria, *The Future of Freedom: Illiberal Democracy at Home and Abroad* (New York: Norton, 2003).

13. On the idea of a new "concert of democracies," see Ikenberry and Slaughter, "Forging a World of Liberty Under Law," Appendix A: Charter for a Concert of Democracies.

CHAPTER 9

1. Kevin Phillips, *The Emerging Republican Majority* (New Rochelle, N.Y.: Arlington House, 1969). In this and the following section, I have adapted some material from an earlier essay, "An Emerging Democratic Majority," in Stanley Greenberg and Theda Skocpol, eds., *The New Majority* (New Haven, Conn.: Yale University Press, 1997), 221–37.

2. For this and related arguments about why the political system has tilted so far to the right, see Jacob S. Hacker and Paul Pierson, *Off Center: The Republican Revolution and the Erosion of American Democracy* (New Haven, Conn.: Yale University Press, 2005).

3. Ibid., 38–44. Some analysts point to polls showing that more Americans identify themselves as conservatives than as liberals, but this has long been the case. For example, the proportion self-identifying as liberal was about the same in 2002 as in 1964, the year of Lyndon Johnson's landslide. See James A. Stimson, *Tides of Consent: How Public Opinion Shapes American Politics* (New York: Cambridge University Press, 2004), 86. Self-identification is also not the only index of ideological support. There is a

crucial difference between "symbolic" identification with an ideology and "operational" support for policies that correspond to that position. Many Americans who identify themselves as conservative nonetheless support liberal policies. Using cumulative data from the General Social Survey and setting aside moderates, Stimson finds that about 22 percent of Americans are symbolically conservative but operationally liberal, while only 2 percent are symbolically liberal but operationally conservative. From a symbolic perspective, the conservatives are the larger group; from an operational perspective, the liberals predominate. Ibid., 90–91. Stimson argues that, in general, swings in public opinion shape politics; Hacker and Pierson offer an explanation of why American politics in recent years has swung far to the right without a corresponding shift in public opinion. In a related controversy, Thomas Frank has argued that the Republicans have used moral appeals to get working-class Americans to vote against their economic interests, but Larry Bartels has shown that the data on trends in voting by education and income don't support that interpretation. See Thomas Frank, *What's the Matter with Kansas: How Conservatives Won the Heart of America* (New York: Metropolitan Books, 2004), and Larry M. Bartels, "What's the Matter with *What's the Matter with Kansas*," *Quarterly Journal of Political Science* 1 (2006): 201–26. The common thread tying together Hacker and Pierson's work and Bartels's argument is that change in politics has far outrun change in public opinion.

4. See chapters 2 and 5.

5. U.S. Bureau of the Census, "U.S. Interim Projections by Age, Sex, Race, and Hispanic Origin," available at: http://www.census.gov/ipc/www/usinterimproj/ (last revised August 26, 2004).

6. Emmanuel Saez and Thomas Piketty, "Income Inequality in the United States, 1913–1998," *Quarterly Journal of Economics* 118 (2003): 1–39; Edward N. Wolff, *Top Heavy: Inequality of Wealth in America and What Can Be Done About It*, 2nd ed. (New York: New Press, 2002).

7. Larry M. Bartels, "Partisan Politics and the U.S. Income Distribution," available at: http://www.princeton.edu/~bartels/income.pdf (revised February 2004).

8. William G. Gale, Peter R. Orszag, and Isaac Shapiro, "The Ultimate Burden of the Tax Cuts: Once the Tax Cuts Are Paid for, Low- and Middle-Income Households Likely to Be Net Losers, on Average," Center on Budget and Policy Priorities, available at http://www.cbpp.org/6–2–04tax.htm. (June 2, 2004).

9. *Health Insurance Coverage in America: 2004 Data Update*, Kaiser Commission on Medicaid and the Uninsured, available at: http://www.kff .org/uninsured/upload/Health-Coverage-in-America–2004-Data-Update-Report.pdf (November 2005).

10. See Chris Mooney, *The Republican War on Science* (New York: Basic Books, 2005); James Gustave Speth, *Red Sky at Morning: America and the Crisis of the Global Environment* (New Haven, Conn.: Yale University Press, 2004).

11. This idea and words to the same effect echo through much recent liberal writing: "Common sense by itself should teach us that we are all in this thing together"; Mario Cuomo, *Reason to Believe* (New York: Simon & Schuster, 1995), 73; Paul Waldman, *Being Right Is Not Enough: What Progressives Must Learn from Conservative Success* (Hoboken, N.J.: John Wiley, 2006), 164–67 (citing a speech by Barack Obama at Knox College in 2005); and Michael Tomasky, "Party in Search of a Notion," *The American Prospect* 17 (May 2006): 20–28.

Index